BEYOND BODIES:
RAINMAKING AND SENSE MAKING IN TANZANIA

For over a century, the Ihanzu of north-central Tanzania have conducted rainmaking rites. As with similar rites found across sub-Saharan Africa, these rites are replete with gender, sexual, and fertility motifs. Social scientists have typically explained such things as symbolizing human bodies and the act of procreation. But what happens when our interlocutors deny such symbolic explanations, when they insist that rain rites and the gender and sexual motifs in them do not symbolize anything but rather aim simply to bring rain?

Beyond Bodies examines Ihanzu sensibilities about gender through a fine-grained ethnography of rainmaking rites. It considers the meaning of ritual practices in a society in which gender is not as bound to the body as it is in the Euro-American imagination. Engaging with recent anthropological and gender theory, this book calls crucially into question how social scientists have explained gender symbolism in a host of ethnographic and historical studies from across Africa.

(Anthropological Horizons)

TODD SANDERS is an associate professor in the Department of Anthropology at the University of Toronto, and a visiting professor in the Department of Social Anthropology at the University of Trondheim, Norway. His recent co-edited books include *Anthropology in Theory: Issues in Epistemology* (Blackwell), *Transparency and Conspiracy: Ethnographies of Suspicion in the New World Order* (Duke), and *Magical Interpretations, Material Realities: Modernity, Witchcraft and the Occult in Postcolonial Africa* (Routledge).

ANTHROPOLOGICAL HORIZONS

Editor: Michael Lambek, Unviersity of Toronto

This series, begun in 1991, focuses on theoretically informed ethnographic works addressing issues of mind and body, knowledge and power, equality and inequality, the individual and the collective. Interdisciplinary in its perspective, the series makes a unique contribution in several other academic disciplines: women's studies, history, philosophy, psychology, political science, and sociology.

For a list of the books published in this series see page 263.

Beyond Bodies: Rainmaking and Sense Making in Tanzania

Todd Sanders

UNIVERSITY OF TORONTO PRESS
Toronto Buffalo London

© University of Toronto Press Incorporated 2008
Toronto Buffalo London

www.utppublishing.com

Printed in Canada

ISBN 978-0-8020-9149-9 (cloth)
ISBN 978-0-8020-9582-4 (paper)

Printed on acid-free paper

Library and Archives Canada Cataloguing in Publication

Sanders, Todd, 1965–
    Beyond bodies : rainmaking and sense making in Tanzania / Todd Sanders.

(Anthropological horizons)
Includes bibliographical references and index.
ISBN 978-0-8020-9149-9 (bound)
ISBN 978-0-8020-9582-4 (pbk.)

1. Rain-making rites – Tanzania – Iramba District.   2. Isanzu (African
people) – Rites and ceremonies.   3. Iramba District (Tanzania) – Social
life and customs.   4. Sex role – Tanzania – Iramba District.   5. Social
epistemology. I. Title.   II. Series.

GN473.6.S27 2008   305.896′390967826   C2007-903856-5

This book has been published with the help of a grant from the Canadian
Federation for the Humanities and Social Sciences, through the Aid to
Scholarly Publications Programme, using funds provided by the Social
Sciences and Humanities Research Council of Canada.

University of Toronto Press acknowledges the financial assistance to its
publishing program of the Canada Council for the Arts and the Ontario
Arts Council.

University of Toronto Press acknowledges the financial support for its
publishing activities of the Government of Canada through the Book
Publishing Industry Development Program (BPIDP).

Contents

Illustrations

Figures and Tables

Preface

This book has been written with the student reader in mind. Each chapter provides an ethnographically grounded guide to and through a particular set of debates in anthropology. My hope is that readers will learn something about Tanzania – specifically, about the men and women in one part of it called 'Ihanzu'; something about rainmaking, ritual, and symbolism; something about gender; and something about the challenges anthropologists face when going about the business of explaining our data.

This book focuses on Ihanzu rainmaking rites and the gender, sexual, and fertility 'symbolism' that informs them. These concerns will likely get the book placed alongside others that employ an interpretive and/or symbolic framework, which in some ways is fine. However, this association is not straightforward, since one of the book's central claims is that Ihanzu rainmaking rites do not mean or symbolize anything beyond themselves; rather, they are geared towards acting upon the world in order to change it. For the women and men of Ihanzu, rain rites 'mean' because they do things; which is to say, villagers find them meaningful because they bring rain. Thus, if this book is about Ihanzu rainmaking and gender 'symbolism,' it is also about anthropological and local explanations and the complex relations between the two.

Things might have been different, of course. I might have written a book on Ihanzu rainmaking that considered, say, how differently situated social actors relate to rainmaking rituals – that is, the everyday conflicts, fissions, and fusions that surround them – and/or examined rainmaking rites as resistance to colonial or postcolonial regimes. These are all worthwhile topics and have already been written about by others.[1] Except in chapter 2, this book does not ask or seek to answer questions about the politics of precipitation. Instead, it aims to make sense of Ihanzu rainmaking and its inherent gendering in terms of the Ihanzu's own epistemological concerns – in other words, in terms of Ihanzu theories of knowledge of the world and its workings. But how does one come to write such a book in the first place? Why rainmaking? Why gender? And why epistemology? Answers to these questions spring directly from my own anthropological placement and entanglements in 'the field.'

When I first arrived in Tanzania in June 1993, I spent two months in the city of Dar es Salaam, a hectic time of studying Swahili, the nation's lingua franca, by night, and sorting out visas, research and residence permits, and a Land Rover by day. With paperwork in order, and a rudimentary grasp of Swahili, I drove west to the place I had read about called 'Ihanzu' in northern Iramba District. Driving directly takes a very long day, much of it over bad roads. This particular trip took much longer, however, since researchers are required to deliver letters of introduction from the highest to the lowest levels of government: from the national research office in Dar, across the country to the Provincial Commissioner; from there to the District Commissioner; then to the Ward Executive Officer in Ihanzu proper; on to the Village Executive Officer in Matongo village; and finally to the ten-cell leader in Kirumi village, where I would live for the next two years. If this three-day odyssey ensured that an astonishing number of government employees knew of my presence and plans to do research in Ihanzu, it did little to inform ordinary Ihanzu villagers, who were caught largely unaware by my arrival.

My arrival in Ihanzu coincided with the dry season and harvest. And an excellent one it was: food, locally brewed sorghum beer, and the celebrations that accompanied both were everywhere in evidence. Naturally enough, people wanted to know why I had come, how long I would be staying, and what I intended to do there. Moreover, with the harvest over, it was the ideal time of year to sit and discuss such matters over sorghum beer. Fortunately, these conversations were possible, for even if my Swahili was still mediocre, villagers' grasp of the language was excellent. This was because nearly all Ihanzu men and women have done migrant labour in other parts of Tanzania, where Swahili is spoken, and because nearly everyone has attended at least a few years of primary school, where Swahili is the language of instruction. My initial

meeting and conversations with some of the men and women of Ihanzu
– at public beer parties, with pleasant weather and little work to do –
could hardly have been more welcoming or enjoyable.

One thing I discovered early on in these discussions was that men
and women of the area had vivid and fond memories of another foreigner – Virginia Adam, a British social anthropologist then working
under the auspices of the East African Institute of Social Research in
Uganda, who had lived in Ihanzu between 1960 and 1962 (see Adam
1961, 1962, 1963a, 1963b). Others who were too young to know or
remember her had often heard stories about Nya Adamu, as she was
called. For several reasons, this was my good fortune. For one thing,
many already shared particular understandings of what an anthropologist should do: collect life histories and interviews, attend weddings,
funerals, markets, government meetings, rainmaking rites, ancestral
offerings, and divination sessions, join in herding, fishing, and farming
whenever possible, all the while taking photographs, recording songs,
drawing maps, and scribbling fieldnotes. A tall order, for sure. In this
context, 'participant observation,' 'interview,' 'oral history,' and indeed
'anthropology' required little explanation. Many already 'knew' what I
was up to. Such local knowledge made it easy for villagers to train
their new anthropologist, and, on balance, made for a less traumatic
entrée into the field, and people's lives, than might have otherwise
been the case.

My association with Nya Adamu had other unexpected benefits.
Through those initial summer months, over beer, many people insisted
that I was quite obviously Nya Adamu's son, following in her foot-
steps, as any good son might. I was, after all, about the right age. And I
was the only other white foreigner to have come to live in Ihanzu for
an extended period and to want to do things anthropological. The logic
was impeccable – except, of course, that I was not her son.

It was only months later that I began to realize my mistake – Nya
Adamu was in fact my 'mother.' This new understanding developed
with my growing comprehension of Ihanzu kinship, and crucially,
what people mean by the term 'mother.' For every Ihanzu has many
mothers: most of them 'clan mothers,' to be sure, but mothers all the
same. Thus, after first denying that I was related to Nya Adamu, I
eventually conceded that she was my clan mother (*iya kwa ndūgū*), our
clan in the United Kingdom being 'Anthropologists.' In this way –
unbeknownst to herself – my 'mother' helped place me in Ihanzu, for
which I am very grateful.

Shortly thereafter, women and men began suggesting that since my mother had been a member of the royal *Anyampanda* rainmaking matrilineage, so as her son was I. Everyone I spoke with, in fact, was delighted by this prospect and found it a great source of amusement. Over the weeks, months and years, I was playfully fitted and refitted into a complex social matrix of siblings, mothers and fathers, mothers' brothers and sisters' sons, cousins and grandparents, children, grand-children, and jesters. Each meeting required an appropriate greeting, which in turn required a rapid working out of various kin linkages between me and everyone else around me. While initially taxing, this process of personal kin reckoning allowed me to participate actively in one of the activities Ihanzu villagers enjoy most, and one they engage in on every possible occasion. Strangely, thanks to my 'mother,' I had 'become' a royal rainmaker.

During those initial months I continued to study Swahili, mapped nearby villages and households, drew kinship diagrams and even con-ducted a partial village survey in Kirumi – those things, in short, that anthropologists sometimes do in such situations.[2] As I came to know my new surroundings and relations and to make friends, I was increas-ingly invited to funerals, beer brewings, weddings, meals, and peanut-shelling get-togethers; I took part in house building, communal farm-ing and herding, and most anything else. As my fluency in Swahili improved, I began systematically to study the local language with the help of a Kirumi woman named Halima. We worked entirely through the Swahili language, in part because neither she nor anyone else I met in the area spoke English, in part because there were no vernacular grammar books or dictionaries. Everyone in my village and beyond was particularly delighted that I was trying to learn their language, and only wondered why my mother had not taught me more. Since my competency in Swahili has always surpassed my competency in the vernacular, most of the complex discussions I had during my stay were in Swahili. This might have proved more problematic were it not for the fact that virtually all villagers command both languages, readily translating and retranslating terms and concepts between them in everyday life, and that neither language can be seen as a storehouse of unadulterated, authentic meaning.

During this initial period I met Shabani, a middle-aged man from Kirumi, who would become my research assistant and good friend. Shabani could explain to me, in plain Swahili, the complexities of the kinship networks in which I was increasingly entangled; he could quickly fathom the (often silly) questions that anthropologists ask, and the disciplinary sense we sometimes make of the answers given; and he was a master of argumentation and eloquent summation, skills he routinely deployed at large village gatherings. Shabani also possessed what can only be described as an implausibly large mental Rolodex of anthropological contacts: whatever topic we wanted to investigate, he had a good idea who to speak with and, of equal importance, where that person could be found. His social networks spanned most of the eighteen Ihanzu villages, and we rarely had any difficulty locating dozens of people of different social categories to speak with on any given topic.[3]

Shabani participated in most of the interviews or, better, directed conversations I had with Ihanzu villagers, except for those I had with Ihanzu women about women's initiation and rain rites, and other 'women's topics' about which men are ostensibly unaware. I say 'ostensibly' because in practice such knowledge is widely shared (at least in outline form), even among local men; and in my case my patent maleness made little to no difference to the data I collected about 'women's issues.' This is because other social categories – ethnicity, colour, nationality – trump gender in this particular research setting, a fact equally attested to by the richness of the data my 'mother' collected in the 1960s on supposed 'men's issues.' Being a white foreigner determined the parameters and possibilities of my research far more than being male.

Arriving when I did during the dry season meant that I watched and waited, as did everyone, for the rain to arrive. By November and December, people's earlier relaxed attitudes had turned to concerns, one might even say obsessions, with the weather, drought, famine, and rainmaking. 'Obsessions' is not quite the right word, for it implies an unhealthy or unnatural fixation, which it was not. When the weather is everything – when it determines, in ways that nothing else can, what will grow and how much, whether and how long people will do migrant labour, whether it will be a feast or a famine year, whether some will live or die – it is unwise not to take such things very seriously. If my own urban upbringing meant this was not immediately obvious to me (as surely it must be to farmers the world over) this oversight was very quickly corrected.

By early February that first season, though a few light showers had come and gone, it was plain to all that the year was going to be a bad one. Villagers planted and farmed sporadically, but with little hope of seeing much of a harvest. They had carried out rain rites at the season's outset, but that had done little to please the spirits or bring rain. Throughout the season, they organized rain dances and ancestral offerings. Later they ferreted out rain witches. Many able-bodied men and women left the villages to do migrant labour in other parts of the country. In time, famine would follow. Regrettably, the next season I spent there, from 1994–1995, offered a depressing repeat performance. As a result, during those years, more by accident than design, I spent more time involved with villagers in rainmaking activities and discussions than in anything else. I have returned to Ihanzu for several summers since then, and these issues remain crucial today. The central preoccupation in my research, and this book, thus became Ihanzu rainmaking and the sense that Ihanzu men and women make of it.

I attended many rain rites during those two initial years in Ihanzu, most of them in Kirumi village where I lived. One particularly striking feature of those rites was the blatant or latent gendering of nearly everything relating to them: I found 'male' and 'female' rainstones, sticks, pots, hoes, spirits, celestial bodies, deities, and much more. Furthermore, in whatever form, male and female were said to possess certain characteristics and capabilities that could, when properly joined, bring rain. Even the rains, I was told, come in differently gendered pairs. (I later discovered in the library back home that such gendering is common across the continent.) I gradually came to see that the Ihanzu inhabit a cultural, social, and moral universe that is both permeated and animated by male and female forces and their joint transformative capacities: a rather different world, in certain respects, from my own. For the Ihanzu, gender is not just concerned with women and men. It is much more. How this is so is the subject of this book.

The ideas and practices surrounding Ihanzu rainmaking and gender discussed in this book are broadly shared by men and women, 'rich' and poor, young and old. This is not to say that all people in Ihanzu are the same, or hold identical beliefs, or do exactly the same things. That would be ridiculous. It is simply to claim that rainmaking rites and their inherent sexuality and gendering constitute the a priori world-as-it-is within which everyday life unfolds. They constitute an episteme, in Foucault's (1972, 1973) sense of the term, in that they frame knowledge and its conditions of possibility. This book takes as its subject this broad episteme rather than the everyday discussions that surround it (and that take place at a different analytic level). While it might have been anthropologically more de rigeur, just now, to dwell on discussions, disagreements, and debates, showing how 'individuals' have their own distinctive ideas that obstinately refuse to add up to anything shared, it is worth noting that people must agree at some level about the world-as-it-is – what it is, how it works – else they have nothing at all to discuss or disagree about in the first place. A world without some such form of agreement would be an utterly chaotic one.

Anthropologists do not simply report 'the facts'; they also, in so doing, unavoidably serve up explanations of them. Thus, my encounters with gendered rainmaking eventually led me to reflect on how anthropologists report and thereby explain 'gender symbolism' in Africa. None of the common explanations, however, was entirely satisfactory. One reason is because Euro-American understandings of gender are inextricably bound up with particular historical experiences surrounding women and men and their bodies – epistemologies, in a word, that guide social science enquiries, analyses and explanations in fundamental ways. The problem, this book suggests, is that such understandings have no social currency in Ihanzu; clearly, then, they cannot be meaningfully and straightforwardly used to 'make sense' of all peoples in all places. How do the women and men of Ihanzu understand and experience gender? What would gender look like if dislodged from its corporeal, bodily moorings? How are we to understand gender within and without bodies? What are the implications for anthropological theorizing and explanation? These are some of the questions addressed in the chapters that follow.

It is probably worth raising, up front, one obvious question about Ihanzu rainmaking rites: 'Do they work?' While not a question anthropologists normally ask, others, within the academy and without, often feel compelled to ask me whether Ihanzu rainmaking rites actually bring rain. I am never quite sure how to respond to this somewhat predictable, seemingly straightforward question, since many of the rain rites I attended (all of which were conducted in the rainy season) were, in fact, followed by rain. My usual response is: 'How should I know?' Rain rites appear to produce what they promise on at least some occasions – rites were performed; within minutes, hours, or days it rained – and in any case they fare no worse than do capitalism, psychoanalysis, and some prescription medicines at delivering on *their* promises. Those singularly obsessed with 'ultimate truth' should consult with analytic philosophers, theologians, and positivists, who largely share this preoccupation, and who operate within specific metaphysics that allow them to believe that definitively answering such questions is possible.

On a final note, though I claim sole authorship of this book, there are many others wittingly and unwittingly implicated in its production. First there are the many Ihanzu men and women who graciously devoted their time and effort to educating as best they could a rather unpromising outsider on life, the universe, and everything. Second, I thank the staff at the Tanzania National Archives (Dar es Salaam), Rhodes House (Oxford), the British Library of Political and Economic Science (London), and the Public Record Office (London), who assisted me during four months of archival work for this project. I also gratefully acknowledge a number of institutions for financing the book's research and writing over the years: the U.S. National Institute of Health (National Service Award), the University of London (Irwin Fund), the London School of Economics and Political Science (Malinowski Memorial Research Fund), the Royal Anthropological Institute (Radcliffe-Brown Trust Fund), the University of Cambridge (Fortes Fund), the Wenner-Gren Foundation for Anthropological Research (Richard Carley Hunt Fellowship), and the Canadian Social Science and Humanities Research Council (Subvention Grant). For allowing me to reprint portions of my previously published materials, I thank *Africa*, the International African Institute and Edinburgh University Press (chapter 3), *Journal of the Royal Anthropological Institute* and Blackwell Publishing (chapter 5) and *Cahiers d'études africaines* (chapter 6); and I thank the Nordic Africa Institute and the Scandinavian Institute of African Studies for allowing me to reprint a map from *Peoples and Production in Late Precolonial Africa* (Koponen 1988) which appears here as map 2.1. At the University of Toronto Press, I wish to thank Virgil Duff, who has been a pleasure to work with. And for assistance with photographic images, I owe thanks to Alison Dias at the University of Toronto. For their insightful comments and suggestions on various parts of the manuscript, all of which have improved the book immeasurably, I thank Misty Bastian, Pat Caplan, Lisa Hall, Henrietta Moore, Knut Myhre, Michael Lambek, Charlie Piot, Pat Sanders, Albert Schrauwers, Katherine Snyder, James Woodburn, and the anonymous reviewers for the University of Toronto Press. As ever, I alone am responsible for any remaining shortcomings.

Language and Orthography

Two principle languages are spoken in Ihanzu: Swahili, Tanzania's lingua franca, and the vernacular, Kĩnyihanzu. Both are classified as 'Bantu' languages. All Ihanzu grow up speaking the vernacular, and then learn Swahili in primary school. In everyday situations, villagers prefer their own language to Swahili, but they readily switch between the two in different contexts. Swahili is used exclusively at government meetings, in government offices, in courts, at church, and in the mosque. Swahili is also the preferred language for courting, (sometimes) for arguing, and for speaking to cattle and dogs.

There are five vowel sounds in Swahili and two additional ones in the Ihanzu language. These I represent as *a, e, i, o, u*, and *ĩ, ũ*. The first five are pronounced as they would be, say, in Spanish or Japanese. As D.V. Perrott says on the first page of her excellent *Teach Yourself Swahili*:

A is something like the *a* in *father*, but not quite so deep.
E is like the *a* in *say*, without the final sound we give it in English by slightly closing the mouth.
I is like the *e* in *be*. When unstressed it is the same sound as we make at the end of the English words *say* or *I*.
O is like the *o* in *hoe* before we begin to close the mouth at the end; very much like the first *o* in *Oho!*
U is like the *oo* in *too*; it is never like the *u* in *use* unless preceded by *y*.

The final two vowel sounds, which I write as *ĩ* and *ũ*, are not present in Swahili, only in the Ihanzu language. The use of tildes over these two additional vowels follows the Kikuyu language model. Thus:

Ĩ is like the *i* in *it*.
Ũ is like the *oo* in *cook*.

The consonants in the Ihanzu language are the same as in English, with a few exceptions. There is no *q* or *x*. As in many Bantu languages, there is no distinction between an *r* and an *l*, the sound being somewhere between the two, a midway point between an English *l* and a Spanish *r*. For consistency with earlier Ihanzu documents, anthropological and otherwise, I use an *l* to represent this sound.

The *ng'* sound (that is, *ng* with an apostrophe), common in Swahili and more so in the Ihanzu language, is pronounced like the *ng* sound in the word *sing*, and never as in the word *wrangle*.

The letter *z* in the Ihanzu language is normally pronounced as if it has a soft *d* before it, as with the *dz* sound in the English word *adze*. There is no hard *ch* sound in Ihanzu as in the English word *church*.

The stress in the Ihanzu language, as in Swahili, is normally on the penultimate syllable.

Finally, when I use apostrophes in the Ihanzu language (with the exception of the ng,' see above), I do so to indicate that a letter has been removed to render the transcription nearer the spoken language. For example, grammatically speaking the prepositional phrase 'to Ihanzu' would be written *kū Ihanzu* but it is heard as *Kihanzu*, which I therefore write as *k'Ihanzu*, to indicate the missing *ū*.

BEYOND BODIES:
RAINMAKING AND SENSE MAKING IN TANZANIA

Introduction: Rainmaking, Gender Epistemologies, and Explanation

Africa is an arid continent. Or at least this is true for vast expanses of it. Small wonder, then, that rainmaking practices have long proved crucial to countless people who live there, in the most diverse settings and circumstances. Yet for more than sixty years – since the 1943 publication of the Kriges' *The Realm of a Rain-Queen*, to be precise – anthropologists have largely forgotten this fact. This neglect, I hasten to add, is only partial. A few monographs on African rainmaking have appeared in recent decades.[1] But their number is negligible. For whatever reasons, and in spite of its ongoing importance for many ordinary people, rainmaking has not excited the minds or thrilled the hearts of anthropologists as many other topics plainly have. Indeed, compared with the vast corpus of anthropological writings on everything from African kinship to kingship, postcolonialism to neoliberalism, one could be forgiven for thinking that the weather and its practical management simply do not matter. This book focuses on rainmaking as the Ihanzu of Tanzania know it. As such, it serves as a reminder of the importance such practices have for many across Africa today.

The Ihanzu are a 30,000-strong Bantu-speaking people who are, in the main, farmers.[2] They live across eighteen villages in north-central Tanzania, the northernmost part of Singida District, an administrative area locals call 'Ihanzu.' Like many agricultural communities in Tanzania and beyond, the Ihanzu are entirely dependent on the rain for their survival. That the rain begins promptly and falls regularly each season – indeed, that it arrives and falls at all – is, quite literally, a matter of life or death. Without rain nothing grows. And without growth, people and animals wither and die.

Because the Ihanzu have long depended on the rain for their very *recent?*

existence, it is not surprising to discover that rainmaking is central, both conceptually and practically, to their everyday lives. They have two royal rainmakers – one male, the other female – whose joint job it is to ensure the rains arrive on time and fall properly each year. Ihanzu rainmakers have done this for more than a century. Through varied rain rites carried out each year in the central village of Kirumi, royal rainmakers regulate the annual movement from the dry 'male' season (*kīpasu*) to the wet 'female' one (*kītikū*) and back again. These rites take on varied forms, as we shall see in the chapters that follow, and are crucial to men and women across the land.

I knew none of this when I began my research; rainmaking, quite simply, was not on my academic radar.[3] When I first arrived in Tanzania in the early 1990s, my aim was to write a rather different book, a book on Ihanzu spatial organization. I planned to explore how cultural meanings are attributed to spaces and how those meanings are (re)produced, negotiated, and altered through everyday and ritual practices (Thornton 1980; H.L. Moore 1986; Cohen and Odhiambo 1989; Parkin 1991). These concerns arose from particular Western academic debates about 'structure' and 'agency' and how we theorize the relationship between them. That book never materialized. Instead, as sometimes happens, everyday life got in the way.

As the months passed in Ihanzu and my skills at negotiating day-to-day life in the local languages sharpened, my attention gradually and irretrievably turned from spatiality and Western academic debates about the locus of historical change towards other matters that were clearly more pressing; more pressing, that is, for the men and women of Ihanzu. These were drought and rainmaking.

Drought is common in Ihanzu, as across the region (Brooke 1967; Maddox 1986, 1988, 1990; Rigby 1969, 20–1; Ten Raa 1968). Both years I lived there were drought years. For this reason, the issue of the weather was difficult – actually impossible – for me or anyone else living in Ihanzu at the time to ignore. Many men and women left the villages during those years to carry out long- and short-term migrant labour in other parts of Tanzania, something they and their neighbours have done since colonial times (Adam 1963a; Iliffe 1979, 161). Other villagers stayed. And those who did so spent enormous amounts of time discussing the rain, or more correctly, the lack of rain. When would it arrive? How and where would it fall? From which direction would it come? How long would it last? What type of rain would it be?

This ongoing conversation, I eventually came to understand, was far from the familiar, prosaic weather-talk so common among Americans and the English. Rather, the Ihanzu speak of the weather not because of its virtual irrelevance to the grander scheme of life, but due to its overriding influence on human affairs. For the agricultural Ihanzu, weather matters.

But rain was not merely worth discussing. It was also something that could be acted purposively upon, something the many rain rites I attended constantly impressed upon me. If, during those years the lack of rain drove people from the villages in search of work in distant parts of Tanzania, it also compelled those who remained to conduct rain rites with increasing fervour, and with increasing despair. Rain rites at the royal rainshrine (ch. 4), women's rain dances (ch. 5), ancestral offerings for rain (ch. 6), and rain-witchcraft trials (ch. 7) – all of these occupied increasing amounts of villagers' time and resources. Under the circumstances, to ignore the rain and rainmaking rites would have been both difficult and disingenuous – all the more so, I might add, when one considers people's typical reaction to my presence in the villages.

When I explained to men and women that I had come to learn and to write a book about them, many spontaneously launched into histories of Ihanzu rainmaking, royal rainmakers, the rites they conducted and the powers they held and hold today (ch. 2). It soon became apparent that for the people of Ihanzu, rainmaking is much more than mere rituals that purportedly cause water to fall from the sky. It is also inextricably linked to a host of other issues: good and evil, the living and the dead, human and divine, royals and commoners, male and female. In short, however one looks at it, rainmaking features centrally in the Ihanzu cultural imagination and forms a practical part of their daily lives (cf. Feierman 1990, ch. 10; Packard 1981). So if it is true, as Evans-Pritchard (1940) would have us believe, that one cannot properly understand the Nuer without also understanding cattle, then this may equally be said of the importance of rainmaking for understanding the Ihanzu. For the many women and men of the area I have come to know through the years, to write a book about the Ihanzu is to write a book about rainmaking. It can scarcely be otherwise.

Consequently, from its early stages, this book has been guided more by Ihanzu sensibilities than anthropological fixations. Concerned first and foremost with Ihanzu rainmaking, it is, above all, a book that would please the people of Ihanzu themselves – at least that is my hope – were they to read it.[4] In this sense, my particular narrative is not just 'a pretext for a comment about something else, some other place, some other people' (Mbembe 2001, 3). It is, I believe, a book that many Ihanzu themselves might have written had they the time and inclination, and had they shared my own anthropological and theoretical preoccupations (cf. Strathern 1988, 309). It is a book that would 'make sense' to them.

Rainmaking and Sense Making

Be that as it may, Ihanzu sense is not anthropological sense. Nor can the two be rendered identical. Thus, if this book is about Ihanzu rainmaking, it must also be about the different explanations or projects of sense making that surround the topic. These include both anthropological and Ihanzu projects, dissimilar though they are, and crucially, how the latter can productively complicate the former. First, a bit about anthropological explanations.

The ways Africanist anthropologists have made sense of rainmaking – their concerns, questions, and answers – have varied a good deal through the years. This means that the 'really interesting question' about African rainmaking, whatever it has been at whatever time, has not remained constant, but has changed and kept pace with broader disciplinary concerns. Naturally, so, too, have the explanations given and the senses produced.

In the early 1900s, scholars asked whether people involved in African rainmaking were rational, or simply following customs that through some minor miracle had been caught in a time warp and catapulted into the 'modern,' colonial era. Some attempted to make sense of rainmaking by suggesting that it was characteristic of primitive, magical thinking that misunderstood cause-and-effect relations. Others disputed this. By the 1930s and 1940s, scholars had lost interest in such questions and the answers they invited, particularly following the publication of Evans-Pritchard's *Witchcraft, Oracles, and Magic among the Azande* in 1937, which demonstrated that supposedly 'primitive' thought was, in fact, rational all along.[5] Today, no right-minded anthropologist would argue that African rainmaking points to an 'irrational' or 'primitive' mindset. The suggestion, rather, would be that African rainmaking differs little from other religious practices such as, say, praying to Jesus or Allah for rain.

From the 1940s, attempts to make sense of African rainmaking shifted focus from (ir)rational mentalities to functional contexts. The most outstanding example along these lines is undoubtedly Krige and Krige's (1943) tome. This book details, like no other, nearly everything under the sun about the South African Lovedu: landscape; subsistence activities; economic, political, and legal systems; social organization; childrearing; marriage and social structure; illness and health; witchcraft and sorcery; 'tribal' attitudes; culture contact and change; and, of course, rain rites and beliefs (among other topics). In this context, rainmaking made sense because it formed part of a broader set of everyday relations and practices in which everything was connected to everything else. Everything, as it were, 'functioned.'

The concept of 'function' no longer occupies the position it once did in anthropology. Nor, these days, does it serve as an adequate anthropological explanation for rainmaking (or for that matter, for anything else). Anthropologists and others today employ different theoretical frameworks, ask different questions, and give different explanations for African rainmaking.

Some attend to the politics of precipitation, raising questions about how rainmaking is implicated in or serves as an idiom for politics, conflict, and historical change (Packard 1981; Lan 1985; Feierman 1990).[6] In so doing, in various ways, these scholars attempt to make sense of rainmaking through political and historical contextualization, while engaging in broader debates in the social sciences about the relation between structure and agency, change and stasis, the symbolic and the material, among others. Other recent scholars have focused on the symbolism and cosmologies that surround and underpin rainmaking practices. While speaking to, among other things, Durkheim's problem of the relationship between society and religion – a problem that arguably has never left anthropology – these scholars suggest that rainmaking makes sense because it forms part of a broader system of cultural meanings and values (e.g., Jacobson-Widding 2000, 178–97; Kaspin 1996).[7]

Yet, whether from yesterday or yesteryear, and whatever the type of 'sense' or explanation on offer, writings on rainmaking have often been compelled to grapple with one issue in particular: gender, sexual, and fertility symbolism. This is because African rainmaking is and always has been pregnant, so to speak, with gender, sexual, and fertility motifs. In many cases and many places, rainmaking implements of all sorts – pots, drums, statuettes, sticks, and stones – are described as 'male' and 'female,' and their ritual combinations are said to produce rain. Specified sexual relations are required or prohibited before, during, and/or after rain ceremonies. Rain songs, dances, and ancestral addresses employ 'obscene' behaviour and commonly play on themes of gender, sexuality and fertility. Cosmologies and ecologies that encompass varied rainmaking practices are gendered through and through. In some locales the weather, the seasons, and the rains themselves are considered 'male' and 'female,' and their appropriate cooperation and combination is required to ensure fertility. To be sure, in different anthropological works at different moments these themes come in and out of focus, and take on greater or lesser analytic importance, depending on the exact questions scholars have asked and attempted to answer. But the motifs are nevertheless ubiquitous. Rainmaking, however one slices it, goes hand in hand with sex, gender, and fertility all across sub-Saharan Africa.[8] The Ihanzu case is no different.

For Africanists this is probably unremarkable. This is partly because rainmaking rites are fertility rites, and it would be strange indeed if fertility themes did not feature conspicuously in them. But it is equally because Africanists – especially Africanist anthropologists – have long noted such motifs in a host of ritual and everyday realms all across the continent. Be it in initiation or healing rites, in culinary practices or homestead design, in life forces or life courses, themes of gender, sexuality, and fertility – as far as most Africanists are concerned – were always already there. In this respect, rainmaking is not unique and bears directly on a broader problem in the social sciences of how we make sense of the blatant and latent gender, sexual and fertility symbolism found in a range of ethnographic and historical settings.

Contemporary Africanists, including anthropologists, have generally explained such things in two ways. Both explanations turn on contextualization of a certain kind, which analysts produce by demonstrating connections between realms that at first glance seem quite distinct. And for both types of explanation, the 'really interesting question' and therefore the answers it elicits, springs from broader anthropological and social science sensibilities of the moment. Today these revolve around bodies and metaphors.

The first type of explanation begins with human bodies, their physiological properties and potentialities, and suggests that these are mapped onto other realms or domains by means of metaphor, metonym, and/or symbol (e.g., Taylor 1992; Broch-Due 1993; Devisch 1993; Werbner 1990; Willis 1991, 272; Emanatian 1996). We all have bodies, so goes the argument, and we thus use them – or rather the bodily understandings we derive from inhabiting them – to create and give meaning to the cultural worlds in which they exist. Through metaphor, we link 'the realm of ideation with those of affect and feeling' (Beidelman 1993, 6); we map our bodily knowledge onto the world around us (e.g., Lakoff and Johnson 1980). It follows that because women and men can together produce children, and because this is a well-known fact, procreation serves as a base metaphor – a 'procreative paradigm,' in Eugenia Herbert's (1993) words – for other transformative acts and activities. By this logic, African rainmaking with all its sexual, gender, and fertility symbolism makes sense because it 'evokes bodily experience' (Feierman 1990: 82) and mimics sexual reproduction.[9] This type of explanation has much in common with those of earlier anthropologists who also argued that the body, sexual relations, and procreation served as a privileged domain of symbolic classification (Turner 1967; Needham 1973).

Another way Africanists have made sense of gendered rituals and life worlds has both continuities and discontinuities with the first. On the one hand, these scholars are less persuaded by the idea that bodily experiences can precede other experiences in and of the world. The difficulty here is, because we all inhabit and come to terms with our world simultaneously, it is hard to imagine how anyone, anywhere, might apprehend one cultural domain – such as the body or procreation – prior to any other (see, e.g., Bourdieu 1990). This means that the body cannot serve as the origin of symbolic classification; people do not come to know their bodies first, and then simply transpose those understandings onto the world around them. Accordingly, while these second sorts of explanations attend to the body, they refuse to see the body as primary, as something that precedes all else. This point aside, these explanations are similar to others in their attention to how metaphor, metonym, and/or symbol, link different domains and, in so doing, 'explain.' Many thus situate the body and human sexuality within a broader set of relations in which everything is homologous, metaphoric, or symbolic of everything else within a particular universe of values and meanings (e.g., Comaroff 1985; H.L. Moore 1986; Weiss 1996; Feldman-Savelsberg 1999; Jacobson-Widding 2000; Gausset 2002).[10] By this reasoning, human sexuality and rainmaking can be 'explained' by their relations within broader social and cosmic schemas: human 'physiological conditions make more sense in light of the corresponding cosmological conditions' (Kaspin 1996, 570), as well as the reverse.

As many such writings convincingly show, there are plenty of places across sub-Saharan Africa where the body reigns supreme and where our interlocutors say so; and places where people explain, in so many words, that making iron, pots, and rain, and other things is homologous, symbolic or metaphoric of human procreation and that this in fact 'explains' them. We know, after all, that in some contexts metaphors work. A difficulty arises, however, when – as happens in Ihanzu – our interlocutors flatly deny such explanations.

On one hot mid-January day in 1995, in discussion with a middle-aged Ihanzu woman from Ibaga village about rainmakers, rainmaking, and 'traditions,' I asked why there were 'male' and 'female' rainstones or rainsticks at all. 'To bring rain,' she tersely replied, as if this were obvious. Unperturbed, I leadingly asked whether these might somehow be related to men's and women's anatomical differences and human sexual reproduction, whether this is why they 'made sense.' 'No,' she replied. 'They are different. One makes rain. The other makes babies.' I persisted, pointing out a number of other 'symbolic' or 'metaphoric' links that any anthropologist might reasonably draw between differently gendered celestial bodies, rainmakers, rainstones, rainsticks, and so on in order to 'explain' them. Might these have something to do with why there are male and female rainstones and rainsticks? 'That's an interesting idea,' she replied noncommittally. 'I guess there are similarities.'

Over the years, I have had many similar conversations with many people in Ihanzu. These conversations suggest, time and again, that women's and men's understandings of gendered and sexualized rainmaking rites concern gender, but lie beyond bodies. Of course some villagers like the woman above will, when pressed, agree to parallels between non-human gendered productive processes and human sexual reproduction. Yet this does not 'explain' anything in that context. For the men and women of Ihanzu, rainmaking does not make sense because it symbolizes, metaphorizes, or evokes other things. Gendered rainmaking implements are not rendered locally sensible because they are 'like' sexed bodies; their combinations do not evoke, symbolize, or metaphorize sexual intercourse or procreation. Rather, in Ihanzu eyes, rainmaking makes sense because it brings rain; and its gendering and sexual combinations are the means by which this is accomplished.

If this sort of 'sense' appears tautological, banal, and therefore anthropologically uninteresting, it also points up the very real chasm that sometimes exists between local and anthropological projects of sense making. For even when our interlocutors insist that male and female rain horns *are* male and female and together bring rain (Berglund 1976, 54), or that rainstones *are* male and female and are themselves 'capable of reproducing' (Avua 1968, 29), our anthropological sensibilities can lead us to deny such claims, to seek out a more sensible sense beneath the apparent nonsense. Indeed, an entire social science vocabulary serves this purpose: such statements are said to serve as idioms for, to evoke, symbolize, metaphorize, dramatize, resonate with, speak to, and so on. These vocabularies and their theoretical entailments insist that our informants' statements simply cannot be true. They must mean something else. After all, everyone knows that male and female bodies are real, as are their reproductive capabilities, whereas anything else gendered is but a pale imitation. This book's heresy is to entertain the idea that, when my Ihanzu interlocutors say and do things about rainmaking rites and the non-human gender forms that infuse them, they actually mean it.[11] To say as much raises serious questions about how we understand African epistemologies, as well as the extent to which anthropologists and other social scientists have been (un)able to think beyond bodies and metaphors in our analytic frameworks – when necessary – in an effort to understand non-human gendering and reproductive processes.

Ihanzu Gendered Worlds

As we shall see throughout this book, the Ihanzu world is permeated and animated by masculine and feminine forces – in a word, by 'gender.' This, however, is not simply to state the obvious: that Ihanzu women and men live together and thus constitute, quite literally, the social and cultural universe they inhabit. Much more than this, it is to point out that Ihanzu notions of male/masculine (*gohaa*) and female/feminine (*sũngũ*) and the relations between them provide villagers with a practical framework that both structures their world and allows them to act meaningfully upon it. Integral to this world are differently gendered pairs: seasons, spirits and celestial bodies, rainmakers, rituals, rainstones, and rains. And much more. Clearly, gender in this context is not synonymous with women and men or with cultural constructions of them. Rather, it concerns itself with broader male and female principles and with relations between the two that go well beyond and subsume such constructions. Male and female are features of and between human bodies. But they are also features found within and without those bodies. Crucial here is the fact that while male and female bodies form part of an Ihanzu gender epistemology, they are not central to it. All genders, human and non-human, are of a kind and feature equally alongside one another. Bodies, in this vision, do not provide the ultimate reference point for all else.

Because the Ihanzu world is permeated by male and female forces in various forms, it is fertile and productive. When male and female combine, things happen. But not any combination will do. Male and female evince themselves in different ways in different contexts, and the Ihanzu hold no monolithic views on gender relations: the relations between male and female are never once-and-for-all decided. Instead, particular gender configurations come to the fore in particular contexts and moments. Sometimes male is considered superior to female. Other times the reverse is true. Yet when it comes to unleashing the genders' joint generative powers – and this applies to producing rain, children, pots, iron, and other things – only the equal and complementary combination of male and female will do. This latter productive combination I call 'gender complementarity,' and it is key to understanding all Ihanzu rainmaking rites.

Gender complementarity, then, is about productive mixing or transformative combinations. And it is the same for all gendered, generative practices, human and non-human alike. During rainmaking rites, participants attempt to combine male and female as equal and complementary parts of a pair; each gender comprises half of a potentially productive, transformative whole. When joined as complementary equals, male and female in the form of bodies and/or ritual artefacts can change the world. They can bring rain.

Because an Ihanzu epistemology of gender encompasses human and non-human forms alike and does not prioritize one over the other, non-human gender forms do not 'explain themselves' vis-à-vis men's and women's bodies. Nor does the genders' ritual combination 'symbolize,' 'metaphorize' or 'dramatize' sexual intercourse – not, at least, from a local point of view. In fact, in Ihanzu eyes, the gender and sexual symbolism (so-called) that gives definitive shape to rain rites does not in practice represent or mean anything at all. It is the real thing. The question one must therefore ask is not simply what and how gendered material objects represent, but *whether* they represent. For here, quite simply, they do not. Anthropological explanations surrounding material objects have often failed to ask such questions, in part owing to an overreliance on analytic models that privilege language and meaning (see Keane 2005; Myhre 2006); and given a number of pretheoretical commitments that underpin Euro-American understandings of the body, gender, metaphor and the nature of explanation itself.

I am suggesting, first, that the Ihanzu do not come to know bodies prior to anything else, and that bodies do not sit central to an Ihanzu gender epistemology. Bodies therefore are not and cannot be mapped onto other things – such as rainmaking rites – in order to 'explain' them. Second, the men and women of Ihanzu do not find homology, metaphor, or symbolism adequate 'explanation' for why rainmaking rites are gendered through and through. Nor, in Ihanzu eyes, do the notions of metaphor, symbol, or homology 'explain' much about why the genders' combinations are potentially productive; why, that is, they can bring rain. Instead, non-human gender forms and their complementary combinations make sense not because they stand in particular relation to other similarly gendered material forms, but because they do what they do.

Explanations of this sort are referred to as teleological. They contextualize and hence explain not by demonstrating interconnections or congruences among gendered bodies and material objects and the known world, but by pointing to causal links between gendered rain rites and their product: rain.

Yet fertility, sexual, and gender 'symbolism' has been conceptualized, recorded, and theorized in Euro-American scholarship according to a different logic. This logic starts and ends with the body and metaphor. It works in the present, linking disparate gendered forms in a fragmented world in order to 'explain.' Such projects of contextualisation, understanding, and explanation are underpinned by a particular 'style of reasoning' (Hacking 1982; also Hastrup 2004), one that springs from a specific set of Euro-American certainties surrounding the body, gender, metaphor, and explanation.[12] These certainties have made it difficult, sometimes impossible, for social scientists to make sense of 'gender' and 'gender symbolism' in Africa without thinking of and through bodies. In order to think about gender beyond bodies, as the men and women of Ihanzu do, we must first unravel the Euro-American epistemology of gender that underpins and informs much social science theorizing and explanation.

Euro-American Gender Epistemologies and Analytic Negativities

> Talking about gender for most people is the equivalent of fish talking about water. Gender is so much the routine ground of everyday activities that questioning its taken-for-granted assumptions and presuppositions is like thinking about whether the sun will come up.   (Lorber 1994, 13)

> Gender, like beauty, is often in the eye of the beholder.
> (Oyewumi 1997, xv)

Gender, like other concepts, forms part of an ongoing intellectual and social project anchored firmly in Europe and North America and, increasingly, in other parts of the world (Manuh 2007; Amadiume 1997; Grosz-Ngaté 1997, 9; Visweswaran 1997). Consequently, the study of gender has been dominated by a Euro-American epistemology with its own categories and concerns. But how useful are these Euro-American certainties for making sense of other epistemologies from different times and places?

Oyèrónké Oyewumi raises this question in *The Invention of Women: Making an African Sense of Western Gender Discourses* (1997; see also 2003, 11ff). In precolonial Yorùbá land, Oyewumi argues, 'the social categories "man" and "woman" were nonexistent, and hence no gender system was in place' (1997, 31). Precolonial Yorùbá social organization was based on seniority, not gender; and 'precolonial Yorùbá cultural logic did not use the human body as the basis of social ranking' (Oyewumi 1997, xii). Bodies were just bodies, no more. Oyewumi then suggests that gender was 'invented' for the Yorùbá through the colonial gaze and policies, since Western social thought is underpinned by 'body-reasoning' or 'bio-logic': Euro-American epistemic reasoning or logic wherein bodies are seen as 'the site and cause of differences and hierarchies in society' (Oyewumi 1997, 7–8).[13] In this way Oyewumi challenges the Euro-American epistemic assumption that sex everywhere constructs gender. The corollary is that scholars who subscribe to a Euro-American episteme have mistaken western cultural concerns for universal truths and in so doing have invented the very category – gender – they seek to explain.

Oyewumi's argument is not without its problems (see Peel 2002; Boris 2007, 193–4; Matory 2003). Among other questions, we might ask how anyone, anywhere, at any time, could possibly apprehend raw biological bodies unfettered by sociocultural blinkers. Yet her insis-

tence that we seriously consider the implications of differing epistemological frameworks for understanding gender has significant heuristic
value.

Marilyn Strathern is another anthropologist who has long been
engaged in such destabilizing projects. Using insights derived from
Melanesian ethnography, she has repeatedly critiqued Euro-American
analytic concepts and commonplaces, probing the analytic metaphors
we live by, showing how such metaphors can hinder our understandings of alternative ways of knowing and ways of being in the world. In
The Gender of the Gift (1988), she deftly deconstructs key anthropological concepts such as 'society,' 'individual,' 'gift,' 'commodity,' and
'gender,' arguing that these are ill-suited metaphors for theorizing
known social worlds that are not premised on the same metaphors.
Though Strathern's project is not without precedent – anthropologists
have long admonished one another to see things 'from the native's
point of view' – she has taken this longstanding project to new heights,
seeking continually and creatively to forge an epistemic space at the
analytic crossroads of Melanesian, anthropological, and feminist
projects of sense making.

At the core of Strathern's project sits a series of negativities or
negative strategies (Strathern 1988; 1990). These sometimes manifest
themselves as familiar anthropological negations: for instance, her
suggestion that Hageners of Highland New Guinea do not share with
Westerners a nature/culture divide (Strathern 1980); and that they do
not define the sexes, as do other Melanesian societies, through initiation or puberty rites. Yet such suggestions provide Strathern with a
starting rather than an ending point to raise more profound negativities
about metaphorization in metropole theory and the production of
anthropological knowledge. These negativities are not meant simply to
say 'they don't do it like we do.' They instead aim to disrupt and dis-
place our own ways of thinking and theorizing about the world. By
exploring Ihanzu rainmaking and gender epistemologies, and by questioning certain pretheoretical commitments that are central to the Euro-
American episteme, this book follows such a Strathernian strategy of
negation. One of its primary goals is to stop us thinking and theorizing
in particular ways about gender. There are several Euro-American commonplaces about gender in Africa that call for such negations, and to
which we must now turn our attention. To demonstrate persuasively
that such thinking underpins a Euro-American epistemology, not just a
remote corner of it, requires a broad sweep across a range of scholarly
concerns with gender.

Gender as Women and Men

Much has been written about gender in Africa, if by this we mean – as many do – women and men and the relations between them. Gender, as a topic of academic inquiry, has become more prominent since the 1960s and 1970s: a time when feminism, civil rights, and other social movements for equality in Europe and America were increasingly pressing themselves onto public agendas. Such movements sparked interest in assessing a number of issues, key among them, the roles and status of African women and men, women's position in society, women's subordination, power, and agency (Hodgson and McCurdy 1996; Hoehler-Fatton 1996; Mikell 1997; Kaplan 1997; Geiger 1997; Turshen and Twagiramariya 1998; Berger and White 1999; Agbasiere 2000; Hassin 2003; Kolawole 2004; Tamale 2004; Cliggett 2005; Kachapila 2006).[14]

Of late, some Africanist scholars have taken issue with earlier feminist scholarship, noting that '"gender" has tended to be conceived as synonymous or coterminous with "women"' (Lindsay and Mieschev 2003; Ouzgane and Morrell 2005; Manicom 1992, 443; Beidelman 1997, 22; Gutmann 1997, 385). The danger here, some have noted, is the tendency both to essentialize 'women' and simultaneously to ignore other social categories that can be equally relevant to explaining structural inequalities. This is why many poststructuralist Africanist scholars no longer focus on gender in isolation – as women and/or men and the relationship between them – but rather on how it articulates with and is conditioned by other social categories such as ethnicity, 'race,' nationality, class and generation (Declich 2000; Greene 1996; Hodgson 1999, 2005; Sunseri 1997; Goheen 1996).

Euro-American assumptions that gender must somehow be about women, or about women and men and the relationship between them and other social categories, pose particular problems. For one thing, such presumptions frequently mean that the categories 'man' and 'woman' are treated as ontological givens rather than as categories that require explanation. Gender appears to be about bodies and to be housed unproblematically within those bodies. It also appears to be about power relations, usually of an asymmetrical ilk, between men and women. Yet an Ihanzu gender epistemology invites us to imagine what gender might look like if it were not confined narrowly to women's and men's bodies or to the relationship between them. For the Ihanzu, male and female forces, while always relational, can operate within *and* without human forms. They can evince themselves at different moments as dual genders within single bodies, as single genders within opposite-sexed bodies, and as genders without bodies. To assume a priori that gender must somehow be about men and women and/or the relationships between them is to disallow such understandings. One negativity that the Ihanzu case therefore advises is that we 'stop thinking that an opposition between male and female must be about the control of men and women over each other' (Strathern 1988, 15). Ihanzu men and women, of course, can and do exercise certain powers over each other. But to limit an exploration of gender to an exploration of these powers would be unnecessarily restrictive and would seriously miscast alternative metaphysics of gender. For the Ihanzu, gender is more than mere bodies and how they control each other.

Gender, Sex, and Bodies

Another way Africanist scholars have broached the topic of gender is through Euro-American preoccupations with the relation between gender, sex, and bodies. In its own way, for its own reasons, this strain of literature also summons its own negations.

The story that anthropologists and other social scientists tell about sex and gender is a familiar one. In the 1970s and 1980s, feminist anthropologists and other scholars distinguished between 'sex' and 'gender' (Ortner and Whitehead 1981b; MacCormack and Strathern 1980; Reiter 1975). The idea was that differently sexed bodies provided the natural biological basis upon which cultural constructions of gender were built. The body – sex – was everywhere the same. The cultural sense that people made of bodies – gender – was not, and varied from one society to the next. Sex did not determine gender. It did, however, provide the physiological foundation for gender's multiple cultural elaborations. Built on the natural facts of biological differences between men and women, gender concerned itself with what society made of those facts: with men's and women's roles and statuses in society and their various symbolic elaborations. These understandings of sex and gender became the prevailing orthodoxy across the social sciences throughout the 1970s and 1980s (Moore 1988).

Ifi Amadiume's well-known *Male Daughters, Female Husbands: Gender and Sex in an African Society* (1987) provides a good Africanist example of such a project, even if she wishes to deny the influence of Western scholarship on her thinking. In precolonial times, Amadiume argues, the traditional Igbo of eastern Nigeria distinguished between biological sex and gender constructions. This allowed for a degree of gender flexibility where, depending on one's social status and achievements, a woman could become male gendered, a man female gendered. With the advent of colonialism, however, ethnocentric and racist British colonialists (and later, ethnocentric and racist Western feminists and anthropologists) imposed biological reductionist views on the Igbo, collapsing and concretizing what was formerly a fluid sex–gender system. Thus sexed bodies were conflated with gender constructs of them and 'a woman was always female regardless of her social achievements or status' (Amadiume 1987, 119). Westerners impoverished and fixed the categories 'man' and 'woman' by reducing gender to biology.

More recently, poststructuralist scholars have recast sex–gender debates in a more Foucauldian light by reversing earlier commonplaces. If feminist scholars previously argued that sex created gender – however indirectly – then it was suggested in the 1980s and 1990s that biological sex was itself a product of the cultural imagination, the result of a particular discursive formation. Thus, no longer can the human body be seen as an acultural artefact around which people then spin webs of gender significance. Rather, 'almost everything one wants to say about sex – however sex is understood – already has in it a claim about gender' (Laqueur 1990, 11; Yanagisako and Collier 1987; cf. Douglas 1982 [1970], 70). From this poststructuralist perspective, sex or bodies are produced by gender, not the reverse (Butler 1990; 1993; Butchart 1998). Sex was gender all along, even if an earlier generation of feminist scholars failed to realize it.

Although on balance, Africanists have shown little enthusiasm for feminist debates about gender, sex, and bodies, much Africanist scholarship has been predicated on poststructuralist sensibilities about gender, even prior to the advent of poststructuralism in the social sciences. This is clear from an older literature on woman-woman marriage and homosexuality (Evans-Pritchard 1951, 1970; Herskovits 1937; Krige and Krige 1943); as well as from writings on initiation rites that suggested decades ago that bodies, gender, and personhood are socially created rather than biologically given; that they are not the natural product of life but the social product of life-cycle rituals (e.g., Richards 1956; Turner 1969; S.F. Moore 1976). Recent Africanist writings on initiation, morality, and power raise similar issues – albeit in novel lexicons – surrounding the production of social identities and/or gender subject formation. Such de-essentializing projects aim to show how gendered identities and subjectivities are ritually (re)defined and (re)negotiated; how they are worked at, configured, transformed, and given meaning in specific sociohistorical settings (Kratz 1994; Broch-Due 1993; Blystad 1999; Power and Watts 1999; Heald 1999; Beidelman 1997). Other projects have detailed how gender intersects with other social categories such as ethnicity, race, class, and generation, and/or (from a more Foucauldian viewpoint) how men and women are variously created, conditioned, and colonized by specific regimes of power (Comaroff 1985; Goheen 1996; S. Greene 1996; Hodgson 2001; Hodgson and McCurdy 2001; H.L. Moore and Vaughan 1994; Stambach 2000).[15]

In Africa or elsewhere, such theorizing on gender, sex, and the body has not taken place in a vacuum. Rather, it has produced and been produced by a series of ongoing concerns in the social sciences and has been underpinned by a set of pretheoretical commitments that derive from a Euro-American episteme. These projects routinely begin with the body and gender representations and plumb the relation between the two. In the process, they implicitly or explicitly speak to familiar Western binaries: nature and culture, essentialism and constructivism, material and moral, social and symbolic, real and ideal, among others. What is more, the arguments around such binaries are commonly framed as arguments about origin points (Errington 1990, 10): where 1970s feminist scholars aimed to show how sex created gender, poststructuralist scholars argue the opposite. Collectively, this literature tends to identify 'real' material bodies – sex – and 'ideal' cultural constructs of them – gender – and to argue about which produces which in a complex world.

These analytic preoccupations have had two unfortunate effects on our ability to theorize gender in Africa. The first is to render 'gender' as something ethereal: as a discourse, a representation, an ideal or cultural construction of something else. The second is the insistence that that 'something else' is and must be the human form. Gender, it follows, is only interesting insofar as it can be causally related to women's and men's bodies, even if scholars disagree over what exactly that causal relationship is. The Ihanzu epistemology complicates such assumptions.

The Ihanzu cultural world comprises many non-human material gender forms, especially when it comes to rainmaking. Consider, for a moment, male and female rains. These are just as real and material as are male and female bodies. And it is not obvious that Ihanzu villagers apprehend bodies and their biological potentialities prior to other cultural artefacts such as gendered rains. The reverse could equally be true. Ihanzu boys and girls, after all, grow up understanding that male and female rains productively combine and jointly ensure fertility long before they understand the minutiae of human sexual intercourse and reproduction. For a time, in other words, gendered rains are meaningful and potent *not* because they evoke sexed bodies and sexual intercourse but because they *are* male and female and potent in their own right. The relation between the human form and other things gendered is not, in this case, the issue of interest. Indeed, there is no such relation to be established.

The noteworthy point is that in Ihanzu eyes, bodies need not sit conceptual centre stage to understand gender; non-human gender forms need not be 'explained' by their relation to human bodies; gender can be materialized in many artefacts, of which human bodily forms provide but one example. Thus by insisting that gender only has meaning in relation to sexed bodies, it appears that many scholars have mistaken Euro-American preoccupations for universal ones. As Oyewumi (1997) has noted, not everyone is equally vexed by questions of whether sex creates gender or gender creates sex. From an Ihanzu viewpoint, gendered rains are meaningful quite independent of sexed bodies. So while social scientists, including anthropologists, may invent such questions and relations as analytic fictions in an effort to 'explain' such things, we must remember that these explanations make self-referential sense within a Euro-American epistemic framework but not necessarily within alternative metaphysics.

The fundamental negativity that we must apply to this literature, then, is to stop ourselves from thinking that gender is an ethereal construction of more foundational material bodies, or a discourse impressed onto them. The Ihanzu epistemology of gender detailed in this book raises the possibility of thinking about material gender forms without thinking of or through male and female bodies. In this sense, the book aims to decentre the body from our analytic frames: no simple feat, to be sure, given the multifronted efforts in recent years to recentre it through concerns with subjectivities, embodiment, and agency, among many others, as refracted through phenomenological, poststructural, practice, and praxis lenses (see Bourdieu 1977; Blacking 1977; Lock 1993; Stoller 1995; Sharp 2000; Geurts 2002; Wolputte 2004). From an Ihanzu perspective, gender is not simply an ideal construction of something more material, foundational, and 'real,' such as bodies; nor is it a discourse imprinted onto bodies; rather, it is itself material and constitutive of that reality – within and without bodies. Indeed, as we shall now see, it is the genders' very materiality that enables them to combine and makes things happen, not just between human bodies but also within and without them.

Reproduction, Symbolism, and Metaphor

If a Euro-American epistemology of gender and its pretheoretical underpinnings has shaped anthropological projects on women and men, sex and the body, it has also dominated anthropological sensibilities and projects concerned with gender and sexual 'symbolism,' and ritual in Africa. The Ihanzu case suggests that certain negativities be applied here as well.

Africanists have long known that gender, fertility, and (re)productive processes feature conspicuously across the continent. Whether in initiation rites (Richards 1956; Beidelman 1964; Krige 1968), circumcision rites (Marwick 1968; Sanderson 1955), dances (Johnson 1954, 140; Ten Raa 1969), rites for twins (Cory 1944) divination (Campbell 1968; Eiselen 1932; Watt and Warmelo 1930; Laydevant 1933), or rainmaking (Sanders 2002), gender and reproductive 'symbolism' were always in evidence. Contemporary Africanists, too, continue to show how gender forms part of a complex interweaving of natural, social, and cosmological forces and worlds (Devisch 1993; Feldman-Savelsberg 1999; Beidelman 1993, 1997; Berglund 1976; Comaroff 1985; Kratz 1994; H.L. Moore 1986; Bourdieu 2001; Green 1999; Sheridan 2002). For whatever else Africanists have wanted to say about ritual, culture, and cosmos, they could scarcely have avoided the topic of gender. For this reason, most would probably agree that gender provides a key – if not the key – organizing principle and base metaphor for countless cosmologies and ritual practices across the continent (Herbert 1993; Moore, Sanders, and Kaare 1999; Jacobson-Widding 1991, 17). At issue, however, is how Africanist anthropologists explain the gender and sexual 'symbolism' found in ritual, and its precise relation to material artefacts in the world, including women's and men's bodies.

In considering gender and other ritual symbolism in Africa, anthropologists frequently raise two questions, implicitly or explicitly: What does gender symbolism mean? And how, through ritual, does it do what it does? The answer routinely given to both springs from a Euro-American epistemology of gender and often relies on a notion of metaphoric links to bodies.

One of the first to write extensively on these matters was Victor Turner. From his work with the Ndembu of Northern Rhodesia (today Zambia), Turner suggested that dominant symbols are multivocal, each with a sensory (or 'orectic') and an ideological pole. Clustered at the former pole are natural, physiological phenomena and processes derived from primordial psychobiological experience (e.g., milk, blood, semen, birth, coitus, death). Clustered at the latter pole are a set of referents to moral and social facts (e.g., reciprocity, respect, obedience; matriliny, age-grade organization, kinship) (see Turner 1967, 90). Turner argued that dominant symbols become meaningful and efficacious when, through ritual performance, these two poles are collapsed. This is the work of metaphor: an 'instantaneous fusion' (Turner 1974, 25) of two different poles or realms of experience. Ndembu ritual participants thus metaphorically (con)fuse real bodies with cultural elaborations of them, energizing the latter with borrowed vitality, meaning, and reproductive powers from the former. To put it differently, because 'the human organism and its crucial experiences are the *fons et origo* of all classification' (Turner 1967, 90), they provide the material basis for the gender and sexual 'symbolism' found in certain rites of transformation.

Interestingly, Turner's views closely resemble those held by 1970s feminist scholars who argued that sex creates gender. For the body and its natural reproductive potentialities provide the origin and ultimate reference point for all non-human gender forms. But there are also important differences, especially when we consider the issue of materiality.

While feminist scholars distinguished categorically between material bodies and symbolic elaborations of them, for Turner this binary proved more complicated. This was due to his abiding concern with ritual performance and his commitment to empiricism. Together these led him to argue that Ndembu gender symbolism – indeed all symbolism – is anchored in everyday, material experiences. For Turner, symbolism was not simply an ethereal matter confined to Ndembu minds; rather, it concerned itself with practical, sensuate engagements in the world. This being so, then Ndembu non-human gender and sexual symbolism could not be explained simply as ideological elaborations of sexed bodies and human reproduction. It was somehow more concrete and complex.

Here Turner recognized for the Ndembu what is equally apparent for the Ihanzu: that 'symbolism' and the attendant ritual practices are less about philosophy than they are ways of acting on the world to change it. The Ihanzu do not use gender- and sexually-laden rainmaking rites 'to symbolize the conceptual categories into which they divide the universe and make it orderly' (MacCormack 1980, 116); nor are their rain rites a mechanism through which 'a society experiences and expresses its symbolic understanding of life' (Swantz and Wild 1995, 59). If this were all that were at stake, it would remain a mystery why villagers bother 'symbolizing' their world continuously and through so many different rituals. Rather, Ihanzu rain rites and the gender, sexuality, and reproductive processes that underpin them are concerned, above all, with the *practical* management of the social, cosmic, and natural worlds. This is not an issue of symbolic representation, but of animating the cosmic and divine powers of the universe in order to transform it. Only through the ritual manipulation of very material objects and physical processes – in this case, gendered ones – can the Ihanzu gain some degree of human influence over ancestral and divine powers. Thus, when men and women say that combining male and female artefacts brings rain, they are not *really* talking about something else, like bodies and coitus. They mean what they say.

Turner instinctively understood such things for the Ndembu. However, his theory of symbolism, meaning, and ritual efficacy was nevertheless underpinned by more familiar Euro-American epistemic propositions – sensory/ideological, nature/culture, material/symbolic, body/gender – that made it ultimately impossible to imagine gender, even when manifest in non-human material objects, as anything other than a symbolic or metaphoric projection or representation of more basic, foundational material forms in the shape of men's and women's bodies. For Turner, then, non-human gender forms and their combinations were meaningful and powerful because they symbolically or metaphorically evoked sexed bodies and human reproduction.

For many contemporary Africanists, Turner's views remain persuasive. Today it is commonly suggested that the physical body is 'the source of myriad creative images' (Broch-Due 1993, 53); that 'African transformative processes invoke the human model as the measure of all things' (Herbert 1993, 5); that 'sexual reproductivity [is] the model of the most powerful forces in the universe' (S.F. Moore 1976); that 'procreation beliefs are key symbols in Bangangté culture, summarizing and elaborating understandings of how the world works and what threatens it' (Feldman-Savelsberg 1994, 464); and that 'the body provides the most immediate and tangible frame of reference within which the individual constitutes and interprets himself in relation to the social and the natural order' (Devisch 1991, 283–4; see also Werbner 1990; R. Willis 1991, 272). For many, too, the notion of metaphor continues to bear a heavy analytic burden, and it is commonly used to 'explain' non-human gendering and reproduction.

René Devisch is one recent poststructuralist scholar who has developed a theory of metaphor and metonym, albeit a theory he sees as antithetical to Turner's (Devisch 1993, 34). Devisch considers healing cults among the Yaka of southwestern Zaire (who share many similarities with the Ndembu), aiming to make 'major dimensions of Yaka culture accessible within the framework of its own arrangements, within the terms of its own epistemological locus' (Devisch 1993, 3). To this end, he explores in exquisite detail how Yaka human and non-human gender categories and relations are intimately intertwined with birth, death, and generation, and how regenerative processes, properties, and potentialities are woven through Yaka natural, social, and cosmic worlds. Yaka and Ihanzu gender worlds have much in common.

Devisch criticizes Turner on several grounds, but most vehemently for his semiotic thinking and for his use of metaphor to explain the meaning and evocative power of symbols (Devisch 1993; cf. Kratz 1994). Inspired by theories of practice and phenomenology that Turner's work anticipated, Devisch goes further, insisting that Yaka ritual symbolism is less about metaphorically representing the world than engaging with it. In this sense, 'knowledge in ritual is primarily practical rather than declarative' (Devisch 1993: 50; Comaroff 1985; H.L. Moore 1986; M. Jackson 1989; Bourdieu 1990). This is an important point for thinking about gender and reproductive processes in Ihanzu and across sub-Saharan Africa, since it underscores their sheer materiality, as well as their non-reducibility to verbal exegesis.

Devisch's disinterest in metaphor as representation leads him to propose an alternative theory of metaphor, one that is linked to practice and embodied performance. He suggests that symbols, including gender and sexual symbols, are made meaningful and efficacious not because they collapse poles of a dominant symbol through ritual, but because ritual performance allows them to range metaphorically and metonymically across previously unrelated experiential domains (Devisch 1993, 37; also Beidelman 1993, 1997). For the Yaka, these domains are the body (*luutu*), life-world (*n-totu*), and group (*tsi*) (Devisch 1993, 30) or, in anthropological parlance, body, culture, and society.

To the extent that Devisch's critique allows us to imagine gender, sexuality, and reproductive processes as material, meaningful, and potent in practice, it provides a useful framework to explore Ihanzu gender epistemologies. Yet Devisch's approach, like earlier approaches, highlights a difficulty characteristic of many Africanists' explanations of non-human gender, sexual, and reproductive processes: the presumption that such things only make sense when linked metaphorically and/or metonymically to human bodies. But *must* such things symbolize, metaphorize, or evoke the human form in order to make sense? And whose sense, exactly, are we talking about? What if we took seriously our interlocutors' statements that gendered objects bring gendered rains, and that sexed bodies and human reproduction are unrelated to this fact?

In many ways, the Euro-American epistemology of gender has dampened the anthropological imagination regarding alternative gender truths that do not revolve around metaphor, symbolism, and bodies. It has made it next to impossible to imagine a world in which non-human gender forms – what anthropologists often dub 'gender symbols' – are just as obvious, just as material, just as potent, and therefore just as real as we believe men's and women's bodies and their reproductive potentialities to be. It has made it problematic to contemplate, let along theorize, nonhuman sexual transformative processes as reproduction in its own right and not simply as a something that signifies, symbolizes, or metaphorizes 'real' sexed bodies and human reproduction. In short, if anthropologists have had lots to say about how and why gendered ritual 'symbols' are meaningful and efficacious, much of which turns on varied notions of metaphoric links to bodies, they have spent far less time considering the possibility that the meanings and ritual powers sometimes vested in non-human gender forms could lie elsewhere, somewhere beyond their metaphoric or symbolic associations.

Metaphor and symbolism share certain similarities. Both, in different ways, are about reducing one category or domain to and/or explaining it vis-à-vis another. Gendered rainmaking rites are ostensibly 'explained' by suggesting that they are really about something else: human bodies and sexual reproduction. Of course, casting non-human gender and sexual reproduction as metaphoric or symbolic may make sense within a Euro-American epistemology, since these things can be 'explained' (away) as representing, standing for, dramatizing, evoking, or resonating with other more 'obvious' things such as bodies and human reproduction. But such explanations must be seen for what they are: questions and answers arising from a particular Western metaphysic that assumes there is 'real' human reproduction on the one hand, and everything else on the other. They provide little theoretical purchase over alternative metaphysics of gender that do not share such visions.

The Ihanzu epistemology invites us to imagine another possibility: a world in which *all* gender forms are meaningful, material, and potent because they form part of a universe in which all power comes in masculine and feminine forms. Male and female bodies and artefacts are meaningful and powerful not because they somehow reflect, represent, symbolize, or metaphorize one other. This is no explanation – or at least, no explanation the men and women of Ihanzu would buy. It is, rather, that all evince and participate equally in a grander cosmic design of gendered mixing, mingling, and transformation: of gender complementarity. Bodies are but one aspect of this innately gendered reproductive world, and they do not sit central to it. All gendered forms and their transformative powers are therefore the same, though they manifest themselves at multiple levels: within bodies, between bodies, and without bodies. These manifestations are a question of scale, not of kind. Akin to the logic of fractal geometry, then, there is no real relation to be established between parts and whole, as each is part of the whole set and is simultaneously a scaled down version of it.[16] For the Ihanzu, non-human gender forms *are* male and female; they do not represent or symbolize them. And non-human reproduction *is* reproduction, not a representation of it.

This brings us to our final negativity, which is this: we must stop believing that non-human genders and reproductive processes are only meaningful and potent because they somehow represent, symbolize, or metaphorize 'real' bodies and human reproduction. Naturally, if we wish, we can invent such analytic fictions. Many have. Given anthropology's lengthy engagement with such issues, many will no doubt continue to spin their symbolic wheels. But refusing to think beyond symbols, metaphors, and bodies – or at least to entertain the possibility of doing so – ensures that we remain analytically and theoretically ill equipped to deal with alternative 'languages of life,' to employ Mbembe's (2001, 15) phrase, surrounding gender. Until we can treat seriously and sometimes literally our interlocutor's statements, until we can think beyond bodies, we will fail to capture alternative metaphysics of gender that – as in Ihanzu – place all masculine and feminine forms and powers on equal epistemological footing, casting both human and non-human reproduction as instantiations of broader principles of mixing, mingling, and transformation.

What this book seeks to develop, then, is an alternative set of conceptual tools that will allow us analytically to extricate the body from gender – or rather, gender from the body – while simultaneously maintaining gender's manifest materiality in our analytic sites. This will allow us to problematize Western social science commonplaces about the material and the symbolic, the real and the ideal, as well as to think meaningfully and materially about gender through, across, and beyond bodies.

Chapter 1

Ihanzu Everyday Worlds

Tanzania is located in East Africa, bordering the Indian Ocean between Kenya and Mozambique (see map 1.1). The former British protectorate of Tanganyika, Tanzania gained independence in 1961.[1] The nation covers just over 945,000 square kilometres, an area about four times the size of Britain, and has a population of around 38 million. Tanzania's landscape and climate vary: tropical along the coast, temperate in the northern and southern highlands, and semi-arid to arid across the central plateau. Different climatic zones support different types of agriculture, which form the foundation of Tanzania's economy. Agriculture accounts for around half the national income and more than three-quarters of exports, besides employing around 90 per cent of the nation's workforce. Important staples include maize, sorghum, and millet; the main export crops are coffee, nuts, cotton, tobacco, tea, and sisal.

Commentators often note that Tanzania has more than 120 ethnic groups and as many languages. Swahili is the nation's lingua franca, and virtually all Tanzanians speak it fluently. This Bantu language is also spoken in Kenya, Uganda, Democratic Republic of Congo, northern Mozambique, and southern Somalia, as well as in parts of Malawi, Rwanda, and Burundi. National statistics suggest that 40 to 45 per cent of Tanzanians are Christians and 30 to 35 per cent Muslims; the remainder practise 'traditional religion.' Yet figures can deceive. For one thing, some self-identified Christians and Muslims also practise some form of 'traditional religion.' For another, it is not entirely clear to what 'traditional religion' refers, given the enormous range of beliefs and practices that are often subsumed under it, not just in Tanzania but across the globe.

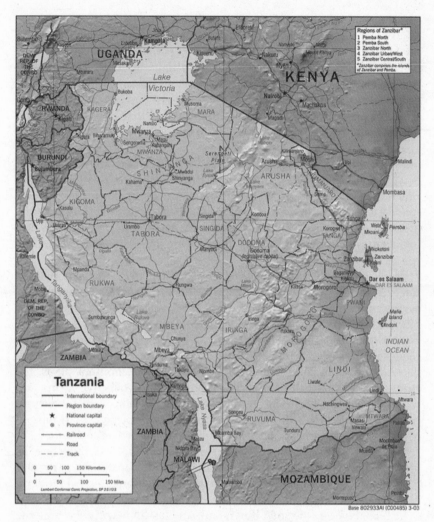

Map 1.1. Tanzania

Tanzania is a multiparty parliamentary democracy. It also has a free market economy. These, however, are relatively recent developments. Before independence, Tanganyika was run by British and (prior to the First World War) German colonial administrations. In 1954, Julius Nyerere formed Tanganyika's first political party, the Tanganyika African National Union (TANU), which was instrumental in guiding Tang-anyika to and through independence. Beginning in the early 1960s, Nyerere and TANU forged and followed a path of 'non-Marxist social-ism' (Tripp 1997, 62) known as *ujamaa*. While uniquely African in cer-tain respects, in practice *ujamaa* followed a Chinese model of state centralization, wherein administrative powers were strongly concen-trated in the central government and delegated to lower-level authori-ties in diminishing amounts. The entire nation formed – and still forms – a political pyramid that included all Tanzanians from the most remote village to its thriving urban centres. These hierarchical political arrangements, themselves informed by earlier colonial divisions and practices, remain today. At its broadest, Tanzania comprises twenty-five regions. Each of these encompasses several districts, within which are divisions, wards, villages, subvillages, and – at the smallest level of inclusion – ten-household cells. Political power is delegated from the top down.

From the 1960s until the 1980s, the single-party state nationalized major commercial, financial, and manufacturing industries; imposed severe import restrictions on foreign goods and currencies; and emphasized manufacturing and agricultural production within the nation, for the nation. Self-reliance was the goal. In a country largely made up of farmers, it is not surprising that agriculture formed the backbone of *ujamaa* and the nascent nation's development plans: the rural, agricultural base, properly organized into collective farms and modern villages, was expected to propel the nation from poverty to prosperity. Nyerere was widely admired and respected, both nation-ally and internationally, for his *ujamaa* vision. However, for a range of reasons the experiment eventually went sour, negatively affecting all sectors of the Tanzanian economy. In the end, Tanzania's particular form of African socialism failed to deliver what it promised: a modern, self-reliant socialist nation.

In 1985, Nyerere stepped down and Ali Hassan Mwinyi became the Republic's second president (see Tripp 1997: ch. 4). This signalled the advent of a new official paradigm, a specific vision and set of practices that was meant to put Tanzania, at long last, back on the golden road to development. This was neoliberalism. Mwinyi's government adopted wholesale the International Monetary Fund's and the World Bank's structural adjustment program, together with the rhetoric that sur-rounded it. The IMF and the Bank assumed that less government inter-vention in the economy is better; that economies work best, and most efficiently, when propelled by market forces rather than by bureaucrats. And both have, by fair means or foul, been foisting such ideas on the global South for some decades.

Consequently, in recent years the contours of Tanzania's postcolonial landscape have been changing in remarkable ways: the country's bureaucracies have been rationalized and reduced, and its borders and economy have been opened to regional and global markets. In the 1990s, the ruling Chama Cha Mapinduzi or CCM, an amalgam of TANU and Zanzibar's ASP, loosened its stranglehold over the media. The three officially sanctioned, government-owned newspapers now circulate in the cities alongside a multitude of locally produced newspapers, tabloids, and magazines, not to mention any number of international news sources. The single state radio station has, of late, been joined by manifold others from near and afar; urban and rural listeners tune in to keep up with the news, soccer matches, and other broadcasts of interest. Additionally, mainland Tanzania saw its first television broadcast in 1994. Today, city dwellers can watch the private network ITV, which broadcasts local and foreign serials and newscasts as well as American sitcoms and action movies. Furthermore, some urbanites now have access to cable and satellite systems, which offer programming from around the globe. Several international banks, such as Standard Charter and Barclay's, following their post-independence expulsions, have re-established themselves or are actively taking steps to do so. Foreign exchange restrictions no longer apply; foreign currencies can now easily – and legally – be bought and sold at any number of exchange bureaux. Land borders with neighbouring countries, at one time tightly controlled (when not closed entirely), have all been flung open, and everyday and luxury consumer goods (once controlled by the state) are today flowing en masse across them.

In the early 1990s the CCM allowed independent political parties to register; currently, there are nineteen. In 1995, Benjamin Mkapa was elected the republic's third president in the country's first multiparty elections; he was re-elected in October 2000. Like Mwinyi before him, President Mkapa and his government enthusiastically supported Tanzania's neoliberal turn. In 2005, Jakaya Kikwete was elected president, and through him, the neoliberal revolution lives on. 'Good governance,' 'anticorruption,' 'hard work,' 'poverty reduction,' and 'unleashing market forces' are all the rage – at least, I hasten to add, in government circles.

Recent reforms have been nationwide in their reach, and no Tanzanian, urban or rural, is unaware of them today. In the cities the informal economy is booming (see Tripp 1997). Privately owned shops are bursting with consumer goods. Street markets bustle with urbanites, young and old, buying imported radios, CD players, and name-brand clothing. After decades of shortages under *ujamaa*, enterprising Tanzanians have today filled their cities with mountains of consumer goods and goodies – as well as dreams for a better future. '*Ujamaa* is dead,' one Dar es Salaam street vendor enthusiastically told me in 1999. 'Today, if we try, we can have anything!' But such dreams can just as easily become nightmares. And they do. For as wealth in some shops and amongst an élite class of individuals increases, so, too, across a much broader segment of the urban population do relative poverty, envy and untenable dreams of a vastly better future. On this score, plenty of Tanzanians and Tanzanianists now recognise that economic liberalization has come with devastating costs: it has created religious and ethnic tensions and forced 'a majority of people [in Dar es Salaam] to use the informal sector as a survival strategy' (Lugalla 1997, 440; also Lugalla 1995; Mbilinyi 1990; Kaiser 1996; Sanders 2001a).

Neoliberal reforms have served rural Tanzanians no better. Many villagers these days are 'growing more crops, risking more in marketing them, spending more in cultivating them, and earning less for their sale' (Ponte 1998, 339). This is true where soils, climate and infrastructure allow for increased production and marketing of crops in the first place. In other areas – Ihanzu is one of them – villagers cannot grow more crops due to inadequate rain, soils and technological capabilities; they cannot sell them due to the lack of local markets or transport to move them elsewhere; and they cannot perform more than the full-time labour they already put in. But this does not mean that recent reforms have passed them by. Instead, the deleterious effects of neoliberal reforms have made themselves felt in other ways: namely, through the ever-present disconnect between promise and practice.

Like their urban counterparts, villagers are only too aware of the wealth that some Tanzanians have managed to accumulate through the free market (*soko huria*). Moreover, they are constantly being told – through government functionaries, the radio, and everyday discussion – that they, too, can succeed if only they try. Yet for many rural Tanzanians, success in the free market economy is unlikely, because of structural constraints that disallow it. Without local markets and adequate roads, they cannot sell anything. And without reliable rains, they cannot grow enough to sell anyway. Thus while the free market has promised the world, it has simply failed to deliver in cities and villages alike.[2]

Such conclusions are inevitable, it would seem, in a country where per capita income is around US $120 annually and where nearly two in five Tanzanians live on less that $0.65 per day.[3] Neoliberal cheerleading notwithstanding, Tanzania remains one of the world's poorest countries. This is why many, perhaps even most Tanzanians would say that the IMF- and World Bank-led neoliberal agenda has failed the nation. For a great many Tanzanians, these are times of austerity, not prosperity. This is certainly true for the people of Ihanzu.

Placing Ihanzu

Ihanzu is in Singida Region, and forms the northernmost part of Iramba District, bordering Shinyanga and Meatu Districts to the north and Mbulu District to the northeast and east (see map 1.2). Although officially known as *Tarafa ya Kirumi* (Kirumi Division), one of seven such divisions that make up Iramba District, I follow local conventions and refer to the area as 'Ihanzu.' The Sibiti River, which flows northwards from Lake Kitangiri and empties into the southern end of Lake Eyasi, forms the northern boundary between Shinyanga Region and Ihanzu. Ihanzu's western border is formed by a tributary of the Sibiti called the Duromo. To the south, an administrative boundary divides Ihanzu from the rest of Iramba, but there are no distinctive geographical features to support this divide and Ihanzu flows imperceptibly onto the Iramba Plateau. From south to north Ihanzu is about twenty-five miles, and about the same from east to west. The place people today call 'Ihanzu,' then, covers roughly six hundred square miles and is firmly embedded in the modern Tanzanian nation-state.

The Ihanzu live in one of the most ethnically diverse regions in Tanzania.[5] Within Iramba District, to the south and west, live the Iramba, another Bantu-language speaking agricultural people with whom they share close social, cultural, and linguistic affinities. In Mbulu District to the east, atop part of the Rift Valley escarpment, live the Southern Cushitic-speaking and agro-pastoral Iraqw, who practise a mixture of pastoralism and intensive agriculture. Immediately to the north, in Meatu and Mbulu Districts, live the Sukuma and Hadza. The former are the largest single ethnic group in Tanzania, the latter one of the smallest. The Sukuma practise a mix of herding and agriculture, with a strong ideological emphasis on the former. The Hadza speak a 'click'

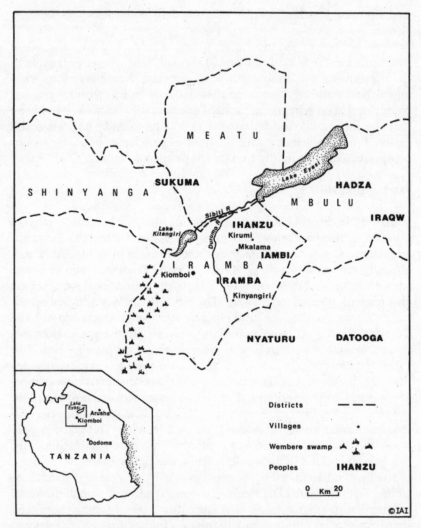

Map 1.2. The Ihanzu and their neighbours

language of indeterminate origin, and their economy, unlike others in
the area, is based largely on hunting and gathering. None of this is to
imply, of course, that these varied peoples are utterly distinct from one
another, that they remain squarely within administrative boundaries,
or that there is no mixing at the margins. This would be foolish. Never-

theless, the striking differences in livelihood strategies, historical experiences, languages, and cultural imaginations between neighbours give
sharper definition to the conceptual and practical boundaries between
them than one finds in many parts of the country.

Ihanzu, like the areas that surround it, is well off the beaten track
and is peripheral to Tanzania's major political and economic centres. If
buses did the route directly, which they do not, it would be two days'
drive from Dar es Salaam and about ten hours' drive from Arusha.
Ihanzu's marginal position within Tanzania – geographically, politically, economically – has been a long time in the making.

In colonial German and British administrators' eyes, Ihanzu was
always 'the back of beyond.'[6] In the early 1900s, German administrators considered their Ihanzu-based fort at Mkalama one of the most
remote and undesirable postings in the whole of Deutsch Ost-Afrika.
Ihanzu was (and is) rife with debilitating and life-threatening water-
and vector-borne diseases. At least one German officer died and was
buried there. When British forces occupied the fort after the First
World War, they fared little better. By 1919, no fewer than nine British
political officers had come and gone due to the 'notoriously unhealthy
climate.'[7]

The weather also posed challenges for colonial regimes. Ihanzu is
classified as semi-arid. Rain – or rather, lack of it – is an ever-present
problem. This, combined with Ihanzu's sheer distance from colonial
power centres, meant that neither German nor British administrators
ever considered Ihanzu a plausible site for large-scale, intensive cash
cropping.[8] Land is also relatively barren. Thus, throughout the colonial
era, only minimal efforts were made to improve the local infrastructure
and economy. The 'primitive' people of Ihanzu, as administrators often
cast them, were instead treated as a de facto labour reserve for more
fertile parts of the country. This is why many Ihanzu men (and these
days, women) have been compelled to trek long distances in search of
labour – to urban centres like Singida and Arusha – since the Germans
first imposed taxes in the area around the turn of the last century
(Adam 1963a; Iliffe 1979, 161).[9]

Colonial visions and impositions concerning local (non)develop-
ment and migrant labour have had lasting effects in the area. And
postcolonial reforms, whether early or recent, have done little to
change this. The nearest town, Singida, is a one-day walk. No major (or
even minor) highways run through Ihanzu, or nearby. Ihanzu's few
roads are unsealed and rarely graded. In the dry season a few buses

move between Ihanzu and Singida, a four-hour drive, twice a week; in the wet season the roads are often impassable. There are some small, privately owned shops that sell things like cooking oil, kerosene, and women's clothes, a few of which have boomed since the early 1990s. But there are no permanent markets where villagers might sell home-made goods or crops. Ihanzu has no electricity, no telephone access, and only a handful of working water pumps. The few government dispensaries in the area are poorly stocked and often have no medicines at all. There are primary schools, and thanks to *ujamaa* policies, literacy rates are high; nearly everyone has been to school for a few years.[10] However, schools are often collapsing, figuratively and literally speaking. The local economy is geared towards subsistence agriculture, except for sunflowers, which provide cash income for some. Through such sales and other means (see below), some villagers might realize Tanzania's per capita annual income of US $120. But for most, this would be unexpected and borderline miraculous.

With all this, some might be tempted to see Ihanzu as an isolated, out-of-the-way place, disconnected from both history and the modern world. So let me be clear: it is not. Ihanzu has long been entangled in regional and national affairs and is very much the product of ongoing engagements with specific historical, political, and economic forces and relations (cf. Tsing 1993; Piot 1999). While this book does not dwell on those engagements, which are many and varied, it is important not to mistake 'marginal' for 'isolate': the former implies unequal relations while the latter improbably implies no relations at all.

Seasons, Subsistence, and Sociality

The 30,000 women, men, and children of Ihanzu live in eighteen villages spread across the land. These are known as *ujamaa* villages, so designated in the 1970s by Tanzania's then-socialist government. Each is composed of a number of subvillages. Village populations are large and often span vast expanses. The central village of Matongo, for instance, has around four thousand residents, who are spread across several miles and a small mountain range. This makes Matongo, for all practical purposes, an impractical village. Truth be told, this is so for all Ihanzu villages and for most things that matter to villagers themselves, including herding, farming, house building, and beer brewing. With the exceptions of tax collection, polling, and compulsory village labour, it is the subvillages (*vitongoji*), rather than the larger *ujamaa* wholes, that function as everyday social units. For simplicity's sake I thus refer to subvillages as 'villages' throughout this book.

Ihanzu today comprises two distinct geographical areas: a central, boulder-strewn 'homeland' plateau, and the more recently inhabited undulating plains that surround it. The plateau forms part of the Rift Valley wall, which rises in some places to over five thousand feet. To the north, west, and east, there are drop-offs to the plains below, some of them sharp indeed. The terrain in this area is rugged. Enormous granite boulders – some of them reaching several stories into the sky – pepper the mountainous landscape, forming an abundance of natural caves (plate 1.1). Some of these caves are used for ancestral offerings. Others contain rock paintings or large drums from a bygone era.[11] Villages and village-sections are permanent and are often divided by the land's distinctive rocky contours. Homesteads tend to be close together, sometimes twenty or thirty yards apart, and fairly evenly spread throughout the villages. Because the plateau land is so thoroughly broken up by large boulders, plots are relatively small and farming is done principally by hand. In the past, this meant using hoes made by local smiths or traded from elsewhere; today, Chinese-made hand hoes are the norm. Soils in this central area are sand loam (*iselwe*). And because they have been farmed the longest – this is the area where the original migrants settled – they are also the least fertile in Ihanzu: plots here normally require substantial fertilization by cattle manure to ensure adequate harvests. The plains surrounding this plateau offer different possibilities.

Beginning in the early 1900s, but especially after the British arrived, some Ihanzu men and women began gradually to migrate from the highland plateau to the lowland plains surrounding it. The plains consist of undulating flats sloping gradually and imperceptibly to the north. On the extremities, a few seasonal rivers flow north, eventually into Lake Eyasi. The enormous granite boulders that are such a distinctive feature of the highland landscape are virtually absent from the plains. Besides some rolling hills and a few slight valleys, most of these areas are flat (plate 1.2). Farther north they become monotonously so. While hand hoes are commonly used to farm in these areas, the expansive rock-free fields also allow villagers to use cattle ploughs. The soils – black cotton soils (*ikūlūhī*) to the east, grey soils (*mbūga*) to the north, and rock soils (*ihangahanga*) to the west – are marginally more fertile but still poor. The villages are spread farther apart.

The Ihanzu are primarily farmers. What is more, unlike many of

Plate 1.1. View of Kirumi, central Ihanzu (December 1994)

Plate 1.2. View from Ilongo village on the western plains (August 1995)

their neighbours, they prefer to imagine themselves as such. While there are a few non-agricultural livelihood options in the area – diviner, smith, or basket weaver; pastor or potter; shop owner or government functionary – all such people also crucially depend on farming. The staples are sorghum (*ilo*), millet (*ũele*), and maize (*akĩmpukile*), grains that are ground and cooked into a stiff porridge called *ũgalĩ*. Ũgalĩ forms the basis of all meals and is eaten with relish (*nyanyi*) of various sorts, most commonly, wild greens.[12] Sorghum and millet also provide a significant source of cash income for households – in fact, they underpin the local economy – when made into beer. Sweet potatoes, peanuts, cassava, beans, tomatoes, and onions are commonly grown in small amounts for relishes. Some villagers also grow sunflowers as a cash crop. These are sold to one of the few small shops in the area; or to entrepreneurs from other parts of the country, who in good years arrive on prearranged days in large lorries and pay cash.[13] Going rates are invariably low, but given local conditions, farmers have few alternatives.

Successful farming requires successful rains, which is why farming in Ihanzu has never been easy. Drought and famine visit the region about one year in five. There are two seasons: a wet, 'female' season (*kĩtikũ*) and a dry, 'male' one (*kĩpasu*). The rainy season normally begins around December and ends in April or May. The months between June and October typically see no rain at all. Seasonal changes from wet to dry and back again are dramatically marked on the landscape, by a movement from the often lush, green months to the invariably dry, dusty, brown ones. But even in 'good' years, rainfall is far from certain. Heavy showers may come early and sweep away all the seeds. Showers may come late, be excessive, and prevent crops from maturing properly. Or, as more commonly occurs, the rain may be delayed or patchy so as to cause drought and famine over the whole area. Annual rainfall averages – a meagre twenty to thirty inches – do not paint an accurate picture. For even in those years with seemingly sufficient rainfall, it is never evenly distributed. From the central highlands, standing say in Kirumi village where I lived, one can see rainclouds moving across the plains below, showering heavily on one village while skipping altogether the next. Even within the same village, two nearby plots can receive different amounts of rain, causing one harvest to succeed while a neighbour's completely fails. With no year-round rivers and few working water pumps, irrigation is not a farming option. Small wonder, really, that villagers devote so much time and energy throughout the year to subsistence activities, activities that have a recognizable seasonal rhythm.

During the wet season, villagers are widely dispersed through the villages and the bush and have little time for anything but farming. This is the least social time of year, with labour largely centring around individual homesteads.

Prior to the onset of the rains, usually in late September or early October, individual homestead members begin raking up and burning the sorghum, millet, and maize stocks that remain on their plots from the previous year's harvest. A husband and wife (or wives) and their children carry out this work; if any other dependants are present, such as sons-in-law carrying out brideservice, or elderly parents, they will help (I will say more about household composition presently). People then wait for rain. Quick rainshowers known as *hongela* come and go during this period, but rarely amount to much. Prior to and in between these sporadic showers are the blisteringly hot, aptly named 'shit-in-the-shade' (*kīnia mũ mpepo*) periods. This is an anxious time, a time during which people drink lots of beer and endlessly discuss their hopes and fears about the year to come.

Once the rains begin in full force, following a one-day farming prohibition (*ikali*), villagers begin hoeing their fields in earnest. Again, as with other farming activities, all household members – men, women, and older children (those who are not at school) – participate. A man and his wife hoe from early morning to late afternoon, every day, once the rains begin. As the hoeing proceeds, men and women scatter their seeds over the field. Hoeing is an ongoing process. The larger the area and the more plots one successfully plants, the more likely one is to obtain a reasonable harvest. On average, most homesteads farm between five and ten acres of land. Some homesteads (22.6 per cent) farm only one plot, and others have three (19.3 per cent) or more (6.3 per cent), but most (51.8 per cent) farm two plots.[14] Those with multiple plots have them in different locations, usually one at home and others at more distant locations in the bush, further to guard against the weather's uncertainties. During these planting months, grainstores dwindle. January marks the beginning of the 'hunger months.'

In February villagers stop hoeing and planting and return to the first plots they planted to remove the weeds (plate 1.3). Again, both men and women do weeding, and they do so progressively over several months. Planting and weeding in stages offers some security, as it ensures that the crops do not all ripen at once. If the rains prove to be

Plate 1.3. Woman weeding a plot, 1962 (photo by V. Adam)

very long, then the crops planted first may rot; but if they stop early, the early crops may survive. Crops planted last, if the rains endure, will provide a good harvest when others have failed.

By the end of April, weeding stops. Further planting is pointless, since by this stage the rains will not continue long enough to result in adequate crop maturation. The challenge now is to guard crops against theft by animals and humans. Baboons and birds plague plots by day; pigs and hyenas by night. The members of the homestead guard their plots round the clock: in the daytime, the women and children scare off birds and baboons; at night, the men sleep on their larger plots, bow and arrows at the ready, to guard against wild pigs and the occasional maize-eating hyena.[15]

Some maize can be harvested by April, thus ending (if temporarily) the hunger months. Maize harvests, however, are rarely large, serving merely to tide people over until the 'real' harvest – sorghum and millet – a few months later. In April women begin sun-drying wild leaves, tomatoes, and onions for later in the year when these foods are not otherwise available (plate 1.4). The preparation and storage of dried foodstuffs is of decided importance; these foods, once reconstituted, make up the bulk of the diet between October and February.[16]

On balance, during the wet season, husbands usually put in slightly longer hours farming than their wives. Wives, for their part, spend a good part of their days collecting leafy greens, cooking, and fetching firewood and water to keep their households running smoothly. The wet season – especially in drought years – is also the time when men and, today, some women, do migrant labour in other parts of Tanzania. Arusha – in particular, the tea and coffee estates that surround it – has long been a destination for Ihanzu labourers (Adam 1963a).

While for most people most of the time the wet season is relatively asocial, there are exceptions to this. Funerals, for instance, require village-wide attendance no matter what time of year a death occurs. Additionally, some years some villagers sponsor communal work parties, of which there are two types. The first, called *shama*, is based on common residence in a village. Each village has a formal, hierarchically structured *shama* organization, complete with office holders. If a man or woman in the village wants to sponsor a *shama*, he or she informs the *shama* Chair, who then sets the machinery in motion.[17] On the designated day, villagers show up at the sponsor's plot. The sponsor must bring a 20-litre bucket of beer (*ntūlī*), a bucket of unstrained beer (*miha*), and the same of non-alcoholic sorghum drink (*magai*) for

Plate 1.4. Woman picking wild greens, 1962 (photo by V. Adam)

the workers, who hoe from morning to midday. They then go to the sponsor's home, where they receive their payment proper: one large earthen vat of beer; or one goat, a 20-litre bucket of sorghum drink, and flour to cook *ũgalĩ*; or one cow. The first of these – 100 litres of beer – is the most common form of payment. *Shama* are infrequent, since to produce this amount of beer in the middle of the hunger months is, for most villagers most years, impossible.

The second type of communal work party is called *kongolesi*. *Kongolesi* is more common than *shama*, since it is considerably cheaper and allows for more flexibility. *Kongelesi* has no rigid organizational structure. A man or woman wishing to sponsor a farming day on his or her plot simply invites a few friends, neighbours, and/or kin. Unlike *shama*, which involves an entire village's labour, *kongolesi* works best and is normally carried out with six to ten people. Workers are not necessarily from the immediate neighbourhood and may even come from other villages. Since it is not always possible to pay workers at the time of their work – farming is, after all, done in the lean months, when there is often little food or beer to give – the sponsor may pay after the harvest or even the following year. Even so, a few things are expected of the sponsor on the day. First, in the morning, he or she must provide workers with a half-gourd of sorghum beer 'to taste' (*kũonza*). Later, the sponsor must provide more beer, normally a gallon, 'to take away the thirst' (*kiheje nyota*). Finally, when they have finished farming, usually around noon, the workers return to the sponsor's homestead, where they are given a 20-litre bucket of beer. This means that for a five-member work crew, each worker receives about a gallon of beer for his or her labour.[18]

With these few infrequent exceptions, wet season activities and the forms of sociality they entail tend to turn on individual homestead labour. In the dry season, all of this changes.

By June the rains have usually stopped and the homestead members have begun to harvest their plots. Harvesting and threshing (*kũpula*) are done by wives, their husbands, and sometimes children (plate 1.5). Winnowing (*kũpeta*), on the other hand, is done entirely by women, usually a woman and her unmarried daughters. Grain is carried from the plots to the homestead, sometimes by donkey, where it is put into the grainstore. From the time the harvest begins until all the grain is in the grainstore may, in a good harvest year, take up to three months, with the process ending as late as August. This gives those who are not cutting new plots a month or so to relax before they begin preparations

Plate 1.5. Women and children threshing grain in Kirumi, 1995 (photo by T. Sanders)

for the next farming season. In many years, however, harvests are more modest and the same tasks may be completed in less than two months.

In the dry months following the harvest, social life in the villages thrives. People criss-cross the villages to spend time with relatives and to attend weddings and funerals (plate 1.6). With grain comes food and beer, and with beer the Ihanzu economy springs to life. Each day in each village, one, sometimes two women brew beer (plate 1.7). The first question that circulates around a village each dry season morning is, 'Magai kũng'wa kwa nyanyu ilelo ĩyĩ?' (Who's got beer today?)[19] Though men and women often drink in their own villages, it is not uncommon for them to walk for miles to another to enjoy beer and the company of friends, relatives, and sometimes even anthropologists. If asked, people say that anyone can drink with anyone else, which in certain respects is true. In practice, though, people at drinking parties tend to congregate based on age, sex, and/or locality. Beer parties are often held at people's homesteads (plate 1.8). Each village also has a public drinking house, which villagers can book in the local government office to sell beer on a particular day. In either location, beer is sold by the gourd and 20-litre bucket. To give some idea of the scale of home beer brewing, in 1994 around half the households in the central Matongo area brewed beer at least once during the year.[20]

The dry season is when men weave and repair their grainstores (plate 1.9). A smaller number weave beer strainers and walk to markets in other parts of the district to sell them (plates 1.10 and 1.11). Some young and older men (usually in small numbers) hunt small game and birds in the bush during the dry season.[21] Others go in small groups for brief periods to fish in the Sibiti River. In July, cichlids are available in abundance; in August (at least in rainy years), freshwater catfish abound.[22] Fish are dried, and are later bartered widely for other foodstuffs or sold in Ihanzu villages. During the dry season, fish are an important part of the diet. Women spend the dry season cutting and stockpiling firewood and picking and drying relishes for the months ahead. They also spend much of their time brewing beer, a task reserved almost exclusively for women. While an unmarried man may brew beer either to drink or to sell – this is vary rare, however – any married man who did so would be viewed with suspicion and probably treated with derision.

One of the most important communal dry season activities is building houses or *matembe* (sing. *itembe*). A man wishing to build a house is

Plate 1.6. Women at a funeral, Matongo village, 1994 (photo by T. Sanders)

Plate 1.7. Women brewing beer (photo by T. Sanders)

Plate 1.8. Beer party in Matongo village (photo by T. Sanders)

Plate 1.9. Man from Kirumi weaving a grain store (photo by T. Sanders)

Plate 1.10. William Kali weaving a beer strainer, 1962 (photo by V. Adam)

Plate 1.11. Men walking to Iramba to sell beer strainers (photo by T. Sanders)

responsible for its walls: he must make the bricks, which means pouring mud into wooden moulds and leaving them to sun-dry.[23] It takes a few months of steady work in warm weather to amass enough bricks to build the walls. A man must also cut all the house posts with which to erect the roof. Since mud houses only last for five to ten years and occasionally, with bad weather and bad luck, collapse even sooner, men are more or less constantly cutting, shaping, and storing house posts in preparation for the inevitable. Once the mud blocks are in place and sufficient house posts are on hand, a date is set for the communal roof building. The man's wife, with the help of other women in the neighbourhood, will begin brewing a large amount of beer for the day.[24] A man with the means will make sure he has a goat or two to slaughter, though this is not, unlike with beer, strictly required.

House buildings are big events. On the designated day, hundreds of men and women – many from the village, some from elsewhere – arrive in the morning hours. Women come with 20-litre plastic buckets, men with shovels and hoes. Men belong to one of four neighbourhood-based building groups, each of which is associated with a particular part of the house and is entitled to specific beer (and, if available, meat) payments (see Adam 1962, 9ff).[25] The elderly men (*anyampala*), often with other groups' help, dig postholes around the existing structure, into which they place heavy, vertical posts (*mapandwa*; sing. *ipandwa*), which will bear the roof's weight. Other groups place the horizontal support posts (*makana*; sing. *lūkana*) on these. Normally there are three such posts, one on either side and one down the centre, and they run the length of the house. The two junior groups then place rafter beams (*malo*) across these. Smaller branches (*kūgūnī*) are then laid perpendicularly across these supports; and atop this layer the youngest groups place small, leafy branches (*zaningala*). The work is arduous.

Women have no named work groups like the men; even so, they are instrumental to house building: they brew beer and fetch water. While the men place the posts, beams, and rafters, a handful of women finish pouring the beer through reed strainers (*mahuzo*; sing. *ihuzo*) to filter out the dregs (*miha*). When the men are finished, the women dole out beer. They then begin fetching water at the nearest waterhole, and return to the house to fill large earthen vats. Since houses are built during the dry season and waterholes are few and far between, this takes time. Once everyone is rested and the vats are full, the women begin carrying buckets of water to the rear of the house and pouring them onto the ground. A few men from the two youngest building groups climb onto the house's flat roof while the rest remain below, at the rear of the house. The latter mix the water into the earth. Once the area has been turned into an enormous bog, the men begin throwing shovels-fuls of mud onto the roof (plate 1.12). Those atop the house spread the mud, which eventually sticks and, once dry, forms a hard surface. Shovelling is extremely hard work that can last for more than an hour. All the men present except the elders take a turn, each turn lasting for only a few minutes. When the roof is a foot or so thick with mud, the work is done. The men and women return to drinking beer for the remainder of the day.

Not a dry season passes without a number of houses being built, or rebuilt, in each village. For this reason, house building is one of the most common forms of dry season sociality, second only to beer drink-ing. In practice, though, the two cannot be easily or profitably sepa-rated. Men and women, when asked of their plans for the day, usually say 'I am going to drink beer,' and only later does it transpire that the reason beer was available in the first place was because someone was building a house. House building, then, might best be seen as a free beer party where a house happens to get built in the process, rather than the reverse. Whatever the case, house buildings are large, public, and often festive occasions (albeit demanding hard work from men and women alike), and most villagers treat them as events not to be missed.

A few daily activities continue the year round, their forms changing only slightly from one season to the next. The most important is herding.

Many Ihanzu villagers own animals. The most common are cattle, fol-lowed in order of frequency by goats, sheep, and donkeys. Some own chickens, dogs, and cats as well. Animals are privately owned; there are no corporate herds, nor, so far as can be established, have there ever been.[26] Both men and women may own animals, though men tend to own considerably more. Domestic animals are important for several reasons. Cattle, sheep, and goats serve as stores of wealth: they are used for bridewealth payments and to pay taxes as well as fines (if found guilty, say, of adultery or witchcraft).[27] Cattle and sheep are slaughtered for ancestral offerings (including those for rain) and at weddings and funerals. Donkeys are used to carry crops home from people's fields; cattle plough fields and provide milk and manure. Livestock (except for donkeys) are sometimes slaughtered for food. This, however, is rare, especially for cattle. It is not uncommon for a man to walk for two days into neighbouring districts to work for a bucket or two of grain before he would slaughter one of his own beasts.

Plate 1.12. House building (photo by T. Sanders)

Many men own at least a few head of cattle, and those with more than ten are considered wealthy (also Adam 1962, 2). Many others, and sometimes women, also own a few goats and/or sheep. Much as women are responsible for beer brewing, men are responsible for herding. Male heads of homesteads sometimes herd their cattle, sheep, and goats alone; more commonly, though, neighbourhood herding groups, which form on an semipermanent basis, jointly herd neighbourhood livestock. All villages have such groups, which are based on common residence rather than kinship or other ties. How many people are involved in a herding group depends largely on how many cattle are being herded; the optimal number is around fifty head, no more. All homestead heads who wish to participate in such a group are responsible for taking a herding rotation from time to time. The schedule for each group is different. A herding group that includes, say, five homesteads will have five rotations, with each member perhaps responsible for a three- to five-day period during which he must herd all the cattle in that group. A male homestead head is ultimately responsible for his rotation, though in practice it is usually a man's children who do the actual herding while he himself farms.

During the wet season, from about March until after the harvest, cattle, sheep, and goats are taken to graze in the bush, far from villages and people's crops. If cattle are many, they are herded separately from sheep and goats. During this period, villages become off limits to livestock grazing and any violations of this are met with heavy fines. *Ndobida*, as it is known, is the wild vegetation in the villages that is reserved and preserved for livestock during the dry months. During the dry months, men herd livestock closer to home in the villages. There they graze on the previous year's maize, sorghum, and millet stocks, as well as the *ndobida*.

Overall, then, seasonal changes in Ihanzu, from wet to dry and back again, set the rhythms of everyday life. Wet seasons tend to be less social than dry ones, with daily labour revolving around individual homesteads. In contrast, dry-season activities following the harvest are more social as the local beer economy thrives. Food supplies, too, wax and wane with the seasons. Some activities, like herding, continue throughout the year with only minor alterations. This seasonal ebb and flow of weather, food supplies, and labour is summed up in table 1.1. The noteworthy point, above all, is the centrality of the weather to the flow of day-to-day life in Ihanzu. Not only do everyday activities move in time with the seasons. More than this, the state of the rains

Table 1.1. Calendar of seasonal activities in Ihanzu

				MEN		WOMEN	
Ihanzu months	English equivalents	Weather	Food supply	Farming	Other seasonal activities	Farming	Other seasonal activities
Mīlekana	December	Moderate rains	Grain stores declining; no fresh greens.	Sowing sorghum, millet and maize	Hunting	Sowing sorghum, millet, and maize	—
Ng'weli wa mūmbīlī	January	Heavy rains	Hunger month (low grain)	Sowing sorghum, millet and maize	—	Sowing sorghum, millet, and maize	—
Ng'weli wa mūhatu	February	Moderate rains	Hunger month (low grain); wild greens ripen	Weeding	—	Weeding	—
Ng'weli wa mūnī	March	Heavy rains	Hunger month (low grain); wild greens plentiful	" "	Migrant labour	" "	—
Ng'weli wa mūntano	April	Moderate rains	Early maize ripens	Small harvest (maize); guarding plots at night (against pigs); begin clearing new fields	" "	Small harvest (maize); guarding plots in day (against baboons and birds)	Sun-dry wild greens and tomatoes
Ng'weli wa mūtandatu	May	Rains decreasing	Ample maize	" "	" "	" "	"
Ng'weli wa mūpungatī	June	Rains stop; very cold	Sorghum and millet plentiful	Harvest sorghum and millet; guard harvest	—	Harvest millet and sorghum	"
Ng'weli wa mūnanaa	July	Very cold	" "	Threshing grain	Fishing, house building	Threshing and winnowing	House building
Ng'weli wa mūng'kenda	August	Moderate temperature	Sorghum and millet plentiful; ample leafy greens	Threshing grain; carrying grain home	Fishing; hunting; house building; weaving of beer strainers	Threshing and winnowing grain and carrying home	Weaving mats, baskets; making pots; collecting firewood; house building
Ng'weli wa mūkumi	September	Hot season	Fresh greens decreasing	Cleaning fields; spreading fertilizers	Fishing; hunting; house building	Cleaning fields; spreading fertilizers	"
Ng'weli wa kumi na kang'wī	October	Hot season; early rains	Grain stores declining; no fresh greens	spreading fertilizers	Fishing, hunting	"	"
Mītia mbeu	November	Rains begin	" "	Sowing sorghum, millet, and maize	Hunting	Sowing sorghum, millet, and maize	—

gives definitive shape to any particular season: how much farming can be done and when; how large the harvest will be, or indeed, whether there will be a harvest; how much food and beer there will be as a result; and how much vegetation there will be for livestock.

This does not mean that the weather determines men's and women's everyday lives in Ihanzu. It does not. Nor does it explain what Ihanzu villagers do – why, for example, they have a lengthy history of rain-making. As already noted, even though the Ihanzu and their neighbours live more or less in the same climatic zone, their historical experiences, cultural imaginations, and ways of going about life vary greatly.[28] Some hunt and gather; others tend cattle; still others farm. Some make rain, while others do not. The climate and weather provide the backdrop against which such variations unfold. Though crucial, they neither determine nor explain these variations.

Residence, Generation and Gender

In a place like Ihanzu where everyone depends on unreliable rains to survive, managing uncertainty is crucial. All villagers know this, of course. And all act accordingly, seeking constantly and in myriad manners, wittingly and unwittingly, to secure scarce resources to reduce everyday life's inevitable uncertainties. As is true across the planet, however, these concerns are never simply about unfettered individual strategizing. Rather, negotiating everyday life unfolds within a complex matrix of social relations and cannot be divorced, conceptually or practically, from the rights and obligations that inhere in those relations. For this reason it is necessary to detail some of the structural relations that frame, enable, and constrain everyday decisions, activities, and possibilities. This means, above all, considering kinship relations and residence. Access to and control over specific resources very much depend on one's gender and generational position in the homestead development cycle.

Ihanzu kinship fits the 'Crow' template, as anthropologists describe it, with its characteristic intergenerational skewing: patrilateral cross-cousins ascend one generation (FZS=F; FZD=M), while matrilateral cross-cousins descend one (MBS=S; MBD=D). The Ihanzu divide themselves into twelve exogamous, non-localized matriclans (*ndŭgŭ*). Clan size varies considerably: the largest – the *Anyampanda*, number around 9,000, while the smallest, the *Anyikīli*, number only about 450.[29] As the term implies, matriclan members trace descent through their mother, maternal grandmother, and so on back to a distant (or some-times not so distant) ancestress. Most people – royal clan members are the exception – cannot trace these connections back more than three or four generations. Most matriclans are subdivided into named clan-sec-tions (also called *ndũgũ*), which total thirty. Some of these control tracts of land in central Ihanzu. Clan-sections are further divided into matri-lineages or *maele* (sing. *iele*). These latter groups are often localized on homesteads and in village-sections. Everyone in Ihanzu is born into a clan, a clan-section, and a lineage. A person retains these social ties in life and death; it is impossible to lose them or to become a member of another clan.

Children also acquire specific ties and relations through their fathers. Each of the thirty matriclan sections has (at least) two addi-tional names specific to it: one male, one female. These are called *alongo* (sing. *mũlongo*). At birth, children thus receive one of two sex-specific names from their father's matriclan section. Everyone, then, is a mem-ber of his or her mother's clan, clan-section, and lineage as well as a 'child of his/her father's clan.' *Alongo* groups are not (paternal) mirror images of (maternal) clans or lineages because they do not form descent groups. However, because *alongo* membership passes from fathers to their children, and because fathers and children live for years on the same homestead, *alongo* are localized in ways similar to *maele*. Moreover, people equally evoke and trace connections through clan and *alongo*, mother and father: to share one womb (*itũgo*), to have suck-led from one breast (*maele*), or to be children of a particular clan (*ang'enya a*) are equally common and powerful ways to emphasize con-nections. The homestead in many respects encompasses all of these relations, as when men and women suggest that 'we come from the same homestead' (*ũsese kũũpũmile itando lĩng'wĩ*).

Houses or *matembe* (sing. *itembe*) are rectangular in shape, with flat mud roofs. They are about six feet tall and twenty or so feet long; they have one door located roughly in the centre and sometimes a few small windows. Most have three rooms: an inner room where sorghum, mil-let, and maize are stored and where occupants sleep; a room at the opposite end where small livestock sleep; and an entry room where people may grind, cook, eat, and rest on hot days. However, what makes a house a home – rather, a homestead – is its fenced-in, semipri-vate courtyard or byre (*itando*). It is here that occupants and visitors sit, rest, talk, eat, mend tools, weave baskets and mats, grind grain, shell peanuts, wash clothes, and brew and drink beer. Cattle and donkeys sleep in the courtyard at night. One does not speak of someone's house (*itembe*), but of his or her homestead (*itando*).

Each homestead is made up of between one and six houses; most common are homesteads with one or two. The size of a homestead depends on the stage in its development cycle, and one can fairly accurately deduce the latter from the former. Access to resources including land, food, and livestock depends on one's position on the homestead, which changes through time.

When a man first marries, he builds a house on, and becomes a full member of, his wife's father's homestead. This may or may not be in his natal village. He remains there for at least a year, perhaps two, doing brideservice. A son-in-law doing brideserve is a dependent on his father-in-law's homestead, but is not in an inferior position vis-à-vis his wife's brothers; he is a fully integrated adult from the start, forming a new but integral part of the homestead. A man's father normally pays his son's bridewealth, at least half commonly being transferred before a husband moves onto his father-in-law's homestead. Fathers-in-law usually give sons-in-law a small patch of land (*nzega*) to farm during brideservice, from which they alone reap the rewards: a son-in-law might sell his harvest to his father-in-law for a cow or several goats; or in an especially good year might divide his harvest between his father-in-law and his own father and receive a cow from each. In this way some men begin to build humble herds while doing brideservice. Yet there is really no question about where a man's allegiance lies during this time: he spends the vast majority of his time working towards the common good of his father-in-law's homestead, herding his cattle, farming his fields. A man rarely returns to help his own father during his brideservice.

A new wife, during the same period, continues to live much as before marriage, dependent on her parents for most things, doing daily household labour of farming, cooking, collecting firewood, and fetching water. But she now has new obligations towards her husband. First, she must cook for him. It is essential that she do this, people say, and that all his food be stored in and come from the main house, underscoring his dependent status on the homestead. From the day of marriage, too, a man gains full sexual rights over his wife and they sleep under one roof. A new wife and husband will live on the homestead until the wife bears a child or, failing that, until an agreed-upon period of a year or two has passed.

Following their brideservice, men commonly return to their father's village (cf. Adam 1962, 3). This sometimes means that married men return, with their wives, to live on their fathers' homesteads for a year or two, farming fields their fathers loan them. Alternatively, they might build a new independent homestead and farm their own fields nearby. Men enjoy living in their natal villages, near their fathers and friends, and are always buried there, too, the only exception being those buried in one of the few Christian or Muslim graveyards. (Wives and unmarried children are buried with their fathers.) Following brideservice, it is equally common for a married man and woman to decide to build their homestead in the wife's father's village; when this happens, they tend to do so at a distance to discourage claims on their labour. Of course in some cases a wife's and husband's parents both reside in the same village, in which case the issue of whose parents will become neighbours is a moot point.

It is a husband's job to provide land for his wife or wives, and access to land is sometimes a factor in deciding where to live. This is not normally a major factor, however, since land in Ihanzu is not a scarce commodity. It is not bought or sold. It is not an important item of inheritance. And disputes over land are very rare indeed. This is because – unlike in some parts of East Africa – land is abundant and not very fertile. Rights in land are usufructuary, and a man stands an equal or better chance of securing good farmland by cutting it from the bush rather than relying on already cleared land. In this regard, little has changed since the 1960s: 'There is no great pressure on land, and a man's acreage is not limited by lack of available land but by the amount which he can clear and cultivate.'[30]

No matter what their eventual location, however, a husband and wife who begin their own homestead are no longer expected to work for or contribute to their father's or father-in-law's households – or, for that matter, to anyone else's. Homesteads are meant to be self-sufficient in matters of production and consumption: homestead members farm their own fields, build their own herds, and take care of all their own needs. A wife on her own homestead has her own grinding stone, grainstore, and cooking hearth, and homestead occupants eat separately from those of other homesteads. A husband and wife both contribute to the production and reproduction of their household, though in different ways. For the most part, it is a wife's responsibility to run her household. A wife decides when and what she will cook, when she will fetch water and cut firewood – all tasks that consume considerable amounts of time each day. She is also usually responsible for everyday monetary concerns: taxes and fines must be paid; children's school uniforms, pencils and paper, cooking and lamp oil, soap and clothing must be purchased. Women have disposal rights over many consumables that can be used to generate income to cover such expenses, the most significant of which is grain.

Together, a man and his wife farm their fields. Yet once the grain is harvested and has been safely stowed in their grainstore, the wife gains control over its allocation within and outside the household. It becomes 'hers.' Since grain is the essential ingredient for all meals and beer – never mind the key to dry season sociality – control over it amounts to control over a large sphere of everyday social life. Such control is not merely token. I have seen cases where a man was asked to sell some grain for livestock, or to give some to a needy clan member, but was effectively refused by his wife on the grounds that it would deplete the stock to dangerously low levels. Husbands are often dim about household budgeting and tend to respect their wives' judgments on these matters. With her grain, a wife must budget from one harvest to the next; grain supplies rarely last into a second year. She must decide how much she can spare for needy neighbours, kin, and others and still have enough to provide for herself, her husband, and their children. Wives can and sometimes do sell grain in non-famine years (typically to neighbours, more rarely beyond their own village). However, because everyone grows grain, grain sales generate little direct cash income. Finally, a wife must take decisions about when and how many times to brew beer (*ntūlī*), the single largest contributor to everyday household income and the local cash economy. Women are entitled to all proceeds from their beer sales, which are normally put towards household expenses. An average beer brew of three buckets of grain can generate between 4,000 and 8,000 Tanzanian shillings (about US $7.25 to $14.50). This may not sound like much. Yet when one considers ordinary expenditures – annual personal taxes of Sh1500, cattle tax of Sh60 per head, sheep and goat tax Sh30 per head, a bar of soap Sh100, a pair of tyre sandals Sh200 – one can see that such income goes some way towards covering villagers' everyday monetary expenses.[31]

A wife also has disposal rights over several other food items that helps her run her household, including cultivated cassava, sweet potatoes, and fruits as well as the wild, dried leafy greens she prepares. Government regulations require that every household farm one acre of such foods, and yields can be significant. Even so, there is no cash market for these items locally, and they tend to be bartered for other foodstuffs when necessary. Wives may sell or exchange their leafy greens for other food items in short supply, such as grain; they also control some food items, including beans, peanuts, and sunflowers. However, because the proceeds from cash crops like sunflowers can potentially be substantial, their sale usually requires consultation between husband and wife. Finally, a wife has full disposal rights over the milk from her husband's herd, which she may trade, sell, or use within her own household.

Husbands, for their part, own and control most livestock, the single most important valuable in Ihanzu. These animals are an important store of wealth, and many seek every opportunity to build their herds. Some begin during brideservice; others wait until they have established their own homesteads. Men inherit livestock, use it to pay bridewealth, and make all important decisions concerning its sale and slaughter. Monthly livestock auctions are held in the village of Ibaga, and Tanzanians from surrounding areas often buy and sell cattle there, too. Cattle fetch high prices, anywhere from Sh18,000 to Sh38,000 (between US $32–$69).[32] Thus Ihanzu men can, if they must, sell or buy livestock nearly any time of the year to generate income. They usually do so, though, only under duress, as when, for example, a large fine, tax payment, or hospital bill cannot be afforded from the everyday household budget. On the whole, men are very reluctant to part with their livestock, even in famine years.

Men use cattle to build social ties. Cattle loans are not uncommon, and any given man may look after his own cattle as well as those of a few clan members and friends; others who own no cattle can also take care of those belonging to others, which provides certain material benefits. Key among them, a man who cannot afford to buy his own cattle is entitled to all the milk and fertilizer of those he takes care of and may use them for ploughing his fields. Cattle owners, for their part, gain some degree of security against livestock disease and drought, and strengthen their social ties by dispersing their cattle across their village and beyond.

In sum, while both husband and wife contribute to their homestead's reproduction, they do so in different ways. When it comes to foodstuffs, women have near exclusive control over processes of exchange and consumption. This includes control over the major crops, sorghum and millet, and over several lesser ones as well. Livestock, on the other hand – especially cattle – are seen as 'men's business,' from which women are for the most part excluded. As we shall

see in the chapters to follow, this particular gendered allocation of
resources and their conceptual associations take on special significance
in ritual contexts, including rainmaking.

After some years, a man may decide to take a second wife. He must
then build a house and carry out brideservice on his new father-in-
law's homestead, just as he did on his first father-in-law's homestead.
He divides his time and efforts equally between his own homestead
and that of his new father-in-law, where he is considered a dependant.
Following brideservice, the husband returns to his own homestead,
and his new wife usually follows him. However, she will not live in his
first wife's house; rather, she will usually have her own, and her own
grainstore and firewood, and do her own cooking and farm (with her
husband) her own fields – in short, she will have her own household.
In some cases, second (or third) wives may live farther away in the
same village or even in a different village. In all cases, a husband is
expected to spend equal time at each of his wives' houses. He is also
responsible for finding adequate fields for each of his wives. In the
1960s about one in four Ihanzu men was polygynous, most having two
wives (Adam 1962, 5); today, this practice is less common, and only 7
per cent of married men are polygynous.[33]

As a man ages, so his homestead grows and the number of people
under his authority increases, as do his responsibilities to others. If his
mother or mother-in-law is widowed, either or both may come to live
on his homestead, where they will often have a separate house, field,
grainstore, hearth, and firewood. The same goes for divorced sisters,
who sometimes (especially if their father is dead) join their brothers'
homesteads. Finally, as a man's own daughters grow up and marry, his
new sons-in-law will join his homestead to carry out brideservice.
Some such individuals may come with land and/or livestock. Others
will not. Homestead heads normally provide small parcels of farmland
for all those living on their homestead. If a homestead head has several
teenaged daughters, sons-in-law, and other dependents living on his
homestead, he will be in charge of a considerable labour force, and will
thus be able to clear and cultivate large fields.

A wife (or wives) will wield more power and have additional
responsibilities as her homestead grows, particularly if the additions
are dependants. She will sometimes spend more time fetching water,
cutting firewood, grinding grain, and cooking, and proportionally less
time farming. But she also gains some flexibility over which daily tasks
she performs and which she allocates to others. Sometimes a wife will

alternate household labour with her daughters and other homestead residents; for example, she might farm one day while her daughters or others grind grain, cut firewood, or fetch water.

Thus a homestead can be large at this stage in the development cycle – sometimes with ten or more people living on it – and control considerable resources. From this apex, a homestead steadily declines. Sons-in-law move away, as do married sons and daughters. Female dependants may remarry and relocate. Elderly relatives will eventually die. Individual houses on the homestead fall into disrepair, eventually collapsing and returning to the earth from which they rose. At the same time, the number of plots a man and his wife can reasonably farm dwindles, and with that, so does the size of their harvest. Eventually households are left with a husband and wife alone, for whom self-reproduction is no simple feat. It is not uncommon at this point for some of the couple's grandchildren to move in with them, for short or longer periods, to help them with farming and household chores – one reason why the grandparent–grandchild relationship is so significant in Ihanzu (cf. Adam 1962, 6). Relations between grandparents and grandchildren are characterized by easiness, affection, and mild teasing (maheko). Grandparents do not discipline their grandchildren; that job is left to parents. A child is commonly named after her or his grandparents (if bridewealth has been paid, after the child's father's father; if not, after the mother's father). When grandchildren live with their grandparents, the latter are nearly always dependant on the former rather than the reverse.

Permeating and cross-cutting these everyday living arrangements and the homestead development cycle are two specific – and contradictory – understandings of everyday gender relations. Both are asymmetrical, though in opposite ways: one claims male superiority, the other female superiority. Women and men alike find these understandings compelling at different times and in different contexts.

The idea that male is superior to female animates much of daily life in Ihanzu and informs women's and men's ideas and practices surrounding an array of daily activities; it is also the most common picture Ihanzu men and women provide, when anthropologists press them, to sum up everyday gender relations. This discourse asserts the frivolity of the feminine, suggesting that women are sometimes simple, irresponsible, and lacking in foresight. Many daily activities are justified on these grounds. The whens, wheres, and whats of planting, for instance, are almost always decisions men make, often on the grounds that women cannot understand the complexities of these matters. This is also why, many say, women are dependent throughout their lives on men; first on their fathers, then on their husbands. Similar arguments are commonly made for why men manage livestock.

Such asymmetrical understandings of gender relations similarly pervade everyday politics, where Ihanzu women as a group participate only minimally. When important village matters arise – cattle theft, rain-witchcraft, battles over cattle with neighbouring pastoralists, and so forth – village meetings are called. Men are expected to participate actively. Most do. Women, on the other hand, do not. Though they sometimes attend, they do not speak. Nor, most agree, should they. Economically, too, as we have seen, women are in many respects dependent on men throughout their lives.

Whatever salience this first disparaging discourse and set of practices about male–female relations might possess, it is, in other situations, thoroughly unravelled by its antithesis: the notion that female is superior to male. Thus men and women routinely point out that only women understand their own households and how to run them; and there are plenty of single-female–headed households to bear this out. Of equal importance, women have close to total control over grain and its allocation within and outside the household. Women thus control much of everyday life and the beer-related sociality that is integral to it. Women control beer brewing, and furthermore, some build considerable status and prestige by consistently brewing good beer. Villagers well know which women are better brewers, and will, in the dry season, walk for miles to attend a beer party given by any such woman. Thus, if men gain power and prestige by controlling livestock, women do the same with beer. And no one can say categorically which is, on balance, more important than the other. Indeed, from a local vantage point, when it comes to gender relations, there is no such thing as 'on balance.' It all depends on context.

Everyday discussions reflect this collective indecision about the precise nature of the relationship between male and female. One middle-aged Ihanzu man from Ng'wangeza village, when I asked him, quickly noted that men were superior to women. After a brief pause, he followed his categorical quip by telling me: 'But sometimes women are more powerful than we [men]. We depend on them. [...] A man may live in a house alone but without a wife he is helpless, or at least he has a lot of difficulties. He must fetch his own water, cut his own firewood, cook his own food. He can't! [...] We depend on women like we depend on rain. [...] If you look at it from another angle, perhaps it is really women who are the important ones, the most powerful.'

Women, like men, share similar indecision about the relationship between male and female. Women and men alike find it impossible to sum up everyday gender relations in any meaningful way, even if all can point to specific examples and contexts where there is notional agreement. For Ihanzu men and women alike, then, everyday life is characterized by competing views on the nature of gender relations. The relative status of the genders is situationally defined and varies a great deal. There is no single 'gender system,' if by this we mean a coherent, all-embracing answer to the question, 'What is the relationship between male and female?' What we find instead is a series of answers that changes depending on context. Because the answers given are context specific and contradict one another, establishing the relation between the genders is, in Ihanzu eyes, an unfinished project. As we shall see in the remainder of this book, this project is further complicated by a third understanding of the relationship between male and female: gender complementarity or equality. It is this notion of gender that underpins all Ihanzu rainmaking rites today, and has for more than a century.

Chapter 2

The Making and Unmaking of Rains and Reigns

With little food and no more European goods to give to (and hopefully impress) local leaders, the tired German explorer C.W. Werther, followed by a nearly endless queue of even more tired trunk-toting porters, reached the Wembere swamps just north-west of Ihanzu. The year was 1893. It was the rainy season, and rain there was. Lots of it.

As is common even in dry years, all the more so in wet ones, the Wembere swamps had flooded, making any passage a potentially perilous one. Rather than turn back, the party toiled determinedly for hours to construct a bridge across the Sibiti River, a feat they accomplished in spite of a hippo's savage attack on their temporary structure. After all had safely reached the other side, the bridge promptly collapsed and was swept away by the floodwaters.

Several hours later, Werther entered central Ihanzu, thus becoming the first European to have done so. He sent some of his messengers ahead to the male rainmaker's homestead ('the Sultan,' Werther calls him) to make him aware of their arrival. And to demand foodstuffs. The full party arrived shortly thereafter.

Perplexed by such an oddity, some Ihanzu men looked on curiously as Werther's party set up camp. Recognizing one particularly exquisite bovine with Werther's party as belonging to a man in Sukumaland, one local came forward and asked where Werther had acquired the beast. It was true, the man was assured[1] – it had belonged to the Mwanangwa from Miatu, but had been purchased from him. Curiosity aroused, the man persisted with his questioning.

How had Werther and his party managed to cross the river, given that it was completely flooded? Again, one of Werther's assistants answered: 'The Great Lord here' – gesturing to Werther – 'made a powerful *dawa* [medicine] that made the river drop, we crossed and the waters swelled once again.' This must have been astonishing news, as such medicines were the purview of powerful persons alone, like their own royal rainmakers. Werther, so it appeared, possessed medicines – potent ones at that – that could influence the elements, causing rivers to rise and fall and who knows what else.

Soon thereafter, fierce fighting erupted between the two sides, which eventually led to Werther's and his party's hasty retreat to the east (Werther 1894, 221ff). Thus began the Ihanzu's first contact – and conflict – with Europeans. It would not be the last.

In this initial, tentative Ihanzu encounter with a European explorer, Ihanzu rainmakers and their medicines featured prominently. This would be so thereafter in one way, shape, or form throughout Ihanzu history and into the present. For this reason, it is impossible to speak of Ihanzu history without speaking of Ihanzu rainmakers and the medicinal powers they command. Ihanzu rainmakers played a pivotal role in integrating and regulating certain types of regional, precolonial trade; they also provided the basis for an Ihanzu moral community. Years later, they featured crucially in anticolonial resistance movements. Beginning in the 1920s, they gave specific form to the newly invented Ihanzu 'chiefdom.' And when, in the 1960s, Tanzanian chiefdoms were abolished across the land, Ihanzu rainmakers continued to hold sway. They still do today. In short, throughout a tumultuous history, a period that witnessed sweeping political, economic, and social changes of every imaginable sort, Ihanzu rainmaking and rainmakers have remained remarkably important (cf. Packard 1981; Feierman 1990).

Much of this importance has turned on Ihanzu's two royal rainmakers – one male, the other female – and the powers they jointly command. In Ihanzu eyes, when it comes to rainmaking, one gender without the other is pointless and impotent. Neither the male rainmaker nor the female one can bring rain alone. Thus to speak of rainmaking is to speak of gender. Curiously enough, this fact, so apparent to the Ihanzu themselves, was repeatedly missed or ignored by successive waves of outsiders: by German and British colonials and later by postcolonial administrators. No colonial or postcolonial administration ever formally recognized Ihanzu's female rainmaker, even though she has been pivotal for as far back as oral and written histories take us (Adam 1963b; Kohl-Larsen 1943, 290). As we shall see, this fundamental neglect or oversight has had profound consequences, not least in framing how anticolonial resistance was dealt with; how the Ihanzu chiefship was eventually given its contours; and how postcolonial administrators view Ihanzu rainmaking today.

Early History, Rainmaking and Identity

For the women and men of Ihanzu, rainmaking is inextricably linked to their earliest history, migration, and identity. I have heard only one Ihanzu origin story, the one all Ihanzu know, the one many have told over the years to non-Ihanzu with evident zeal (Kohl-Larsen 1943, 194–5; Adam 1963b, 14–15).[2] The story comes with minor variations, though all versions tell of an ancient migration from Ukerewe Island in Lake Victoria to the Ihanzu's present location. Different clans, driven by famine and drought, made this lengthy journey. During the migration, people say, each clan or clan-section rested or settled temporarily at various sites along the way. These places are remembered by name, and are today used as ancestral offering sites, particularly those within Ihanzu proper.

After some warring between clans and with others en route, the migrants, people say, took refuge in Ihanzu's central mountainous region, an area called *Ihanzu la ng'wa Kingwele* (Kingwele's Ihanzu), named after one of the first *Anyansuli* clan members. The village of Kirumi is the focal point here, Ihanzu's 'sacred centre.' This is a rocky, highland area surrounded on all sides by vast open plains. There, the story goes, they built a large, fenced-in enclosure in which to live in safety. When men or beasts threatened, they could seal up the entrance with a large door made of sturdy poles called *mahanzu* (sing. *ihanzu*). The people thus became known as Anyïhanzu: 'the people of the byre door pole.'

During the migration, each clan allegedly brought particular things with it. Some came with seeds, others with cattle. Few can name all the clans and clan-sections or spell out what, exactly, each supposedly brought with it. People never fail to mention, though, that the first Ihanzu rainmakers also came from Ukerewe, bringing with them their rainmaking knowledge and ritual paraphernalia. For many, this seems to be the point of telling the migration story in the first place – to say, in so many words, 'We came from Ukerewe with our rainmakers, rain medicines, and rain.'

Whether this original migration ever took place we may never know.[3] But fact or fiction, the idea that it did occur has informed

Ihanzu notions of their history and identity since at least the turn of the last century.[4] Everyone I asked about what makes an Ihanzu an Ihanzu – male or female, young or old, 'rich' or poor, religious or not – explicitly noted as much, often pointing proudly in the northerly direction of Ukerewe for added emphasis. It is no doubt true, as Lambek (1996, 239; also 2002) reminds us, that such expressed visions and versions of the past are inextricably linked to their consequences for relations in the present. But it must equally be said, at least for the Ihanzu, that this present has been recognizable for more than a century. The women and men of Ihanzu have long identified themselves as a 'rainmaking people' who, from the very beginning of time, have owned and controlled their own rain.

Precolonial Rainmaking Economies[5]

In the 1880s and 1890s, just before the arrival of German colonial forces, the men and women of Ihanzu lived over a relatively small highland area centred on Kirumi. They were also embedded in an expansive regional economy, warring and exchanging, raiding and trading with their neighbours (see map 2.1).

The pastoral Maasai and Tatog made periodic cattle raids into Ihanzu (Adam 1961, 3, 5; Kidamala and Danielson 1961, 74–5; Reche 1914, 69),[6] and many elders tell of the heroic exploits of Ihanzu men who, hidden among the many boulders and caves in the area, shot and killed Maasai with arrows as they passed through with their stolen Iramba, Iambi, and Turu cattle. From time to time, Ihanzu returned the stolen bovine goods to their rightful owners in the south, sometimes for a profit.[7]

During this period, Arab and Nyamwezi caravan traders passed to the south and north of Ihanzu (Alpers 1969; Roberts 1970). Some Ihanzu men obtained beads from southern caravan traders, and iron for hoes from Nyamwezi traders (Kidamala and Danielson 1961, 77; Obst 1923, 218n, 222; Stuhlmann 1894, 759, 763; Werther 1894, 238). From Sukuma traders to the north, Ihanzu traders acquired iron in return for salt gathered at Lake Eyasi (Obst 1912a, 112; Reche 1914, 84; 1915, 261). The hunting and gathering Hadza, also to the north, provided the Ihanzu with ivory, rhino horns, honey, and arrow poison in return for calabashes, beads, cloth, knives, axes, and metal arrowheads (Obst 1912a, 112; 1912b, 24; Reche 1914, 19, 71; Woodburn 1988a, 51; 1988b).[8] To the north-east, the Ihanzu exchanged goods with Iraqw traders: articles made by their own smiths – arrowheads, knives, hoes,

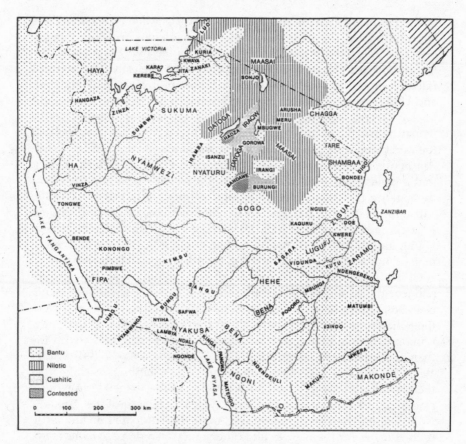

Map 2.1. 'Tanzania' c. 1890 (source: Koponen 1988)

and axes – in return for livestock, red earthen body paint, tobacco, and arrow poison (Obst 1912a, 112; Reche 1914, 69, 71). And as far east as Mbugwe, some Ihanzu traders obtained brass and copper jewellery, since Ihanzu smiths were adept at working with iron but unskilled at working with softer metals (Reche 1914, 84).

Thus, far from being isolated in their mountainous homeland in precolonial times, the Ihanzu – or rather, some men from Ihanzu – ranged far and wide, maintaining extensive trading networks across the region. They were always involved in a broader regional political-economy.

The people of Ihanzu and their royal *Anyampanda* clan rainmakers were renowned for their powerful rain medicines well beyond the boulder-strewn confines of their own land. In the 1890s, and likely earlier, the Ihanzu played a key role in what might be called the regional rainmaking economy. People from Turu, Iambi, Iramba, Sukumaland, and Hadza country made annual pilgrimages to the royal Ihanzu village of Kirumi, bringing tribute of black sheep, among other things, to Ihanzu rainmakers. In return, they were given rain medicines so that the rains would be plentiful in their own lands (Adam 1963b).[9] Royal *Anyampanda* rainmaking powers were considered so potent, in fact, that peoples from Turu and Iramba to the south – who had their own rainmaking traditions, medicines, and shrines – routinely visited the Kirumi rainshrine in harsh years to obtain stronger medicines (Adam 1961, 2; Jellicoe 1969, 3). (During my stay in Kirumi I met several young and middle-aged men who had come from Iramba and Sukumaland to visit the royal rainmakers for this purpose) (see map 2.1).

Others in the region who made no regular pilgrimages to Kirumi still recognized the medicinal superiority of Ihanzu's royal rainmaking clan. Today rainmakers in faraway places derive their authority from their Ihanzu origins. In Mbulu, the Iraqw's *Manda* clan regulates the rain, and people there claim that *Manda* powers originated with the Ihanzu *Anyampanda* rainmaking clan (Thornton 1980, 203–4; Winter 1955, 11; Snyder 2005, 126–7). Similarly, the Wambugwe claim that their royal rainmaking clan had its origins in the Ihanzu *Anyampanda* clan (Gray 1955, 42; 1963, 145; Kesby 1981, 41; Thornton 1980, 216).[10]

Precolonial Ihanzu rainmakers did more than prepare rain and fertility medicines for themselves and others; they also prepared war medicines. Royal *Anyampanda* medicines were so potent, my informants commonly claimed, that Maasai and Tatog were defeated time and time again and eventually repelled from Ihanzu never to return.[11]

For various reasons, then – namely, because they provided rainmaking, fertility, and war medicines – the Kirumi rainshrine, Ihanzu royal rainmakers, and the powers they controlled served as a precolonial focal point for many peoples across an expansive area.[12] If this was true across the region, it was equally the case within Ihanzu itself.

In the 1890s, the people of Ihanzu numbered no more than a few thousand. Villagers farmed sorghum, millet, groundnuts, manioc, sweet potatoes, beans, and tobacco. Domestic livestock included cattle, sheep, goats, and donkeys (*Deutsches Kolonialblatt* 1901, 903; Obst 1923, 218; Reche 1914, 69–70; 1915, 260; Werther 1894, 238; 1898, 72).[13] Ihanzu

men had a reputation as keen hunters[14] as well as competent smiths
(Obst 1923, 218–22; Reche 1914, 84; Werther 1898, 72).[15] In this mountainous area, which was fairly densely populated (*Deutsches Kolonialblatt* 1901, 903; Obst 1912a, 114), men and women worked their fields
together. All lands were owned and allocated by particular matriclans.
When a man cleared the bush in order to farm or live, that land became
his matriclan's property (Reche 1914, 74).[16]

Men and women alike greatly valued ornamental beads, which they
obtained from caravans passing through Turu and Iramba (Stuhlmann
1894, 759, 763; Werther 1894, 238). Blue and white beads were the most
sought after (Obst 1923, 223; Reche 1915, 260), being ritually auspicious
colours and associated with rainmaking (cf. Tanner 1957, 199). The fact
that Ihanzu men wore bead necklaces, and that women wore beads on
their arms and legs, around their waists, and in their hair (see plates
2.1, 2.2, and 2.3), prompted one early German observer to dub them
'the Bead People' (*Perlenvolk*) (Obst 1912a, 115).

Ihanzu villages were fairly independent and largely autonomous
with regard to their own internal affairs. All villages were governed
informally by groups of male elders, who were the final arbiters in village matters. When inter- or intra-village conflicts developed over
murders or adultery, fines were negotiated between the parties
involved (Reche 1914, 85).[17] Movement between villages was sometimes dangerous and often required certain medicinal protections and
precautions (Adam 1963b, 17).

Yet villages and villagers, in spite of some tensions between them,
were connected in practice, in that all recognized the supreme authority of the royal rainmaking clan section: the *Anyampanda wa Kirumi*
(Adam 1963b).[18] There were on any given occasion two royal rainmakers – one male, the other female – known as the 'owners of the land'
(*akola ihĩ*). In the 1890s the male 'owner' was Semu Malekela (Werther
1898, 72–3); Semu's female counterpart was his sister's daughter, Nya
Matalũ.[19]

These two royal owners of the land lived in and rarely ventured
beyond the royal village of Kirumi. They were jointly responsible for
the general welfare and prosperity of all Ihanzu villagers. Semu initiated male circumcision ceremonies (*kidamu*),[20] hunting parties,[21] and
salt-fetching caravans to the northern salt flats.[22] He could also offer
sanctuary to murderers, regardless of the Ihanzu village from which
they came (Adam 1963b: 16; cf., S.F. Moore 1986: 57; Rigby 1971: 397).
Nya Matalũ, for her part, initiated and coordinated women's rain

Plate 2.1. Ihanzu women displaying their adornments, 1911 (photo by E. Obst [1912a])

Plate 2.2. Elderly Ihanzu woman, c. 1934 to 1939 (photo by Kohl-Larsen [1956])

Plate 2.3. Elderly Ihanzu man, c. 1934 to 1939 (photo by Kohl-Larsen [1956])

dances (*masīmpūlya*) in dry years and played an indispensable role in various other rain rites.

Together, this royal duo regulated the Ihanzu agricultural cycle from the first cutting-of-the-sod ceremony (*kūtema ilīma*), which initiated each new agricultural season, to giving the order to begin the harvest (*kūpegwa lupyu*). They also made war medicines together. In a variety of ways, the fertility of the land and the well-being of its inhabitants were in the hands of these two royal owners. This, in turn, gave them a degree of political authority within Ihanzu (Adam 1963b).[23]

Semu and Nya Matalū were assisted in their rainmaking tasks by male and female rainmaking assistants known as *ataata* (sing. *mūtaata*). Each Ihanzu village had at least one such assistant. These assistants exercised no particular power or authority over fellow villagers on the basis of their positions; they functioned more as intermediaries between the two royal *Anyampanda* rainmakers in Kirumi and villagers from other parts of Ihanzu.[24]

In August or September of each year, rainmaking assistants collected grain from their respective villages, which they then brought as tribute to the owners of the land in Kirumi (Reche 1914, 85; 1915, 261; Werther 1898, 99). Some of this grain, informants say, was divided between the two royal rainmakers, blessed, and later returned by the assistants to the villages from which it came to ensure all-round fertility. The remainder was later used by Nya Matalū and her female assistants to brew sorghum beer for the annual rainmaking or *kūtema ilīma* ceremonies.

Semu and Nya Matalū jointly initiated these rites each year in Kirumi, usually in October. Ihanzu rainmaking assistants attended, bringing with them a number of children from their home villages. Rainmaking assistants from outside Ihanzu – those from farther afield who received rainmaking medicine from Ihanzu royals – are also said to have attended these rites. After a 'grandson' and 'granddaughter' cut the sod with special hoes (a long-handled 'male' hoe and short-handled 'female' one), the children, who probably numbered in the hundreds, began hoeing the royal *Anyampanda* fields adjacent to the Kirumi rainshrine. These annual cutting-of-the-sod ceremonies normally lasted a day and a half (cf. Adam 1963b).

The pre-colonial picture of Ihanzu in the early 1890s that emerges is one of a small number of decentralised and largely autonomous villages, clustered around the boulder-strewn centre of the country. Each village was responsible for its own internal political, legal, and economic affairs. Village elders – any men of advanced age – governed their own daily activities. From this highland 'fortress,' some members of the community occasionally trekked over vast distances and were deeply involved in long-distance trading of various goods in neighbouring areas.

There was limited cooperation between villages, occasionally there was fighting. People did, however, share a common purpose in both warfare and rainmaking. And in both instances, villagers looked to the two *Anyampanda* owners of the land in Kirumi for protection and to cure their ills. Indeed, the very flow of day-to-day life throughout Ihanzu – the farming cycle, hunting, circumcision, the rains, and the state of the land itself – hinged inexorably on the powers of the two rainmaking royals.

Unmaking Reigns and Rains

It was into this world of cross-regional trading, raiding, and rainmaking that German military forces made their first forays in the late 1800s. A principal objective of these forces was to 'pacify the natives,' as it were, not least because much 'tribal' hostility was being directed against the Germans themselves. These pacification efforts and local resistance to them are best understood from a regional perspective, since colonial forts and forces in one area often made their influence felt in places farther afield.[25]

For some years, Gogo people had been extracting tariffs from passing caravans (including German ones) – a practice that German colonialists, for obvious reasons, deplored (Peters 1891, 521). Thus, in 1894 they erected a massive fortress in Ugogo (Obst 1923, 303–4; Prince 1895; Sick 1915, 59). Kilimatinde, as the fortress was called, was about thirteen days south of Ihanzu country by caravan, or five days for runners (Admiralty 1916, 326). From Fort Kilimatinde colonial forces tentatively extended their influence to the west and north, into Turu, Iramba, Iambi, and Ihanzu (Sick 1915, 59–60).[26] But not without grave difficulties. They often encountered people who, as one early observer meekly and misleadingly put it, 'did not like the protection of the Germans' (Obst 1923, 304). More to the point, anticolonial resistance and revolts were rife right across the region for decades.[27]

The German military response was often a simple one: to kill as many as was deemed necessary to quell the situation. One popular strategy was to capture and hang local leaders, diviners, and rainmakers, who were seen as roguish and responsible for inciting anticolonial violence. In many cases, German suspicions were patently correct: traditional leaders, rainmakers, and the like were often uniquely situated to unite people against aggressive colonial forces, both locally and across vast expanses (cf. Lan 1985; Jellicoe, Sima, and Sombi 1968; Maddox 1988, 759; Sick 1915, 45; Swantz 1974, 77).[28]

From Kilimatinde, German military patrols made their first large-scale expedition into Iramba and Ihanzu areas in 1899. In Iramba, they swiftly captured some local leaders, some of whom were hanged (Lindström 1987, 38).[29] In Ihanzu, the story was different. The Ihanzu male rainmaker, Semu, who had repelled Werther's party seven years before, had by this time died; his younger brother, Kitentemi, had succeeded him as male rainmaker sometime in 1897 or 1898. Nya Matalũ was still female rainmaker (see figure 2.1). The Germans were either unaware of or unconcerned about these 'leaders.' For instead of capturing and/or hanging them, they simply appointed a *jumbe*,[30] a man by the name of Mũgunda s/o (son of) Nzega, who was to rule over Ihanzu and who would periodically report to them at Kilimatinde.[31]

Somewhat predictably, this proved an unsatisfactory arrangement. People in Ihanzu continued to cause problems. As a result, colonial officials decided to establish an outpost of Fort Kilimatinde, a new fort in Ihanzu proper (Obst 1923, 304; Sick 1915, 60). They chose Mkalama village, just southwest of central Ihanzu. On 26 May 1901, one Sergeant Künster and his troops arrived and built a temporary 'thorn fortress' as well as necessary living quarters for the soldiers. The German-appointed *jumbe* assured Künster that the men and women of Ihanzu, now reputedly under his control, had surrendered completely to the colonial government. Indeed, in certain respects, things were looking up: around a thousand locals showed up at the site, supposedly to make peace with the new administration, and they celebrated well into the night. Not insignificantly, Kitentemi was not among them (*Deutsches Kolonialblatt* 1901, 903).

German forces soon began erecting a large stone fort at the same location. This immense structure, part of which still stands, is perched high atop a hill, surrounded by massive stone walls (plate 2.4). The location, wind-swept though it is, affords a view of much of western Ihanzu and, to the south and west, well into Iramba and Sukumaland. The fortress took eight years to complete, largely by forced Ihanzu and Iramba labour.

Peace dances aside, the Germans' problems did not end in 1901. Not

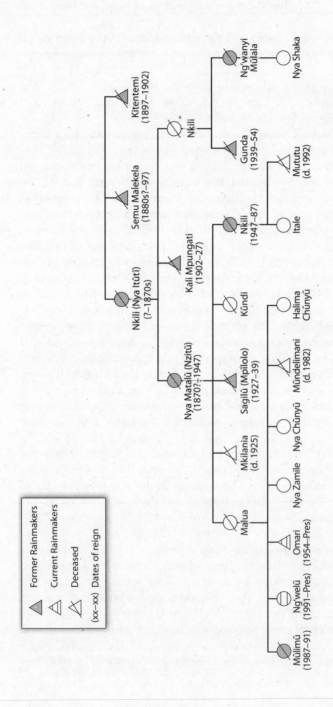

Figure 2.1. *Anyampanda wa Kirumi royal matrilineage*

Plate 2.4. Remains of Fort Mkalama, 1995 (Photo by T. Sanders)

even close. For just after beginning their Mkalama fort – only weeks after the grand 'peace dance,' in fact – there was a district-wide uprising directed against colonial forces and their instruments, the German-appointed *jumbe* (*Deutsches Kolonialblatt* 1902, 587).[32] Revolts barely subsided.

In June 1902, Ihanzu, Iramba, and Iambi forces attacked and annihilated a number of colonial caravans (*Deutsches Kolonialblatt* 1903, 1). Following several such successful campaigns, 'the natives were so emboldened as to send a formal declaration of war to the military post at Mkalama.'[33] Zahn, the German sergeant in charge at Mkalama, dispatched troops to Iambi. They suffered heavy losses at the hands of locals, who had joined forces with men from Ihanzu and Iramba. In the end, many African colonial troops and two European officers were killed in the battle.[34] 'The position was now so serious that Zahn had to retire to Mkalama and call in all his patrols, a move which appeared very necessary when a series of attacks on Mkalama ensued which were repulsed only with great difficulty.'[35] Days later, reinforcements arrived at Mkalama from the German fort at Mpwapwa, and the revamped colonial forces mounted another assault. This time they were victorious (*Deutsches Kolonialblatt* 1902, 587; Thurnwald 1935, 18).

From oral and written sources, it is clear that Ihanzu's then rainmakers, Kitentemi and Nya Matalū, played an instrumental role in these anticolonial battles (Adam 1961, 9; 1963b, 17; Jellicoe 1969, 3). Little wonder, really, since they had already proved themselves and their medicinal powers the previous decade by successfully repelling invasive Maasai and Tatog cattle thieves. Nor was this fact lost on the German administration – or at least half this fact. For this time the rainmaker Kitentemi was captured, hauled to Fort Kilimatinde and hanged.[36] Nya Matalū, for her part, seems to have benefited greatly from colonialists' lack of knowledge about differently gendered rainmaking pairs: she survived the encounter unscathed and, according to informants, continued to prepare rain secretly in Kirumi with Kitentemi's sister's son, the new rainmaker, Kali (figure 2.1). Kitentemi's capture and removal signalled the end of violent anticolonial resistance in Ihanzu.

In Ihanzu today, Kitentemi is a household name. He is remembered not so much for what he did during his brief period as male rainmaker, but for what became of him: he was captured and taken away, never to return to Ihanzu again. During my fieldwork, women and men seemed to enjoy speculating, when asked, about Kitentemi's fate. Some suggested that he might have been taken to Germany to start a rainmaking clan there. Most, however, proffered that Kitentemi's fate is simply a mystery and that we shall never know for certain – this, even though most are well aware that German forces captured and hanged rain-makers, diviners, and leaders from all across the region. It is as if the many men and women who spoke to me about Kitentemi and German colonial history refuse to see the defeat of royal rainmakers or their powers, as if they prefer to cast their own history (at least when it comes to rainmaking) as an open question. What is more, people claim that when German forces stole their male rainmaker, Kitentemi, in so doing they stole the rain. And life turned bad. Very bad.

On balance, the first decade of the twentieth century was not a kind one to the men and women of Ihanzu. The decade saw drought after drought, famine after famine, particularly towards its end. Faced on and off with starvation, many desperate villagers bartered away the few cattle they had for grain in Iramba, Turu, and Sukumaland (Sick 1915, 18).[37] To complicate matters further, the German administration imposed taxes during this period (Admiralty 1916, 19–20; Jellicoe 1969, 10). This was one reason why, during the famine years of 1907–10, many Ihanzu and Iramba villagers began trekking to the northern part of the territory to work on the northern railway and plantations in Moshi and Arusha (Adam 1963a; Iliffe 1979, 161). At home in the villages and beyond, forced labour under German rule became a deplorable fact of life. This included bush clearing, road construction, and fort building at Mkalama. For the latter task, Ihanzu men had to walk to Mbulu District, where they picked up (quite literally) beams and carried them back to Ihanzu. Each trip took a few days.

Everyday resistance, to borrow Scott's (1985) term – foot-dragging, apparent sluggishness, and extreme reluctance to carry out colonial labour of any sort – became part of Ihanzu's everyday political landscape (Admiralty 1916, 80–1).[38] Some men refused to carry out such work at all. Others worked at such an exaggeratedly lethargic pace that some German observers remained in a constant state of anxiety, annoyance, and incomprehension.[39]

But not all stayed to resist the new colonial regime. Many simply left. One elderly man born in Kirumi village said this:

I was born during the period (I don't know the date) when they started building that fort at Mkalama [1901]. After they began building that fort, the Germans gathered people to do the work there. My parents both saw

that the work was too hard and wanted to leave so we moved to Sukumaland. I was only small at the time and was carried on my mother's back ...

When we arrived in Sukumaland, we lived there until I grew up a bit,
and it was then that my father was forced to go and fight in the [First
World] War. His name was Kea. When my father was taken, I was fully
aware of what was going on. I saw my father was going to war ...

After my father was taken off to fight, I went to live with my grandfather who had come with us to Sukumaland. He also wanted to get far
away from those Germans and their fort.

I collected many life histories like this one that attest to the fact that
countless men, women, and children left Ihanzu during this first
decade of German occupation. They did so not just to get food and
return, as happens under other circumstances, but rather to escape the
clutches of the governmental menace at their doorstep. In all directions
they scattered: into Hadza country, Sukumaland, and Mbulu.[40]

It was during these trying, turbulent times, my informants claim,
that the two royal *Anyampanda* rainmakers, Kali and his sister Nya
Matalũ, fled Ihanzu for Hadza country to the north. One of my most
reliable informants, an elderly woman from Ibaga village, gave the
year as 1910, the same year the fort at Mkalama was completed. Their
relocation notwithstanding, the evidence suggests that men and
women continued to see their rainmakers, and not the German-
appointed *jumbe*, as Ihanzu's only legitimate figureheads. A British
assistant political officer based at Mkalama in the early 1920s wrote
that during the transition period, after Kitentemi had been hanged and
jumbe had been appointed, 'the tribal chiefs still controlled their people
and from them permission was still sought for planting, harvesting,
marriage, circumcision, for the cure of ills, the detection of thieves, for
the punishment of murderers and the rectification of tribal ills, while at
the same time they were looked to to produce favourable conditions
through the Sun-God for the year's harvest. The Germans tried hard to
stamp out this system, and the measure of their failure is in the degree
of fidelity with which the people still cling to their hereditary rulers.'[41]

Thus, while German forces may have removed and hanged Ihanzu's
male rainmaker, Kitentemi, in an effort to quell the violence directed
against them – and in this they may have in part succeeded – their
actions also contributed in significant ways to their eventual undoing.
What they failed to see was that, in local eyes, reigns and rains were
inextricably linked; to attack a royal rainmaker was to attack the rain

and hence all Ihanzu women and men. The British administration, whatever else it did, would not repeat this mistake. Quite the opposite.

Making Reigns and Rains

The First World War devastated the whole of German East Africa. Countless Africans fought and died on both sides; and severe drought and famine once again plagued the region. In 1919, F.J. Bagshawe, a British District Political Officer, painted a haunting picture of German East Africa's central region: 'On my arrival in February an appalling state of affairs existed. Excepting for the Masai and Tatoga who are not dependant upon cereal food, and for the Wafiomi, all tribes were practically starving. On every road were to be met thousands of natives with their families travelling – too often unable to travel further – in search of food, ready to barter their last remaining possessions, their children, even their wives, for food ... I do not know how many died, and I have never tried to find out. To look back upon that period is like recalling a nightmare.'[42]

Ihanzu was among the worst affected areas. Villagers starved owing to lack of rain, but equally because German forces throughout the war had shipped vast quantities of grain out of Ihanzu by carrier safaris, and by transport wagons of the Arusha Dutch, to the front in Moshi.[43] Local labour shortages exacerbated an already precarious situation.

Life histories reveal the extent of the tragedy. Many able-bodied Ihanzu men who might otherwise have farmed were, during the war, recruited by both sides – some were enlisted and paid, others were abducted at night – to fight a foreign war they scarcely understood. Some were marched to distant locations to fight or work as porters; others did so closer to home. Towards the end of the war, as the Germans retreated south into Iramba from advancing South African forces, they abandoned their fort at Mkalama and abducted many Ihanzu and Iramba men – any who had enough strength to carry their loads – to hasten their retreat. Many died in the process. German forces pillaged and plundered, taking with them any and all foodstuffs and livestock (cf. Brooke 1967, 15; Ten Raa 1968; Maddox 1988, ch. 3).

Many remember this period as *nzala ndege* or 'the aeroplane famine': a phrase evoking wartime Allied forces' aeroplanes that flew overhead.[44] William Kali, now an elderly man, vividly recalls this monumentally chaotic period. At the time, he was a young boy living in

Matongo village: 'Many people moved out of Ihanzu. Many people. They went in all directions in search of food. Many of those died. Many who stayed died too. We stayed. My father went into the bush, into Hadza country, and learned how to dig roots in the bush. It was hard. We picked some wild fruits and ate roots from the bush. There was no food. None. I even ate baboon meat sometimes! There was nothing. We survived.'

Ali Gimbi, who was born in Ikŭlŭngu la Mpepo village, was the son of a wealthy cattle owner and farmer. He, too, remembers the aeroplane famine: 'We sold all our cattle. We – father, mother, my maternal uncle, the children, everyone – went to Mbulu in search of food, and we stayed there for three years [until the war's end]. It was hard there too.'

At the war's end, dealing with the immediate disaster was among British administrators' top priorities. As part of this process they sought to re-establish 'chiefdoms' across the land, much as they had existed prior to the arrival of the Germans. Or so they believed. (Re)establishing chiefdoms meant, among other things, finding 'chiefs' and making sure they were doing what they were intended to do: ruling over their 'tribes' (Graham 1976; Iliffe 1979, ch. 10). War, forced labour, drought, and famine had sent a flood of 'chiefs' and 'tribesmen' in all directions. Early British administrators took it as part of their task to correct this, to redraw and underscore tribal boundaries and to ensure that people stayed within them: a massive geopolitical exercise, as it were, in reducing to a minimum 'tribal matter out of place.'

British administrators had set up shop at Mkalama in the old German fort. From their earliest days in Ihanzu, they paid close attention to the German-appointed *jumbe*. One thing that quickly became clear was that these 'leaders' were nothing of the sort: they were seen as illegitimate, were highly unpopular, and had little or no influence among ordinary villagers. Many, it seems, had used their positions for personal gain: 'Careful inquiries were made into the methods of each jumbe; as to the number of under-strappers employed by him, and as to their and his actual tribal status. Following this, numbers of jumbes have been charged and convicted of crimes (varying from the concealment of murder to cases of mere petty theft) and five jumbes are undergoing detention at the present moment.'[45]

With most of the *jumbe* in prison, and the need to establish a functioning government, it fell to the new British administration at Mkalama to find and empower local leaders in the district. This meant finding male 'chiefs.' Because the administrators' guiding principle was 'to ignore those jumbes and others who have no status tribally, and to enlist the support of the chiefs and jumbes who, by reason of their hereditary position, enjoy the actual respect of their people,'[46] it took little time to locate the exiled rainmaker Kali Mpungati in Hadza country and return him to Ihanzu as the 'rightful, hereditary chief.' He was one among three chiefs installed in Mkalama District in 1920:

> During this year the hereditary chiefs of the Mkalama tribes were restored to power. The Germans recognised none of them and their influence, which remained never the less at full strength amongst the tribesmen, was a potential source of mischief, instead of being, as now, a useful instrument in the hands of the Government. A change of administrative officers took place during this re-organization, whilst at the same time the Police officer was removed and a native clerk of many years local standing was sent to prison. This combination of events gave an excellent opportunity for trouble amongst the backward tribes of the sub-district: that none at all occurred is, I consider, satisfactory proof that the tribal changes were in the right direction.[47]

The right direction? Perhaps. But Ihanzu royal rainmakers were never 'chiefs' in the sense that administrators imagined: not during German times, not before.[48] For one thing, Ihanzu royals never 'ruled' over 'their people.' Rather, they attracted a certain amount of respect and authority because of the ancestrally sanctioned rainmaking powers they controlled for the benefit of all. For another, the only reason this was possible at all was because royal rainmakers came in differently gendered pairs. Yet British administrators never seemed to realize this; or if they did, their concerns remained elsewhere. While Kali Mpungati was returned from exile and installed as the first 'chief' of Ihanzu, his sister, Nya Matalũ, who is said to have returned with him, was given neither governmental office nor official recognition.

When Kali and Nya Matalũ returned to Ihanzu, so did the rains. The aeroplane famine, at long last, was over. And with rainmakers and rains, Ihanzu itself held new possibilities and promise that had been absent since the Germans first entered the area decades earlier. As a result, by early 1920, 'many hundreds of Anisanzu [Ihanzu], who, during the past years, had fled to neighbouring districts to avoid the impositions inflicted upon them, have now returned.'[49]

One elderly man who, along with many of his relatives, had spent the aeroplane famine far from Ihanzu in Mbulu District, had this to say: 'We got the news that Mpungati and Nya Matalũ had lots of sorghum at home so we returned ... That is how he got his name, Mpungati. It means "someone who brings [people] together." His real name is Kali. Our owners of the land had returned and so did the rains and the food. When we returned, I didn't leave the country again.'

Many female and male elders, like this one, delight in telling dramatic tales of the triumphant return of their exiled royal rainmakers. The stories often involve a motorcar of some sort, in which colonials and rainmakers rode, and a parade of followers on foot. In these stories, it is not just the leaders' physical return that is at issue. Of equal importance is the return of the rain. Two young women told me that as the two rainmakers were driven triumphantly back into Kirumi by British officials, the rains followed immediately behind them as they proceeded, drenching the crowds that followed. Thus, in the Ihanzu popular imagination, early British administrators not only returned the rightful Ihanzu owners of the land to Kirumi, but in so doing – and unbeknownst to themselves, I suspect – returned the rain in the bargain. If the Germans destroyed the rain, the British returned it.

Plus ça Change ...

But British administrators' attitudes towards Ihanzu rainmaking nonetheless remained mixed throughout the colonial era, a promising start notwithstanding. On the one hand, I have found no evidence that the British administration ever actively discouraged Ihanzu rainmaking practices. It is equally clear, though, that administrators lived in perpetual hope that Ihanzu rainmaking beliefs and practices would one day vanish. Hopefully soon. Yet in spite of the many comings and goings of 'chiefs,' administrators, education officers, and missionaries throughout the British colonial era, rainmaking institutions and practices did more than survive. They thrived.

Under Chief Kali, throughout the 1920s, large, public annual rainmaking rites once again took place at the Kirumi rainshrine, as they had before Kitentemi's capture and hanging by German forces. Yet even while his newly created position as 'chief' allowed him, with Nya Matalũ, to bring rain, Kali routinely refused to take on administrative responsibilities with any degree of enthusiasm, and commonly opposed government policies. On Kali's death in 1927, the Singida District Officer reported:

Chief Kali, who died during the year and who was an autocratic and obstinate old man, was the principal stumbling block to amalgamation [of Ihanzu with Iramba]. It may be possible to induce amalgamation or at least a federation with Iramba in the coming year as the present chief, Asmani, does not appear to have the same tribal pride as his uncle. The matter, however, rests to a large extent with the elders of the tribe now that old Kali has gone and their prejudices are not easily broken down. It would, of course, be easy to direct an amalgamation but such a course would be most indiscreet and would probably lead to trouble.

In the Mkalama area the mass of the people and their leaders are steeped in superstition and they have to be handled carefully ... The question of rainmaking in this area is one which must be approached with the greatest caution.[50]

From earlier German experiences, British administrators understood perfectly well the extent to which resistance, reigns, and rains were linked, even if they failed to recognize the central conceptual and practical position the female rainmaker filled for the men and women of Ihanzu.

Sagilū Asmani succeeded Kali in 1927 as 'chief of Ihanzu' and male rainmaker. Nya Matalū, Sagilū's mother, continued as female rainmaker. From the start, Sagilū held great promise for British administrators. He had travelled far and wide and had lived in Tanga and Dar es Salaam while serving in the army. While away, he had converted to Islam (he even took the name Athmani) and had acquired a taste for European fashion and for conspicuous European consumption habits.[51] Ihanzu-based colonial officials thus held high hopes that Sagilū, unlike Kali, would be able to wrench 'his people' from a 'primitive past,' as some other colonial chiefs in neighbouring areas had ostensibly managed:[52] 'The authority, Asmani, comes of a line of rainmakers, but having spent the last seven years in the K.A.R. [King's African Rifles] prior to succeeding to the chiefship this year on the death of his uncle, Kali, it is more than probable that he does not know much about the art which was always jealously guarded by old Kali. As far as can be ascertained, Asmani has not been initiated in accordance with tribal custom. It is anticipated therefore that rainmaking will not play such a prominent part in the tribal life as hitherto.'[53]

Such hopes were not realized. Rainmaking remained central (misguided colonial assumptions about 'tribal initiation' notwithstanding). What is more, Sagilū eventually proved to be one of the most loathed chiefs in the territory, at least among administrators. With his extraordinary annual income of £35,[54] Chief Sagilū was (nearly) able to satisfy his seemingly insatiable desire for foreign goods: my informants claimed that he owned, among other things, a bicycle, a motorcycle, and a rifle, and that he routinely drank beer and smoked tobacco and marijuana. Years later he even purchased a Land Rover. In spite of his dazzling display of material wealth, however, Sagilū never became the 'progressive' chief that administrators had hoped for. Not even close. Only a year after Sagilū took office, C. Lyons, an administrator based at Mkalama, was already longing for bygone days: 'During the lifetime of Kali the old mtemi of Isanzu the court of Isanzu was the best controlled court in Mkalama [District], but with the advent of his successor I regret to say it is the worst. Sagilu (or Asmani as he prefers to call himself) is still young and very inexperienced. It is possible that he is a man of good character and has many latent good qualities, but up to date he has only succeeded in making a bad impression on all who have come into contact with him.'[55]

Elders who can remember, and younger women and men who cannot, relish telling tales of Sagilū's and his mother's defiance of British officials. One popular story tells that when administrators drove from Mkalama to call on Sagilū in Kirumi, instead of humbly greeting them, he remained inside his house with his friends drinking beer and smoking a number of substances, forcing colonial officials to wait inordinate amounts of time, or in some versions, to return on another occasion.

Other commonplace stories tell of the royal rainmakers' impressive displays of ancestrally sanctioned powers in administrators' presence. As Nya Chūnyū, an elderly woman from Kirumi, told me: 'Sagilū was around during British rule and, after asking around at Kiomboi they [some high-up colonial officials] arrived at Sagilū's house by car, saying they had heard he could make rain. He went to his mother [Nya Matalū] and told her the white men wanted some rain and she told him to bring it. He donned his black clothes, his lionskin loincloth, and went to the rainshrine. The British were afraid to enter. There he did his stuff with those pots and the rain began to pour! They said goodbye and went on their way, leaving him there as chief.'

A similar story revolves around colonial administrators' desires to establish chiefly legitimacy – to see, among the three chiefs of the Mkalama Federation, who the 'real' one was. Though I have recorded several versions of this story myself (e.g., Sanders 2001b), I take one

recorded by an anthropologist in 1963 to underscore its historical dura-
bility:

> The 3 chiefs used to meet at Mkalama, with the D[istrict] O[fficer], and
> each had his separate house. The DO decided to hold a competition to see
> who was the greatest rainmaker. He ordered Kingu [of Iramba] to bring
> rain on the first day. The hours passed, and no rain came. He ordered Jima
> [of Iambi] to bring rain on the 2nd day. Hours passed, no rain came.
> Sagilu realised that his turn would come next, borrowed a bike, and rode
> all the way to Kirumi. He told his mother that rain must fall during the
> lunch hour break on the following day. They prepared their medicine,
> and he returned immediately to Mkalama, so that his absence was not
> even missed. When the DO asked him if he could bring rain, he just said
> 'We will see.' The rainclouds gathered in the morning over Mkalama, and
> it grew darker. At noon it began to pour down, and it rained heavily ... It
> was so heavy that many of the tembe roofs caved in. The DO said that
> indeed Sagilu was the greatest of them all.[56]

These well-known, often-told tales of Ihanzu in the late 1920s and
1930s are interesting for several reasons, not least for what they tell us
about submerged subaltern histories of the colonial enterprise and
local notions of power and authority. For present purposes I wish only
to highlight the fact that the women and men of Ihanzu have long
imagined their own rainmakers as more powerful than those of their
neighbours; and that the powers these royals wield do what they do
because they come in differently gendered productive pairs. Only
when male and female rainmakers join forces, when they cooperate,
will the rains come.

If early British administrators were publicly supportive and privately ambivalent about Ihanzu rainmaking, the same cannot be said
for the Augustana Lutheran missionaries, who first opened their doors
in Ihanzu in 1931. As with colonial administrators, both early and later
missionaries cast the Ihanzu and their rainmaking beliefs and practices
as 'superstitious' and 'traditional,' assuming they would eventually
vanish under the weight of modernity. Unlike colonial administrators,
however, these self-designated 'messengers of love' (Ward 1999) positively loathed such things and aimed explicitly at the 'breaking down
of their primitive tribal religion before the advance of civilization'
(Johnson 1934, 23). From this pious perspective, not only was rainmaking seen as 'superstitious,' 'primitive,' and 'traditional'; it was also

understood as irrevocably evil, something that had to be eradicated at all cost.

Ihanzu Lutheran views have changed little in recent years. The local reverend, himself an Ihanzu man, continues to preach on the perils of tradition, including rainmaking, and on the salvation Jesus offers in the form of moral and material betterment. But today, seventy-some years after missionaries' entrance into the area, this missionary message falls mostly on deaf ears: around 80 per cent of Ihanzu men and women call themselves 'pagans' (*wapagani*), and do so unabashedly.[57] Monumental missionary efforts from the 1930s onwards aside, few Ihanzu women and men today have any enthusiasm for hearing The Word of a distant demigod if this means the wholesale abandonment of rainmaking practices and royals.

Chief Sagilũ died in 1939. When he did, British officials successfully steered the royal rainmaking line of succession from a teenaged (and potentially troublesome) rainmaking 'chief' named Omari, to a more congenial character named Gunda.[58]

Gunda was Sagilũ's mother's sister's son and was thus a member of the royal rainmaking lineage (figure 2.1). He remained in office for fifteen years, from 1939 to 1954. In addition to being a greatly respected and gentle man who is said, with his female counterpart, to have controlled the rains admirably and with great skill, he was an efficient bureaucrat and administrator, much as colonial administrators had hoped. Villagers themselves, it appears, could not have cared less about his aptitude for administration, so long as he cooperated with Nya Matalũ and brought rain, which he did each year at the royal rainshrine.

It was during Gunda's chiefly reign, in 1947, that the elderly female rainmaker, Nya Matalũ, passed away, ending possibly the longest reign of any Ihanzu female rainmaker. This ancient woman had managed to outlive all of her own daughters, save one, who immediately succeeded her. Nkili, or Nzĩtũ as she was sometimes known, became the next female rainmaker, and a powerful rainmaker she proved to be over the next forty years.

In 1954, Gunda the regent chief stepped down, and Sagilũ's sister's son, Omari Nkinto, now about thirty years of age, became 'chief.' At the same time, he became Ihanzu's male rainmaker, who with his mother[59] Nkili now conducted rain rites each year.

As far as government functionaries were concerned, Omari was always a difficult man. As with his chiefly predecessors (with the exception of Gunda), his central concern was not with policy or politics, but rainmaking. If Ihanzu men and women appreciated this aspect of his personality, colonial officials by and large did not. Marguerite Jellicoe, a Tanganyika government sociologist, wrote of Chief Omari in the early 1960s:

An apparently young man of very difficult personality. Is variously called [by colonial officials?] lazy, weak, ineffectual, shy. Avoids whenever possible meeting strangers, especially Government officials and Europeans. Is said to be practically illiterate, which fact helps to undermine his present-day position, literacy now being admired. Clearly has an immense 'inferiority complex' coupled with a firm belief in his powers as a rainmaker and his rights as traditional chief. Very touchy and ready to take offence at any imagined slight, but still has great power over the more traditionally-minded of his people, and if he is offended it is difficult to make any headway ... He should on no account be asked about his rain-making rites, until perhaps he is known very well. The best approach is through the history of his clan and of the Masai wars ... Neither should any initial curiosity whatever be shown about the rainmaking house (the *mpilimo*) which can be seen close to the old tumbleddown resthouse. Nor should Kirumi Ridge [Ng'waūngu] be climbed (the rainmaking hill behind the Resthouse), nor any drum cave visited, without the permission of the Mtemi. The Mtemi speaks Swahili.[60]

Jellicoe's comments make plain the extent to which many 'traditionally minded' men and women in the 1960s saw Chief Omari much as he saw himself: first and foremost as a rainmaker. Even if literacy was admired – which it likely was, among a small minority – this had little bearing on whether or not Omari, together with his mother, was respected or brought rain. For at the end of the day, 'In the eyes of most of the Isanzu, the chief is not regarded as a government servant but as the giver of rain' (Adam 1963b, 10; cf. Packard 1981, 169).

Even if administrators failed to notice, the same was true for Nkili, Omari's mother. One anthropologist noted in the 1960s: 'She is a woman who is feared and respected throughout the kingdom ... She succeeded her mother [Nya Matalū], a woman who lived to a great age and outlived all of her daughters except this one. Nkili is said to possess her own rainstones ... People are afraid to thwart her wishes, and she wields great influence over the chief and all the royal family' (Adam 1963b, 17–18).

Omari, who lives in Kirumi today, speaks fondly of his years as government chief: he owned a Land Rover; lived in a palatial, modern government house in Kirumi; afforded imported brandy and whisky; supported five wives and his children; and conducted rainmaking ceremonies with his mother at the Kirumi rainshrine without governmental interference. In fact, Omari is not the only one who tends to remember the 1950s and 1960s as 'the good old days.' So does the female rainmaker, and ordinary villages, too. Those were decades when royal powers were strong, times when Ihanzu rainmaking practices in manifold forms flourished, times when white people – the British social anthropologist Virginia Adam, to be precise – came from faraway places and took special notice (Adam 1963b). Although the two royal rainmakers had conducted rain rites publicly since the 1920s, it is clear with hindsight why these particular years in the twilight of British rule are sometimes singled out as the heyday of Ihanzu rainmaking. This has everything to do with what happened immediately after independence.

Gaining Independence, Losing Rain

When Tanganyika gained independence on 9 December 1961, Julius Nyerere and his Tanganyika African National Union party (TANU for short) ruled the nascent nation.[61] Although some Ihanzu men and women I know played active roles in the process, on balance, independence to many Ihanzu villagers seems to have meant very little. Many with whom I have spoken on the topic, in fact, do not remember with any clarity those particular years. What did make an indelible mark on people's imaginations was the new government's decision the year after independence to abolish chiefdoms across the land.[62] It was not so much that ordinary Ihanzu villagers had, come to love their 'chief' or the 'chiefdom' that the British administration had, over many decades, created. Rather, men and women feared that with the destruction of the chiefdom, Chief Omari and his mother Nkili would be prohibited from bringing rain (Adam 1963b, 15). These fears were not entirely unfounded.

Former chief Omari recalled a meeting that he and the two other former chiefs of the Mkalama Federation had with the new District Commissioner, after being relieved of their chiefships in December 1962:

The DC was really angry, crazy you could say. He told us, 'So you think you are chiefs? Real big men? Well, let me tell you you're nothing. TANU is in charge now. You are just rubbish, savages [*washenzi*]. All of you. There's no place for any of you lot.'

You know, *they* are the savages. Do you know what happened then? We left Kiomboi and returned home, all of us. And the rains did not fall over the whole of Iramba District that year, and the government had to start importing food aid, dishing it out by the cup, to help the people.

Coincidence is a strange beast. With Tanganyika's independence and the demise of her chiefships came the total failure of the rains across the country. The central and northern parts of the nation were particular hard hit, 'causing a famine which was the north's worst since the 1890s' (Iliffe 1979, 576). Many villagers spoke then, as Omari and others do today, in a single breath, of the demise of the Ihanzu chiefdom and the massive drought that ensued (e.g., Adam 1963b).[63] And to the extent they did, and still do, Chief Omari's deposition harks back to a bygone but not entirely forgotten era many decades earlier when German forces captured, hauled off and hanged the male rainmaker, Kitentemi. In both cases the demise of male rainmakers signalled the demise of the rain. Time had seemingly come full circle, the end mirrored its own beginning.

With Omari's removal in the early 1960s, a young and relatively well educated TANU man filled the newly created position of Division Clerk (*Katibu Tarafa*). He was himself an Ihanzu man and a Lutheran, and he had no connection with the royal *Anyampanda* rainmaking clan-section – something that no doubt underscored the desired break between new and older orders (cf. Abrahams 1981, 37). The clerk soon moved to the administrative centre of Kirumi village. There, to make the transition from chiefs to TANU complete, he moved into the former chief's house, a massive and positively ostentatious structure built towards the end of the British colonial era to convey an unmistakable aura of chiefly authority. With the chief now living in a modest mud-brick home near the rainshrine, the grand State House and its single occupant now embodied all the power and hopes of a new but as yet unproved post-independence order.

Some of my informants claim that certain local TANU administrators tried to pressure the Ihanzu royals to stop making rain and, on occasion, tried to stop villagers from giving grain tribute to their rainmakers; such instances, though, seen to have been more the exception than the rule. More often than not, it appears that administrators turned a blind eye to royals and their rainmaking rituals. For some, this was because they had better things to do; they saw rainmaking rites as relics of the past, and they supposed, as did the missionaries and colonial administrators before them, that they would fall by the wayside as the nation modernized and developed. Others ignored such things because they were themselves of Ihanzu origin and understood perfectly well the importance that rainmaking had both for themselves and for all others with whom they lived. It was thus that Omari and Nkili continued to carry out rainmaking rites throughout the 1960s, albeit no longer on the grand public scale that Adam had witnessed in 1961 and 1962 (Adam 1963b).

By the mid-1960s, the devastating drought and famine that had plagued the nation had ended, and the rains of the early 1970s were sufficient. This state of affairs was once again threatened in the mid-1970s by *ujamaa*, or African socialism. This was due to an attack, not on Ihanzu's rainmakers, but rather on their royal home, Kirumi village.

Ujamaa was the most elaborate social experiment ever attempted in Tanzania (save for colonialism, of course). This complex policy turned on the interrelated notions of independence, freedom, and self-reliance.[64] One of *ujamaa*'s central pillars – and it affected millions of rural Tanzanians – was villagization. Its premise was simple: if people lived in close proximity, all would benefit from easy access to roads, transportation, shops, schools, dispensaries, water pumps, and other modern conveniences. The government would provide the raw materials for these ventures; villagers, in the spirit of cooperation, would provide the labour necessary to assemble the greater good. This thinking also extended to large, village-owned collective farms, on which people were urged to work together for the common good. The logistics of such a massive, nationwide relocation programme – millions of Tanzanians were moved into large, centralized villages – were daunting, the final results mixed.

In 1975, district-level officials in Kiomboi decided that Ihanzu would be divided into sixteen *ujamaa* villages (*vijiji*),[65] each comprising several smaller subvillages (*vitongoji*). The criteria for such decisions were straightforward: those villages with more 'modern' amenities that were easily accessible were favoured, while those that were remote, with fewer amenities, were not. (Modern markers here included water pumps, road access, dispensaries, courthouses, schools, shops, and churches). On these grounds, dozens of Ihanzu villages were slated for closure, their residents to be relocated to more 'modern' *ujamaa* villages. Some areas of Tanzania saw confrontations, sometimes violent, between overzealous government officials and reluctant villagers, but there were few signs of open protest in Ihanzu. With one notable exception, that is: Kirumi.

The thought of closing Kirumi disturbed villagers. As far back as anyone could remember, Kirumi had been the rightful home of their royal rainmakers, the place where their ancestral migrants from Ukerewe first settled. It was here that former rainmakers, male and female (except Kitentemi), were buried. And it was here that rainmaking rites had been conducted since at least the 1800s. Kirumi meaningfully connected Ihanzu women and men with their past, and sketched a tentative path into an uncertain future. Having survived Maasai and Tatog raids in the nineteenth century, and having withstood the onslaught of two different colonial regimes in the twentieth, now it appeared that Nyerere's villagization programme was going to destroy Kirumi – and with it, the rain – forever.[66] As one elderly woman from Isene village pointedly put it, 'Closing Kirumi is like closing Ihanzu.'

Zugika Maua, a now-elderly man who was in 1975 the head village representative of Kirumi (*shina wa Kirumi*), explained that there were lots of troubled public meetings that year during which villagers expressed profound concerns about Kirumi's closure. Following one meeting, he said, he wrote a letter of protest on villagers' behalf, pleading that Kirumi be incorporated as a subvillage under a larger *ujamaa* umbrella. The letter went to the Division Secretary, an Iramba man named Welia who lived in Kirumi and who was a staunch supporter of the closure. He paid no attention.

In his letter, Maua suggested that there was no good reason to close Kirumi. It had, after all, some modern facilities: a dispensary, a courthouse, and an almost reasonable road. He did not mention rain in the letter, though he told me that this, really, was what at the time concerned most people. 'To convince the government,' he said, 'they did not want to hear about our problems of rain. We had to use a different approach and show them how modern we were. We told them about roads and dispensaries, not chiefs and rains.' A subtle irony, it would seem, deploying British-built 'modernity' to save Ihanzu 'tradition.' For his efforts, Maua was reprimanded in court and fined 500 shillings (about $1.50 today). Other villagers were ignored.

In the middle of it all, the unpopular Division Secretary, Welia, was unexpectedly transferred from Kirumi and a new secretary, Obedi Lange, took his place. Like his predecessor, Lange was an Iramba man and a Lutheran. Unlike Welia, however, he was sympathetic to villagers' concerns. In fact, little time passed before Lange sided with villagers, arguing at the district level in favour of Kirumi's incorporation under Matongo village.

Eventually, after nearly a year of commotion by villagers, district-level officials abandoned their original position and issued a revised and updated statement: Kirumi would *not* be closed. It would be incorporated as a subvillage of Matongo village. Men and women were elated. In former chief Omari's words: 'That time when the government wanted us to move out of Kirumi to Matongo was a real disaster. They said all of us would go, everyone. But there was one thing that stopped them: that house [pointing to the rainshrine]. In the end they realized that if they moved us from here, they would absolutely destroy our rainmaking traditions and so, in the end, they let us stay. What do you think would have happened if we had moved? All this would be bush, and there would be no rain.'

It is unlikely that rainmaking was the reason district administrators eventually changed their minds. Even so, Omari speaks in tune with most villagers when he points to the significance that rainmaking practices had for most in the 1970s, and indeed have today. That Kirumi village be closed was the only proposal in Ihanzu that raised a public outcry, which lasted for nearly a year. It was also the only village in the whole of Ihanzu that was, once wiped clean from the map, re-drawn by government officials in ink.

Rainmaking in the New Millennium

Today, Ihanzu rainmaking continues to shape encounters with postcolonial administrators, though only, I think, when anthropologists occasion such reflection. For the most part, Ihanzu's royal rainmakers have continued to do what they do in Kirumi, and representatives of Tanzania's modern nation-state show little interest in them.

Iramba's District Commissioner made a brief visit to Ihanzu in 1995 to hold a public meeting about adopting new fast-grow maize seeds, and to persuade villagers that they should 'develop' using 'the free market.' Before the meeting, he asked me how my research was going on Ihanzu 'traditions and customs' (*mila na desturi*), those things generally 'known' to preoccupy anthropologists. He also wanted to know, among other things, why 'the chief' had not seen fit to show up at this particular government meeting, as all villagers are expected to. I replied that I had not seen him that morning, that he might be in Kirumi or, most probably, was on the way as we spoke. Somewhat irritated, the DC made clear his view on chiefs and rainmaking: 'For a long time the chiefs here in Tanzania stopped modernity. They kept people from becoming modern (*watu wa kisasa*). They were against education, against good roads, against business and against change. They only wanted old customs [*mila za zamani*] ... Perhaps it's better that the chief stays there in Kirumi with his rainshrine. He had many years to send modernity backwards [*kurudisha nyuma maendeleo*]. Now they're gone and the government's here. We will develop these people!'

The DC's comments raise a few points. First, postcolonial officials today consider Ihanzu rainmaking and rainmakers (when they consider them at all) to be outmoded relics that have no place in our 'modern' world. These ideas – no, fervent hopes – are informed by a particular unilinear vision of the world, a world where modernity destroys tradition, where the present inevitably overwrites the past. Such ideas or hopes are hardly new. As we have seen, similar notions have underpinned administrative thinking since the advent of colonialism more than a century ago. Second, the DC's comments suggest that postcolonial administrators do not recognize female rainmakers and/or 'chiefs' and the central role they play for locals any more than their colonial predecessors did. Rainmaking chiefs are just men. (This of course is not an issue that concerns them, given rainmakers' alleged irrelevance in and to the modern world.)

These points notwithstanding, Ihanzu villagers remain adamant that rainmaking is not just a thing of the past, but equally something highly desirable in the present, something they actually want, something they actually *need*, and in the particular gendered form it takes. But why? What is at stake?

Claims about 'tradition,' 'culture,' and 'identity,' anthropologists have long known and frequently shown, can serve particular class or clan, generation or gender interests. This is commonly the case, as for instance in northern Tanzania, where there are resources like land, livestock, and labour worth fighting over (S.F. Moore 1986). In such cases and places, what counts as 'tradition,' or what makes one more 'traditional' than someone else, is crucially linked to managing one's livelihood successfully. Ihanzu 'traditions,' however, are not linked to identity politics in the same way, or to the same extent: being more 'traditional' or insisting on maintaining rainmaking 'traditions' provides no obvious material benefits, no privileged access to scarce resources, to specific socially situated actors. Such claims are these days more likely to attract derision from administrators. Truth be told, within Ihanzu, there are no 'traditional' resources worth struggling for: the long-farmed matriclan lands are largely exhausted, and people cut new plots from the bush in preference to them; and there are no 'traditional' corporate herd holdings that villagers might tap into. The point here is that associating oneself with 'traditional' rainmaking is no means to secure scarce resources for oneself, or to deny others.

So why bother? First, by linking rainmaking, 'tradition,' and Ihanzuness, villagers attempt to forge a solid conceptual mooring in an ever-changing world. In this sense, rainmaking provides Ihanzu women and men with the means by which to establish meaningful historical connections with their past, and to concretize their own place-in-the-world at present. 'Rainmaking,' villagers frequently told me, 'is our tradition' (*jadi yetu*). Yet as important as such moorings are – and here is the point to underscore – for the women and men of Ihanzu, rainmaking is first and foremost crucial because it brings rain: a tautology, to be sure, but one that nonetheless captures the essence of what is at stake. For without their two differently gendered royals and the powers and rains they jointly control, all would cease to exist. There would be no rain. There would be no harvest, food, or beer. There would be no animals. There would be no villagers.

Chapter 3

Gendered Life-Worlds and Transformative Processes

Rainmaking rites aim to transform the land from dry and barren to wet and fertile. Central to this process – not only in Ihanzu but across the whole of sub-Saharan Africa – is gender, and the power that male and female together evince. African rainmaking rites are replete with gender and sexual motifs: male and female processes and objects comingle to transform the world. This is true not just of rainmaking, of course, but of countless rites across the continent from initiation to iron production. One issue of interest is how anthropologists explain such gendering.

In Africa and elsewhere, to speak of gender is to speak of women and men and the relations between them. It follows that to speak of 'gender symbolism' – as plenty of social scientists do – is to speak of non-human forms and activities that derive their meaning from what women and men think they are and do. 'Male' and 'female' objects and their combinations, in this sense, are said to be meaningful because they mimic, symbolize, and evoke sexed bodies and 'real' human reproduction. Since Ihanzu rainmaking rites are full of things sexual and gendered, one could argue that these rites take their cues from human bodies and sexual reproduction; and that ritual participants project known corporeal qualities into and onto the social and natural world they inhabit. Thus the social historian Eugenia Herbert explains gender and sexual symbolism in iron smelting in sub-Saharan Africa, arguing that 'African transformative processes invoke the human model as the measure of all things' (Herbert 1993, 5). She is not alone. Many Africanists posit the same relation between gendered objects and processes on the one hand and women's and men's bodies and human reproduction on the other. But to whom, exactly, do such explanations 'make sense'? In this chapter, I will suggest that while such explanations appear plausible to certain academicians and others working within a Euro-American episteme, for the women and men of Ihanzu such 'explanations' explain nothing. Ihanzu rainmaking, with its gendering and sexuality, cannot be adequately explained by suggesting that it symbolizes something other than what it is.

As we saw in chapter 1, Ihanzu notions of everyday gender relations are complex and contradictory. People sometimes claim that male is superior to female, at other times the opposite. Such evaluations depend on context. To complicate matters further, women and men share another understanding of gender relations that evinces itself at other times, specifically, in the context of transformations. This I call 'gender complementarity.' Gender complementarity is inextricably linked to notions of power and transformation. Unlike other Ihanzu gender arrangements, which turn on gender asymmetries of different sorts, gender complementarity places male and female on an equal footing. In this vision, one gender evokes and demands its opposite; one without the other is neither meaningful nor potent. When combined as equals, however, male and female can transform the world – quite literally. Indeed, the equal and complementary combination of differently gendered pairs is the logical prerequisite for the continuation of life in all forms: to (re)produce rain, babies, iron, and many other things, villagers insist that male and female must cooperate (*kiunga*) and reside together harmoniously (*wikĩĩ ũza palũng'wĩ*). Together as equals, male and female can make things happen. In one way, shape, or form, gender complementarity underpins, informs, and gives meaning to all Ihanzu rain rites.

While gender in this sense can be about men and women – as, for example, with the royal rainmaking pair discussed in the previous chapter – this is not strictly required. For in Ihanzu, gendering is also evident in myriad non-human objects and their productive combinations. Ihanzu gendered capacities or forces can and do routinely operate across, within, and without men's and women's bodies. Shelly Errington's comments in a different context are useful here: 'A rhetoric of gender could be used to describe or characterize "male" and "female" cosmic energies, roles, activities, and functions in a particular society, but without a presumption that they either reflect or are anchored in physical differences between men and women, or that sexed bodies or individual men and women are required to fulfil or enact those activities or roles' (1990, 18).

Thinking along these lines invites a particular sociology of knowledge surrounding gender, one in which male and female attributes and forces can be evoked and harnessed within different material forms. We might thus imagine gender as *embodied capacity* that can inhabit human bodies but equally other things, too. Such thinking has several analytic advantages. First, it levels the epistemological and ontological playing fields so that one gendered form or combination is equivalent to the next: male and female are male and female. Whether rainstones or royal rainmakers, gender combinations lead to specific outcomes. To imagine different gender forms, then, is to imagine multiple, non-categorical models of scale. At whatever level of scale, large or small, each model is similarly gendered and potentially transformative. Second, such thinking undermines the idea that some gender forms exist prior to others; and with that, the idea that the body and human sexual reproduction provide the template for all other things gendered and sexual. Seeing gender as embodied capacity instead insists that all Ihanzu gender forms – human and non-human alike – participate simultaneously in the same universe of value and meaning. Finally, such thinking points to alternative projects of meaning making, different explanations that do not hinge inexorably on the human form. Non-human gendered forms make sense *not* because they are 'like' human bodies that ostensibly pre-exist and 'explain' them but because, when appropriately combined, they produce particular outcomes. What 'explains,' in other words, is not some conceptual mapping of bodies onto other things gendered but the fact that gendered combinations, of whatever sort, produce results – be they iron, rain, babies, pots, or something else.

This chapter considers how gender in this sense permeates and animates Ihanzu villagers' cultural, social, and natural worlds, before we consider in the chapters to follow the specifics of how such imaginaries play out in rain rites. I begin with human reproduction and the production of persons, not because this provides the ultimate reference point for all else, but because this topic will be more familiar to readers than other possible starting points.

Producing Persons

In Ihanzu eyes, persons are created through the equal combination of the genders, and each person is consequently composed of a complex mix of male and female elements. All people are said to be composed of the gendered process that produces them. And it is their gendered composition that allows them, in turn, to reproduce. These understandings are refracted through a number of Ihanzu realms of relatedness, including those which anthropologists otherwise speak of as unilineal descent.

Ihanzu matrilineages, or *maele*, are known by the name of their oldest living female member. While each person is born into such a group, and will be a lifelong member of it, there is also a sense in which one's membership is concretized through sharing a common, intergenerational substance – milk – that flows ultimately from the breast of a single ancestress. Women pass milk through the matriline to their offspring. Children of both sexes are thus partially composed of clan milk, which people speak of as a cool, female substance. This given, it is unsurprising that *maele* also means both 'breasts' and 'milk,' and we might for this reason do better to speak of Ihanzu 'milk groups' rather than matrilineages. When people explain, as they often do, how two individuals are related, such links are routinely evoked as those resulting from having come from a single womb (*kūpumie ndaa ĩng'wĩ*) or having sucked the same milk (*kūnkile iele lĩng'wĩ*). Such statements are more literal than metaphoric, and imply being born and fed from the same ancestress. (They need not imply sharing the same biological mother.)

If 'milk group' affiliation suggests that the links and substances derived from and through one's mother are crucial to a person's makeup, it is equally evident that such understandings only become meaningful when juxtaposed with a different set of linkages and substances acquired through a person's father.

While milk passes from mother to child, many Ihanzu claim that children receive blood – which is considered male and hot – from their fathers (cf. Colson 1961, 77). A man's sons, in turn, pass blood to their children. His daughters do not. This arrangement, where certain people share one blood (*sakami ĩng'wĩ*), amounts to a 'blood group' of sorts even if these groups remain unnamed, have no descent groups, and thus do not constitute patrilineages. What is more, because virilocality is common, 'blood groups' are often localized, further stressing patriline continuity through time. Blood is associated with father, masculinity, and the patriline and, like milk, is a necessary component of the person.

Apart from blood, a person gains other crucial aspects of the self from and through the father, including a name, a clan animal, and another clan affiliation. Just as people are members of their mother's matriclan, so too are they considered 'children of their father's matri-

clan' (cf. Colson 1961, 41, 74–9). Based on their father's matriclan affiliation, each person is born into one of several *milongo* groups.[1] Each of
the thirty matriclan-sections has two *milongo* names specific to it – one
male, the other female – and each child receives one of these names.
With these names also comes a clan animal specific to each clan or
clan-section (table 3.1). Thus every Ihanzu, besides being a product
and member of his or her mother's matriclan, is equally produced by
and a child of his other father's matriclan (Beidelman 1963b, 60).

A child therefore is constructed through mother, womb, and milk as
well as through father, father's matriclan, blood, a name, and a clan
animal. A person's constituent parts are distinctive and derive from
mother or father, yet they are said to be of equal importance and to
complement one another. Equally indispensable to a person's make-up
are one's seeds of life. These substances, which each person embodies,
are the result of a person's own conception as well as the source of that
person's future capacity to (re)produce.

Procreation

As elsewhere in Tanzania, when it comes to sexual reproduction, all
Ihanzu I have asked suggest 'that both sides contribute to the child
equally' (Brain 1983, 10). Acting together, male and female bear (*kūtuga*)
children. Ihanzu notions of procreation thus make a powerful and
unequivocal statement about the potency and transformative capacity
of complementary gender combinations.

The Ihanzu have a particular concept of semen or, perhaps better
put, 'fertilizing fluids.' Men and women both possess such fluids,
which come in male and female forms (cf. Broch-Due 1993, 54–5). The
word *manala* is occasionally used to discuss fertilizing fluids but only
in one-to-one conversations, since it verges on the vulgar. Most commonly, if such matters are discussed at all, men and women speak of
water (*mazī*) and seeds (*mbeū*).[2] These terms are used interchangeably
for male or female fluids.

Fertilizing fluids are not generally thought of as flowing through
matrileages or the patriline in the same way as do (female) milk or
(male) blood. They are instead considered unique to each generation.
In some ways, male and female fluids are the same, since both types of
'waters' or 'seeds' are said to contain exactly half of the eventual
attributes of the child they will produce. There is no notion that the
flesh or bones, for instance, derive exclusively from one side or the

Table 3.1. Clan children and animals

Clan or clan section	Male name	Female name	Emblem
1.1 Anyampanda wa Kirumi (Anyanzoka)	Sungwa	Mŭza	Baboon
1.2 Anyampanda wa Kĭnyakambĭ (Iyĭndĭ, Mŭhaĭ or Mpilimaigŭlŭ)	Nkangala	Itale	Bee
1.3 Anyampanda wa Anegaa	Izuligi	Itale	Finch
1.4 Anyampanda wa Igomano	Nkangala	Itale	Bee
1.5 Anyampanda wa Ikela	Nkangala	Itale	Bee
1.6 Anyampanda wa Itiili	Sungwa	Mŭza	Baboon
1.7 Anyampanda wa Ikunguli	Sungwa	Mŭza	Baboon
1.8 Anyampanda wa Matongo	Sungwa	Mŭza	Baboon
1.9 Anyampanda wa Kĭnyĭngogo	Nkangala	Itale	Bee
1.10 Anyampanda wa Nyonyela	Nkangala	Itale	Bee
1.11 Anyampanda wa Magemelo	Nkangala	Itale	Bee
2.1 Anyambilu wa Gŭdali	Igĭmbĭ	Ĭzima	Cattle
2.2 Anyambilu wa Kinyankŭnde	Igwĭla	Sungi or Ilimŭ	Giraffe (male) Rat (female)
2.3 Anyambilu wa Azigo	Iyĭndĭ	Ĭzima	Cattle
2.4 Anyambilu wa Mŭmba	Mĭlĭsita	Mŭmba or Ng'wai	Cattle
2.5 Anyambilu wa Anyankunĭ	Ipŭza	Mĭanzi	Cattle
3.1 Anyankalĭ wa Ilumba / Iyanĭko	Igŭnda	Ng'wanyi	Leopard
3.2 Anyankalĭ wa Ipilinga	Mpinga	Shoga	Lizard (Sections together: sun)
4.1 Anyansuli wa Kingwele	Mŭtĭpa	Mŭlĭma	Wild boar
4.2 Anyansuli wa Mŭkĭlampĭlĭ	Mŭtĭpa	Mŭlĭma	Wild boar
5.1 Anyambeŭ	Ikĭngu	Siu	Cat
5.2 Anyambeŭ	Ikĭngu	Nzĭtu	Sheep (Two sections together: moon)
6 Anyang'walu	Mpanda	Itale	Donkey
7.1 Anyambwaa	Kĭula	Mŭgalu	Dog
7.2 Anyambwaa	Makala	Chŭnyŭ	Dog
8 Anyisungu	Mŭkumbo	Kiliĭ	Parrot
9 Anyambala	Ilanga	Igoli	Goat
10 Asambaa	Mŭgana	Ng'wĭgo	Parrot
11 Anyakumi	Kĭtŭndŭ	Mŭsŭa	Scorpion
12 Anyikĭli	Mŭsengi	Ikĭli	Lion

other.[3] On the other hand, the two fluids differ in one important respect: their gender. This is crucial, people say, because only the combination of male and female is a productive one: neither two female fluids together, nor two male ones, has any generative power.

It is not the case that only men possess male seeds, and only women female ones. Rather, since each person is the product of the complementary combination of male and female fertilizing fluids in the first place, each man and woman houses within him- or herself *both* fluids. Each body – male or female – thus contains within it a dual-gendered generative potentiality that is identical to the gender combination that originally produced it. If male and female bodies must combine as equals to ensure reproduction, the same goes for the differently gendered seeds or waters within those bodies. To reproduce, a man's female seeds must combine equally with a woman's male seeds, or vice versa, to unleash their joint generative powers. Their children then embody the resulting dual-gendered combination. Such understandings productively complicate the commonplace suggestion that human reproduction speaks for itself, and that people simply apprehend it as-it-is and then project onto less-understood cultural realms. Moreover, dual-gendered (re)productivity *within* single bodies raises the possibility of auto-(re)production, a topic we shall consider below in the context of women's rain dances (see chapter 5). For now, we must examine what happens to a person's differently gendered 'seeds' or 'waters' upon death, since this, too, requires a gendered transformation.

Death and Disassembling the Person

Just as parents are said to give life to children by giving them gendered waters or seeds, so are children required to return these life substances to their parents on death. There is, therefore, a heavy ideological and practical emphasis in Ihanzu funerary rites on the deceased's mother (*iya*) and father (*tata*), and a reversed flow of fertilizing fluids and other goods from children to parents.[4] Of course the Ihanzu are not unaware that biological parents often die before their own offspring – a fact that may, for some readers, cast such regressive life-cycle flows in an odd light.[5] But there are no impossibilities here. This is because mother and father in this context and others are as much about mother's and father's clans as they are about biological mothers and fathers. It is, after all, mother's and father's clans that ultimately bear children.

Every Ihanzu knows that a mother and father must wash and dress their child on death. These parents, addressed throughout a funeral as mother (*iya*) and father (*tata*), are, however, always of the same sex. A man's corpse, to give an example, is washed by two men, one of whom must be the deceased's father (i.e., from the deceased's father's clan), and the other of whom must be its mother (i.e., from the deceased's mother's clan). A woman's corpse, on the other hand, is washed by two women, who are similarly said to be 'mother' and 'father.' In both cases, and in spite of the sex of the actual participants, people stress the complementary nature of 'mother' and 'father' preparing their 'child' for burial. Throughout funerals it is these mothers and fathers – there may be several on any given occasion – who must cooperate and carry out specified parental duties in order to ensure the requisite transformations.

Placing a corpse in the grave is done by father, mother, and a jester (see Sanders 1998). In this case, the two parents are always men, but men whom people insist are 'mother' and 'father.' Thus, much as mother and father combine to produce a child, so too do they join gendered forces to take them to their final resting place.

After the burial, for the next few days of mourning, several animals from the deceased's homestead are slaughtered. Stressing once again the dual-gendered contribution from both parents – and here, the need to return those life forces on death – specific cuts of meat are divided between the deceased's mother and father. In this way, life in the form of livestock is returned from child to parents.

Finally, one of the most significant funerary rites is held on the final day of mourning. Seeds are taken from the deceased's grainstore and boiled into a mixture called *mpeke*. It is essential that father and mother be the first to eat this food. At the many funerals I attended, they were. The reason, people say, is that this final funerary act of consumption – ingesting the child's own seeds – returns the original gendered seeds of life, those fertilizing fluids given to the child on conception, to his or her mother and father on death. It is the mother's and father's right to recover, and their child's duty to return, the seeds of life given at conception. This essential returning of seeds from children to parents is known as *kūshusa mbeū*, a practice mirrored in Ihanzu inheritance.

Inheritance

It is common practice at Ihanzu funerals to divide and return inheritance to the deceased's mother and father. In this way the deceased's property, like fertilizing fluids, is returned to its original source. Consider the following illustrative case:

In September 1994, a man in his 90s died in Kirumi village. Masusu, as he was known, was a member of the Anyampanda clan. He was sometimes called Ikīngu, a child of the Anyambeŭ clan, since his father was of that clan. Following Masusu's funeral and return of seeds to his parents, his (clan) parents sought to divide up the property (kūgalana mataho).

Thirteen people took part in the negotiations: three men from his father's clan, all Masusu's classificatory fathers; one man and one woman from his mother's (and of course his own) clan; and Masusu's wife and children.

Masusu's fathers presided over the meeting. The few clothes Masusu had, they divided evenly between mother and father. One pair of trousers and one shirt went to the former; one overcoat to the latter. Underscoring the importance of the gendered division and the regressive nature of inheritance, of Masusu's one pair of shoes, one shoe went to his mother, the other to his father.

A man's bow and arrows are extremely important at such proceedings and every man, on death, must return these things to his father. Unfortunately Masusu's bow had either broken or been lost some years earlier. In its stead, Masusu's son gave his own bow and arrows to his 'grandfather,' Masusu's fathers. Masusu's fathers then gave one arrow to the mothers, as is customary. Two stools and an axe were then handed over to the fathers. Normally a small amount of tobacco must pass from child to father, but since Masusu again had none, his son gave a token amount of money. All these inheritance transactions are fairly typical, and have been for many decades.[6]

Days earlier, during the funeral, Masusu's sister's son was publicly given Masusu's two grainstores, his house, two papaya trees, his wife and a cow. If Masusu had had a plot of his own, which he did not, his sister's son would have inherited this too. It is because Masusu's sister's son shares his own mother's clan that people gloss such practices as mother's inheritance.

It is not unusual for societies with matrilineal groupings to divide inheritance between mother's and father's sides (Beidelman 1993, 44; Colson 1961, 75). The point of interest, however, is that the Ihanzu do this to enable children to return at death that which was given to them by their mother and father in life. Parents inherit from their children.

And children must return to their parents the differently gendered seeds of life that produced and composed them (cf. Lindström 1988, 176). In this sense, counterintuitive though it may seem, Ihanzu inheritance practices and life cycles are regressive.

Considering conception and death together, we may sum up as follows. Through sexual union a man and woman mix their own unique gendered seeds or waters in equal amounts. This complementary combination generates new life, a life that is composed of the differently gendered life forces that create it. On death, life forces must be returned to the parents who gave them. This reversal is explicit, and made manifest both at funerals and in inheritance practices, where everything that was the person – gendered seeds and property – is divided between female and male and given to mother and father. For the Ihanzu, then, persons are produced, disassembled, and reproduced through a transformative cycle of gender combination, separation, and recombination. Mother and father combine as equals to produce offspring composed of male and female; mother and father combine as equals to return their male and female fertilizing fluids to themselves, which gives them the ability further to reproduce. In short, gender complementarity and its transformative properties animate the eternal roundabout of life. This is so for persons and for many other things, too.

Female and Male

So far we have seen how specific notions of gender complementarity and transformation underpin the life cycle from birth to death. The same logic informs certain everyday objects and practices. We can begin to get a handle on how this works by considering two archetypical Ihanzu male and female objects: the bow and the grinding stone, respectively. These two objects are found in virtually every Ihanzu household. Jointly, they embody the essential gendered elements of the household and the necessary transformative qualities to keep it dynamic. They also go a long way towards revealing the 'natural' differences between the genders that many Ihanzu remark on, and how their complementary combination is thought a productive one.

Men use bows (*ūtū*) and arrows (*mīyī*; sing. *mūyī*); women do not. Though today few in Ihanzu hunt, it is common and expected that each man own a bow and arrows (five arrows, to be exact), which should hang over his bed. Moreover, these bows and arrows, as we have seen, are highly significant in inheritance cases, and they must be transferred from sons to their fathers on death.

Many Ihanzu men and women say that bows embody – quite literally – virility and masculinity. Bows are fierce (*taki*) and hot (*pyu*). They are highly mobile and initiators of activities. A bow's work is done in the bush, and varies greatly from no work at all, to sudden and enthusiastic bursts of energy that provide meat, which is an indispensable ingredient to any proper Ihanzu meal.

If bows embody certain Ihanzu male characteristics, then grinding stones (*nsio*), people say, contain within themselves certain female ones. These include permanence, endurance, and domesticity. Grinding stones are used by women, never by men or boys. They are durable female property and are passed through the matriline from daughter to mother. A newly married woman brings a grinding stone with her to her new household. A husband has no right to move, remove, or otherwise touch his wife's grinding stone. It is only on divorce that these stones are removed. Grinding stones, unlike bows, are immobile for as long as a wife lives on her homestead. People say they are gentle, cool (*apolo*), and slow (*polepole*) and that they provide the other indispensable ingredient of every meal: stiff porridge or *ugali*.

The noteworthy point is that male and female in the shape of bows and grinding stones are, when appropriately combined, a source of transformative power. Together they ensure the continued reproduction of everyday life on the homestead through the complementary combination of male and female elements: hot and cold, active and passive, mobility and stability, bush and domestic, leader and follower, meat and grain. Bow and grinding stone are essential to a homestead's short- and long-term reproduction.

Gender complementarity, and the male and female elements that constitute it, must be seen as relational and context dependent. Bows and grinding stones, when discussing the household, are routinely cast as male and female; each evokes its gender opposite. But the same objects, in other contexts, can also become differently or dual gendered.

Take the grinding stone. Each house has at least one such stone, invariably located near the hearth (*moto*) in the entrance room. This room is called *k'iandaa* – the womb – and, as such is a place where transformations occur. It is here that a woman and her daughters spend considerable amounts of time each day grinding grain and cooking, transforming seeds into stiff porridge and beer. Just as male and female seeds are mixed to produce children, so too do grinding stones transform sorghum seeds into the essentials of everyday life. In this context, however, while people say the grinding stone is female, its partner stone that moves across it becomes male. Male initiates, is mobile and hot. Female is immobile and cool. Male is active and on top. Female is passive and beneath. Thus, while grinding stones as a whole are rendered female when juxtaposed with bows and the reproduction of the entire household, in other circumstances the complementary male–female relation and its transformative powers are replicated within the grinding stone itself. This given, it is not surprising that men and women sometimes speak of grinding (*kūsia*) as sex, as well as the reverse. Grinding is necessary to produce porridge and beer, just as sex and mixing gendered seeds are necessary to produce children. Both processes aim to transform the world; and they do so independent of each other, each making sense for the specific outcome it produces. The same holds true for rainmaking and rainmakers.

Royal Rains, Reigning Royals

It is common knowledge in Ihanzu that their two differently gendered rainmakers embody royal 'waters' or 'seeds' from a long line of rainmakers. They thus condense within themselves the generative gendered forces of the Ihanzu cultural universe. Together, and only together, they can make things happen. This is why, people opine, they must cooperate in all that they do, but most especially to bring rain. Iha Mūza, an elderly man from Matongo village, explained it this way. To bring rain, 'our rainmakers must work together. That is, the rain will refuse [to fall] if they just sit there like this [separate], without cooperating. It will just refuse! It really won't rain. If the rain refuses to fall, Chief Omari goes to his sister's [the female rainmaker's] at night and they discuss it very carefully, perhaps all night, until they agree. Then the rain will come.'

Leaving aside the only slightly veiled allusion to royal incest – a topic I take up in the next chapter – there are a few important facets to royal gender complementarity and to the productive capacity it presupposes. These centre on the equal sharing of two things: rainstones, and the esoteric knowledge of how to use them.

Rainstones and knowledge of their use go hand in hand. One without the other is of little value. An unskilled practitioner with only rainstones could not bring rain any more than could a knowledgeable practitioner without rainstones.

As is common across the continent, Ihanzu rainstones come in male and female forms.[7] The gender of individual stones (which are mainly low-value gemstones) is not obvious from their appearance. Each Ihanzu ritual leader owns his or her gendered rainstones. The male leader owns all male rainstones, which he keeps in the royal rainshrine in Kirumi village. The female leader owns all female rainstones, and supposedly keeps them on her person (see Adam 1963b). Rainstones pass through the royal matrilineage, male and female stones to male and female rainmakers respectively.

If rainstones are differently gendered, so, too, is the know-how required to use them. Here again, people say that each rainmaker has at his or her command a particular gender-specific knowledge of rain-making, and this makes this royal pair the ultimate authority on all rainmaking matters. Each is thought to contribute unique, gendered royal wisdom to the process. Because such knowledge is, by definition, a royal secret, non-royals are uncertain as to how exactly male and female rainmaking knowledge might differ. Even so, what is plain to all is that half the knowledge is only half the picture and is therefore fundamentally incomplete. Neither can produce rain alone.

Because the gendered royals own gendered rainstones and knowl-edges, they are also said to own the rain. It is on this basis, in fact, that they hold the positions they do: royals reign because they own the rain (Adam 1963b: 15). Rain, like fertilizing fluids, equals fertility. And rains, like fertilizing fluids, royal leaders, and their rainstones, are gendered.[8]

Rains in Ihanzu are many. They differ in the direction from which they come, in their relative strengths, durations, and seasonal fluctua-tions, and with regard to what time of day or night they fall, as well as where they fall. What is more, people distinguish between and have much to say about different types of rain – unremarkable, perhaps, in a place like Ihanzu where rain is not just advantageous but absolutely essential to life itself. There are named rains that belong to specific Ihanzu leaders of the past, rains that have specific characteristics regarding how they fall, the direction from which they come, their intensity, and so on. There are so many types of Ihanzu rain, in fact, that I found it quite impossible to find even nominal agreement among the many women and men I spoke to about their exact numbers and characteristics. With one edifying exception: gendered rains.

All Ihanzu men and women I have spoken with on the matter draw a fundamental distinction between two all-encompassing, over arching types of rain. These are male rain (*mbula a agohaa*) and female rain (*mbula a asũngũ*).[9] Villagers say that all rains can be placed squarely into one of these two categories. Furthermore, when asked to elaborate, people invariably agree on two points: first, that each leader owns his or her respective gendered rain; and second, that these rains, like their owners, must complement each other if they are to be productive.

An elderly man from Matongo village, Ihanzu's Division Secretary (*Katibu Tarafa*) in the early 1960s, put it like this: 'There are male and female rains ... The two have to go together. That's why there's a male and female chief. It's like a house. Is a house really a house with only a man in it? Of course not. There must be a woman too. It's the same with rain.'

Here, as elsewhere, the genders complement and complete each other. Spouses, rainmakers, and rains only become meaningful and productive when combined as gender opposites. Each is dependent on the other, each forms half of a potentially productive whole.

As with other things gendered, male and female rains are said to possess certain characteristics and combined potentialities. One of them is the sequence in which gendered rains must fall. In one middle-aged woman's words:

> The male rain (they say that is the one of Chief Omari) goes first [*kũtongela*], the female rain (the one of Chief Ng'welu) follows [*kũshata*]. Most times the male goes first, and we [women] follow. For example, a man clears the bush to farm and then the woman comes and works later ... Another time when men go first is at a funeral. It is always the men who dig the grave. Women only come later to wail.

Male and female rains thus fall in specific ways, male preceding female. This sequencing is not accidental, and follows from Ihanzu understandings of transformative processes. One elderly male diviner from Mkalama village explained it this way:

> These rains are different. The male rain must go first; it is fierce [*ntaki*]. He opens the path ... You, the man, must clear the bush [for a field] or you build a house so a woman can be put in it. It is the same with all animals, the male always goes first ... There is one reason this must be so: if some [rain-witchcraft] medicines have been placed somewhere, if that [female] rain called *maembeela* comes, it will not fall because it has no strength. For example, the day before yesterday, do you remember the rain that came that night? It was not good. Lightning was everywhere; moreover, it was

destructive. That was a male rain, because it came to do work. So if either of the other two female rains comes now [after the male rain], it will fall immediately. They will fall gently. There will not be any wind. The water will just fall. Again [it will be] good water. It will soften the ground and saturate it to the core.[10]

Another woman, this one from Kirumi, provided further insights into the genders' productive complementary combination:

You could say that rain and sex are the same. It's always the male who must go first [kūtongela], the female who follows [kūshata]. A man enters [kingīla] a woman and she [later] bears a child. A man builds a house and puts a wife in it. A man first clears the bush, later his wife comes to farm the cleared land. With the rains, the male goes first, it really enters [kingīla] the country with force and prepares the ground for the female rains. The female rains [then] begin, those that endure and are very gentle. No man can have a child without entering a woman. No woman can bear a child without being entered [by a man]. With the rains the same. Male and female must cooperate.

In these accounts the gendered sequencing of rains is grounded in the God-given 'natural' order of things. Male precedes female. Male is fast, fierce, and potentially destructive. Male rain alone will fail to provide the amount of water necessary to soak the land: alone he is too hasty and unwieldy to do any long-term good. If anything, I was told, male rain by himself would *dry* the country. Female rain, on the other hand, is enduring but frail. On her own she is of little value. It is only when male and female rains combine as equals that they can render the landscape fertile and productive.

The idea that gender complementarity is the source of transformations underpins not only Ihanzu understandings of the production of persons and rains but virtually everything in the Ihanzu universe. It is all part of God's grand design.

The Gendered Universe: God(s), Spirits, and Celestial Bodies

God is of decided importance to all Ihanzu, whether self-proclaimed 'pagan,' Christian, or Muslim. I met no one who claimed otherwise. Around 80 per cent of the Ihanzu claim to be pagans (wapagani), 18 per cent Christian, and 2 per cent Muslim. When speaking Swahili, as

Ihanzu Christians do at church, men and women refer to God as *Mungu*. In the Ihanzu vernacular, *Itunda* is the most common God-name. This was not always so. Elders suggest that the term *Itunda* is of Iramba not Ihanzu origin, its advent unmysteriously coinciding with the first missionaries' arrival in Ihanzu in the 1930s. Elders and early written accounts agree that God's previous Ihanzu name was *Lyoa* (Obst 1912a, 115), the word the Ihanzu today use for the sun. As we shall see, God and the sun are both considered masculine.

By whatever name, God – and there is only one such divinity figure – is said to feature centrally in all our lives. Quite unlike Iramba accounts, in which God apparently vanished long ago (Pender-Cudlip c. 1974, 6–9), for the Ihanzu, God is said to be omnipresent and determining in everything we do. Even so, the precise nature of His divine direction and presence remains elusive: it is never clear what He gets up to, how He moves people to do what they do, and what His motives are for doing these things. Nor are such things discoverable through divination, as are, say, the motives of ancestral spirits or witches. Thus even if God plays a pivotal role in all aspects of Ihanzu life, that role is fundamentally perplexing, ultimately unknowable.

People may be vague about why God does what he does. But no one is uncertain about what, long, long ago, He once did. All seem to agree that God, in the beginning, created the world and everything in it: rain, men and women, the land and all the rest.[11] The verbs used to discuss this creation are *kũlompa* and *kũumba*, as, for example, when people say that 'God created rain' (*Itunda ai wĩlompwa ĩmbula*) or the earth (*Itunda ai ũmbile ihĩ*). Such statements imply the creation of something from nothing and are not used to speak of human activities. Mere mortals who 'create' things – rain, pots, beer, food, or children – can only act on already existing, God-given matter. Thus, while royal rainmakers can attract rain (*kũluta ĩmbula*) and 'make,' 'prepare,' 'forge,' or 'fashion' it (*kũnonia ĩmbula*), no one believes them capable of creating it, if by this we mean producing it from thin air. (This is why 'rainmaking' can only be done in the wet season, when God's rain is available to be enticed.) By the same token, people are capable of producing or bearing children, but do not 'create' them as such. God is the only true 'creator.'

When God created the world, He allocated certain tasks, abilities, and responsibilities to certain people. It is commonly held, for instance, that God gave rain and rainstones and the knowledge of how to use them to the first Ihanzu rainmakers.

When God created humans, people reason, he must have done so by vesting each with a soul (*nkolo*), since all people – men and women, boys and girls of all ages – are known to have one. Souls, like their owners, are definitively gendered. Whether male or female, souls are said to reside in bodies, most likely in the heart, which is also called *nkolo*. People say that the soul can be seen in strong sunlight as an ill-defined shadow that surrounds a person's cast shadow.

Souls are ordinarily housed in bodies, but they do not always remain there. They may, and often do, temporarily abandon the body during sleep to visit far-off locales, as well as distant people, both living and dead. (This is how witches can move about at night while ostensibly remaining asleep in their homes.) As someone nears death, the body becomes less able to contain the restless soul. The soul may leave the body and return several times over a period of days or even weeks, causing alternating states of coherence and incoherence, before its final departure from this world and entrance into the ancestral underworld (*ūlūngū*). Only after the soul's final departure from its corporeal container does it becomes an ancestral spirit (*mūlūngū*; plur. *alūngū*) in the full sense of the term.

When, on death, souls take permanent leave of their bodies, they join their fellow souls in the underworld as spirits. Unlike in some parts of Africa where only men's souls become ancestral spirits (Jacobson-Widding 1990), or where male and female spirits dissolve into a genderless collectivity (Bloch 1987, 326–8), in Ihanzu spirits remain differentiated by gender as they move from this world into the next. Gendered souls in life become gendered spirits in death.

In the underworld, male and female spirits are said to exist much as they did while alive, but with one crucial difference: male and female spirits cooperate, at all times, in every respect. Gender inequalities so pervasive in everyday life fade into oblivion. Indeed, this total cooperation between the genders on death is the key to the spirits' control over the powers of their ancestral other-world. And this one. Their world is portrayed as a world of gender harmony and material plenty, a place (usually said to be 'down') where fertility flows in abundance and that is the ultimate source of all this-worldly vitality. The living rely heavily on the dead and the powers they wield, a fact nowhere more apparent than with rain.

By cooperating, spirits can bring rain to this world. Or they can withhold it. The option they choose at any given time depends, in the main, on the living: if the living are 'working together,' 'cooperating,' and 'living together harmoniously,' this bodes well. Spirits will likely see this, be pleased, and bring rain. If, on the other hand, people quarrel, do not cooperate, and so forth, the ancestors will know, be angry, and withhold the rain. In either case, it is only by acting jointly as male and female that the spirits are able to bring the rain or to stop it. Spirits work together to realize their joint productive potential, good or bad. In the world of the dead, as in the world of the living, gender complementarity is the primary transformative force. This applies equally to divinity figures, like Mūnyankalī, who routinely operate in both worlds.

Mūnyankalī is a somewhat ill-defined figure in that men and women rarely agree on who, exactly, he is. For some it is God. For others it is spirits. Many simply do not know. In whatever guise or disguise, Mūnyankalī, whose this-worldly manifestation is the sun, can rightly be regarded as 'a visible and tangible symbol of a supernatural world about which nothing can be known' (Adam 1963b, 22).

Mūnyankalī is central to rain and other ancestral rites, and it may therefore seem odd that Ihanzu men and women speculate so little about him. Yet what they do say, scant though it is, betrays a profound confidence about the cosmos and the forces that operate within it: that ultimate power resides in differently gendered pairs acting in concert.

Today, as in the past, Mūnyankalī is unequivocally said to be male (Kohl-Larsen 1943, 296–7). Not only the Ihanzu but most of their neighbours, too, associate the sun with masculinity (Jellicoe, Puja, and Sombi 1967, 28; Pender-Cudlip c. 1974, 14; Tanner 1956, 51–2; Ten Raa 1969, 28). 'Mūnyankalī is the father of everything,' remarked Sungwa, an elderly man from Ng'wangeza village; 'he is God' (*Itunda*). Like this man, many Ihanzu I have spoken to assume that Mūnyankalī and God (*Itunda* or *Mungu*) differ only in name. Others are less certain. Tellingly, though, whatever one's position, this masculine divinity figure is virtually always spoken of in relation to two other things, both of them feminine.

The first is the moon. Many proffer that the moon is the sun's wife. Thus, if the sun is the father of everything and everyone, then the moon is their mother. This becomes manifest, one middle-aged woman from Ibaga village noted, during solar eclipses, when 'the female [moon] always sleeps under the male [sun].' Others link the moon to female cycles of fertility (cf. Ten Raa 1969). In all instances the sun and the moon are said to work together, each playing an indispensable gender-specific role in the cosmic life cycle. Male is to day as female is to night. Male is hot, female cool. In the context of rain and other ances-

tral matters, it is less the moon than another feminine figure that people most frequently foreground. These are Mũnyankalĩ's two wives.

Mũnyankalĩ, the male sun, moves each day from east to west. In the
process he moves from his senior wife's house in the east to his junior
wife's house in the west. With each of these wives, each day, he unites,
cooperates, has sex. In Ihanzu eyes, Mũnyankalĩ's daily movement
across the sky, and his ongoing sexual encounters, both evince a gendered universe as well as regenerate it. Villagers make this explicit
during ancestral addresses at rain offerings, as we shall see in chapters
to follow.

The east (kũkilya) and morning are associated with birth, growth and
renewal. Mũnyankalĩ has sex and is reborn each morning in the east.
Life-giving rains come from the east. Each year, for the annual rain
rites, the royal rainshrine is opened in the morning when the sun is rising. And divination sessions, which usually occur in the morning, face
east. All ancestral offerings, too, take place in the morning. The west
(kihili), in contrast, is commonly associated with death, downwards,
and decay. Mũnyankalĩ has sex and dies each evening in the west.
Ihanzu graves have east–west orientations, and the head is invariably
placed to the west. When, on occasion, the wind causes rain to fall
from the west, as sometimes happens, people say this is bad rain
(mbula mbĩ) that brings aphids, lightning, and other things unpropi-
tious. And the rainshrine is closed each year in the evening, when the
sun is setting in the west. The west is about bringing to a close important life events, including the grandest of all, life itself. It is associated
less with negativity than with ambivalence and the inevitable consequence of life: death.

The sun's movement across the sky from one wife to the other each
day evinces and enacts a gendered drama of cosmic proportions. He is
hot, active, and mobile. His wives are cool, passive, and permanent.
Husband and wife join forces each day, they come together, cooperate,
and live harmoniously together and reproduce. Each plays his or her
part in the gender bargain, each provides what he or she can provide
as different but equal parts of a pair. For the men and women of
Ihanzu, these daily cosmological occurrences are themselves evidence
of the gendered nature and operation of the universe. Much more than
this, Mũnyankalĩ's daily encounters with his wives not only *reveal* the
powers of divinity but also, quite literally, through continued sexual
activity, *reproduce* them. Heavenly forces unite daily. And the known
world – the entire cultural, social, and natural universe – rejuvenates

itself in the bargain. The God-given universe and everything in it are ordered and animated according to the principle of gender complementarity and its transformative capacities.

Conclusion

From an Ihanzu perspective, the genders and their transformative potentialities are refracted through the entire social, cultural, natural and moral universe: from big to small; from top to bottom; and within and between bodies, rains, and rainmakers, bows and grinding stones, divinity figures, and spirits and celestial bodies, among other things. Together as equals, female and male complete a vision of the world, a world that would otherwise remain imperfect, chaotic, and impotent. In this sense, Ihanzu ideas about the generative powers of gender – what I have called 'gender complementarity' – provide both a way of knowing the world and a means to act purposively upon it. In whatever form, when male and female combine as equals, things happen. Gender in this sense is more than women and men or their bodies. Much more. Moreover, when the women and men of Ihanzu speak of and act on such things, they do so with multiple, non-categorical models of scale in mind (though not, I should add, in so many words). It is not that 'real' sexed bodies are the *fons et origo* and render meaningful less tangible non-human cultural worlds. Nor is it that villagers 'know' bodies and simply 'believe' the rest. Rather, because human and non-human gender forms constitute and participate simultaneously in the world, women and men know that all gender forms, when paired appropriately, contain within themselves the capacity to reproduce and change the world. The evidence is all around them. Each pair makes sense because it is powerful and transformative in its own right, not because it mimics something more foundational and 'real.' Imagining gender as embodied capacity moves us some way towards such understandings.

Chapter 4

Annual Rain Rites

As we saw in chapter 2, annual rainmaking rites (*kũtema ilĩma*) have taken place in the royal village of Kirumi for over a century. These rites usher in each new farming season and are meant to ensure the arrival of the new year's rains. Like other rites in Ihanzu and beyond, these are replete with gender and sexuality in varied forms, in terms of the participants as well as the ritual objects and processes. While the previous chapter considered the issue of explanation, this one considers the related issue of how anthropologists imagine and represent such things in our writings. This requires attention to the relation between local and anthropological models, and ritual processes and practices.

Africanist anthropologists have long known that in rainmaking and other rites across the continent, disembodied gender forms, transformative processes and cosmos go hand in hand. Where an earlier scholarship spoke of African systems of thought, cosmology, and *connaissance* (Forde 1991 [1954]; Molet 1965; Capron 1965; Dieterlen 1965; Lebeuf 1965), more contemporary scholars discuss African folk models, world views, and thought patterns (Jacobson-Widding 1984; 1990; Hammond-Tooke 1974; Berglund 1976). Much of the recent literature has attended to the various binary oppositions – day and night, left and right, centre and periphery, wild and domesticated, nature and culture – that together constitute broader culturally specific symbolic modes of understanding. Within these symbolic worlds, many have noted, the cultural categories 'male' and 'female' or 'masculine' and 'feminine' reign supreme (Beidelman 1964, 1973, 1993, 1997; Århem 1991; Brandström 1991; Berglund 1976; Udvardy 1989; Herbert 1993; Jacobson-Widding 2000).

Such studies have furthered our understandings of gender, ritual, and symbolism in Africa. Yet certain difficulties remain, owing largely to the semiotic models that underpin them. First, there has been a tendency to over-systematize African symbols and symbolic processes. Everything is presented as coherent, as conceptually neat and tidy in the here and now. Second and related to this, many of these writings tend to conflate local and analytic models, thereby downplaying or even denying the inevitable distance between them. Many analysts thus present 'emic' viewpoints – the native world-as-it-really-is – as if the world could somehow imprint itself directly onto the pages of a monograph. It is worth noting, however, that the Ihanzu share no all-embracing 'African system of thought,' no meaningful, totalizing master narrative of 'gender complementarity' simply waiting to be articulated, decoded, and recorded in an unmediated fashion. Nor is there a vernacular equivalent for 'gender complementarity' that locals use, as I have done, to sweep across vast non-contiguous conceptual and social landscapes of transformative processes. Such are anthropological models, analytics, or fictions, not local ones. To echo Marilyn Strathern (1988, 309) they enable us to present an analysis from the perspective of a particular Western anthropological preoccupation of what certain Ihanzu understandings of gendered transformations might look like if our interlocotours shared such preoccupations. For Ihanzu women and men, the transformative power of gender complementarity reveals itself not as a coherent Platonic whole, but rather emerges in strips and patches from very practical real-world engagements. The Ihanzu, I would venture, are not unique.

Finally, many such analyses assume that 'gender symbolism' has 'a meaning' and that informants can discursively formulate that meaning. While it is true, as we saw in the last chapter, that some Ihanzu women and men can and do explain how male and female in varied forms combine to transform the world, we must remember that such decontextualized statements are responses to anthropological questions; they are not, from a local vantage point, 'the meaning.' Nor can we readily assume that such statements are 'symbolic' of anything. In Ihanzu eyes, gender complementarity does not *mean* things so much as it *does* them. Gender complementarity, as a set of culturally constituted practices, is locally meaningful because it makes things happen. Through practical action, it aims to unleash powers in the world and, in so doing, creates the potential to change that world. Ihanzu rainmaking might thus be best considered a theopraxic religious form: one whose principle purpose is to act on rather than reflect upon the world.

This chapter details the practical unfolding and gendered, generative logic that underpins Ihanzu annual rainmaking rites. In the process we shall see how, through one particular set of rain rites, participants attempt in practice to mobilize the gendered forces inherent in the world so as to transform it. I thus aim to render anthropologically meaningful that which is locally meaningful for very different reasons; to give considered attention to Ihanzu sensibilities about gendered transformation – to their own transformative 'language of life,' in Mbembe's (2001) words – while remaining mindful that my lexicons and descriptions are not synonymous with the Ihanzu world-as-it-is.

The central village of Kirumi, where all Ihanzu rain rites take place,[1] is about a mile from north to south and about the same from east to west. The village is bounded to the south, east, and west by massive boulders and small mountains, while to the north the village falls down part of the Rift Valley wall to the former village of Tumbili, which was closed during *ujamaa* (see plate 1.1). There are seventy-one homesteads unevenly spaced across the village, each of which farms a small parcel of land directly adjacent to it. A Byzantine network of paths criss-crosses the village, linking different homesteads and demarcating one person's plot from another's. Kirumi has one dirt road that runs north–south, past a now defunct colonial courthouse and former chief's house, dead-ending at a small, often empty government-run dispensary.

Not far off the main track, mostly obscured by some tall trees, is the royal rainshrine (*mpilimo* or *ĩĩndo*). It is here that annual rain rites take place. An unremarkable structure in many respects, it could easily be mistaken by outsiders for a cattle enclosure. The shrine's outer walls are made of *mĩlama* trees (*Combretum molle*) about ten feet tall and several layers thick, thus making it impossible to see inside. These tree walls form a square about fifteen by fifteen feet. The shrine has no roof. When the shrine is not in use, its doorway, which faces west, is sealed off with a number of sturdy tree poles (*mahanzu;* sing. *ihanzu*). Inside the shrine, against the north wall, is a small mud hut where some of the rainmaking paraphernalia are stored. A number of small, earthen pots (*shũngũ*), 'similar to the ordinary pots used for cooking ugali [stiff porridge]' (Adam 1963b, 5), sit on the ground in the centre of the shrine. These pots are the focal point of men's activities at the rainshrine and have been for decades (Kohl-Larsen 1943, 166).[2] They house the male rainstones and, in the wet season, all rain medicines. Locals consider the area around the shrine, like the shrine itself, 'sacred' (*miko*), and ordinary villagers are forbidden from using the two paths that pass the shrine. Only male and female rainmakers and their assistants may use these paths or enter the shrine.

Annual Rainmaking Ceremonies in the 1990s

During my stay in Kirumi village I attended most of the rites in two annual rainmaking ceremonies (1993–4, 1994–5). The following is based primarily on the former season, supplemented with data collected during the latter.

A number of people participate in annual rain rites today. These include the male and female rainmakers, male rainmaking assistants, and a 'grandson of the shrine.' These days, the male rainmaker oversees these rites. Omari, as he is known, sets the dates for the ceremonies and provides the necessary medicinal know-how so that his assistants can help bring rain (plate 4.1). Until the abolition of the chiefship in the 1960s, both male and female rainmakers played visible, public roles in annual rain rites (see Adam 1963b). Today, men and women insist that, although the male rainmaker is today most visible in these rites, it is only in concert with the female rainmaker (today, his sister) that he can successfully bring rain. Without consultation and agreement between these two royals, the rains, villagers seem to agree, will fail.

Several elderly men called *ataata* assist Omari each year. These assistants, who today total nineteen, live in and represent different villages from across Ihanzu. Rainmaking assistants carry out various duties. They serve as middlemen between the male rainmaker in Kirumi and villagers in other parts of Ihanzu; they collect grain tribute each year for the two rainmakers; and they gather roots and leaves with which to prepare rain medicine at the royal rainshrine. Their positions are unpaid and carry little in the way of status or material benefit. Rainmaking assistants generally do their work because they enjoy it and because they understand its importance for the country.

In addition to these assistants, there is also a man known as 'the grandson of the shrine' (*mizūkūlū a mpilimo*), whose responsibility it is to initiate and carry out certain rainmaking duties. The term 'grandson' here should not conjure up images of young boys, since the Ihanzu kinship system allows grandchildren to be older than their grandparents. 'Grandsons of the shrine' are and long have been elderly men (see Adam 1963b).

Plate 4.1. Rainmaker Omari in front of the rainshrine (photo by T. Sanders)

Apart from these people, no other villagers participate directly in annual rain rites. Even so, most Ihanzu today find their continued performance vital to their own livelihood and well-being. Without them, people say, the ancestral spirits would become angry and the rains would most likely fail. Whenever I visited villages in other parts of Ihanzu during the rainy season, men and women routinely asked about the state of the rains and royal rain rites in Kirumi: whether the sod had been cut yet; whether there were plans to carry out other remedial rites; whether any rain witches had been identified and tried; and so on.

The first rite performed in annual rainmaking ceremonies, one that marks the onset of the new agricultural season, is the night-time cutting of the sod (*kūkumpya lutinde*). This is a secretive rite that, in the 1993–4 season, took place in mid-October just prior to the onset of the rains. The male rainmaker summoned the grandson and a few experienced assistants to Kirumi. Dressed in black, they entered the rainshrine and lit a fresh *mūlama* tree branch on fire. Black is the colour of rain clouds, and people commonly say this is why it is the preferred colour for rainmaking rites. Once the branch caught fire, they threw it into a nearby cave. With that, the sod had been cut. The news spread rapidly from village to village across Ihanzu the following day. Following a one-day farming prohibition (*ikali*) out of respect for the ancestors, villagers could begin to farm.

Later that month came the official opening of the rainshrine (*kūlūgula mpilimo*). Rainmaker Omari normally determines the precise date for this, based mainly on the state of the weather: if the rains appear near, the shrine is opened sooner rather than later. This particular year, there was no great urgency since there were no obvious signs that the rains were near. On a designated day in October, before sunrise, rainmaking assistants began arriving in Kirumi from their respective villages. All wore black. Many adorned themselves with or carried certain ritually significant leaves, all said to be 'cool' and 'gentle,' and all explicitly associated with rain. The most common such leaves are *mūlama* (*Combretum molle*), *mūmbīlīlī* (*Entada sp.*), *mūsūī* (*Sclerocarya birrea*), and *ipolyo* (*Rhoicissus tridentata*). The grandson arrived with a black sheep that he had, a few days previous, acquired from a member of the royal clan-section.

At the rainshrine, as the sun was rising, the assistants removed the shrine's weighty tree door. The grandson, with a sheep, was the first to enter the shrine. There, he forced the sheep to the ground, its head to the west and tail to the east in the manner of all rain-offering sacrifices. The grandson then slit the sheep's throat and, when it was dead, began carving it up. He tossed some of the sheep's stomach contents around the shrine. This, I was told, was to cool (*kūpola*) the shrine, the spirits, and the land.

Outside the shrine, the men roasted and ate the sheep. They then entered the shrine and, with some rakes and hoes from the hut, cleared away the weeds and leaves that had accumulated since the previous year. They removed the rainstones from their pots, carefully anointed them with castor-seed oil (*mono*), and replaced them. The shrine was now officially 'open' for the year. Rainmaking assistants and the grandson socialized at a nearby beer party, and returned to their respective villages the following day. Over the coming weeks, the rainmaking assistants began one of their more onerous tasks: collecting grain tribute from villagers for the two rainmakers.

Each year, the rainmaking assistants collect a token amount of grain (usually a cup or two) from each household in their villages. They may do this alone, but just as often they are assisted by an elderly local woman. All Ihanzu villagers, irrespective of where they live, should pay tribute since all ostensibly benefit from royal rainmaking rites in Kirumi.[3]

By early November, rainmaking assistants had begun to deliver their grain tribute to the two royal rainmakers in Kirumi. Their arrivals never went unnoticed and were sometimes spectacular. Assistants were invariably followed by a silent queue of children and an elderly woman. Rainmaking assistants led the way. The children, sometimes as many as thirty, followed single file, each with a small basket of grain tribute on his or her head. The elderly woman followed behind the children. All wore black or similarly dark colours; many adorned themselves with ritually significant leaves. None spoke.

The years I lived in Kirumi, the total amount of grain each assistant delivered to the two rainmakers varied considerably. Some brought as much as two large burlap bags, others as little as half a bucket. This grain was delivered to the male and female rainmakers and divided equally between them. The rainmakers, for their part, did not keep this grain, but recombined and blessed it, before sending it back with the rainmaking assistants to the villages from whence it came. There, rainmaking assistants put the now-blessed seeds into their own grainstores. People say that this annual division, combination, and blessing of seeds ensures fertility of the land, an abundant harvest, and full grainstores for all villagers. Bringing seeds to Kirumi each year, dividing them between male and female rainmakers, and returning them to the villages is one of the most significant elements of annual rain ceremonies and is never omitted from people's descriptions of them.

Once the grain has been received, blessed, and returned, the next stage in the annual rain rites is to prepare rain medicine (*kŭnonia makota*), something that must be done anew each season. When men prepare rain medicine – something they always do inside the shrine – they do so either naked or in their undergarments. This season, it was an early November morning that rainmaking assistants and the grandson arrived at the rainshrine to prepare the medicines. They opened the pole door and entered naked, leaving their clothes outside. Senior assistants donned their clothes once again and began collecting special 'rain medicines' (*makota a mbula*) from the bush surrounding Kirumi. This medicine consisted of a variety of roots, leaves, and branch shavings, which other assistants, working inside the shrine, ground on a grinding stone into a powder. Once this was done, they mixed the medicine into a large vat of lukewarm water. The grandson immediately transferred this medicinal mixture into the smaller pots that hold the rainstones. As he did so, he addressed Mŭnyankalĩ in a loud, theatrical tone:

Ũewe Mŭnyankalĩ nŭpŭmile kŭ mŭtala wako nŭkŭlŭ n'ŭinzŭ kŭ mŭtala wako nŭnino, wakĩla mŭnŭ m'Ihanzu wahanga kŭkete ipolyo, ipolyo la mpilimo. Ĩmbula nĩng'kŭlŭ! Ĩmailo nĩ dŭ! Akombi atuge nĩ amintŭtĩ! Kŭkete ipolyo la mbula. Ũko n'ŭninzŭ ŭtwale ninza aya ni mabĩ ŭmagŭmĩle mŭ lŭzĩ mŭ Nyanza.

You, Mŭnyankalĩ, who come from your senior wife's house [in the east] and are going to your junior one's [in the west], you have passed through Ihanzu and found we are carrying out an offering at the rainshrine. Let rain pour down! Grain in excess! Let women bear twins! We have a rain offering here. Take good news to the place you are going. As for the bad, toss it into the waters of Lake Victoria.

The moment was highly charged. Assistants listened in silence. When recounting this part of the ritual sequence, participants and others routinely stress that the medicinal water, once placed to the pots with rainstones, begins to boil furiously, without fire. This is due, people say, to the powers activated by the combination of the pot, rainstones, and medicine. People's descriptions of this boiling consistently

suggested something far grander that what appeared to me an unin-
spired fizzle, a consequential point that I return to below.

After the medicinal water has 'boiled' there is normally little else to
do for the season – if, that is, the rains fall regularly and on time.
Regrettably, this particular year they did not. Rainmaking assistants
thus returned to the shrine several times during the season to remix
the medicines and, on one occasion, to prepare entirely new ones.
Given the eventual gravity of the situation, men and women took
other remedial rainmaking measures as well, the topic of chapters to
follow.

There are other rites associated with the shrine that are carried out
more sporadically. During the rainy season, for instance, any conflict
that leads to bloodshed in any Ihanzu village requires certain remedial
rites at the rainshrine. Bloodshed from fighting is known to heat and
endanger the land. This is because it angers the spirits, who may, in
turn, stop the rain or send damaging lightning strikes, or both. Lightning, especially, is said to share commonalities with blood: both are
considered hot (*lũpyu*), fierce (*lũtaki*) and red (*lũkaũku*). Thus, when
brawling blood is spilled, the instigator of the fight must give to his or
her local rainmaking assistant a black, pregnant goat. Rainmaking
assistants slaughter the goat at the rainshrine. Small pieces of the fetal
goat – referred to as 'womb water' (*mazĩ a ndaa*) – are then mixed into
the rain pots with the medicines and stones. People say this pleases the
spirits and cools the land. In the 1994–5 season three goats were sacri-
ficed at the rainshrine as a result of brawling and spilled blood.

When, in June, the wet season's end was drawing near, the rainmaking assistants returned to the rainshrine to close it for the year. This was
done in the evening, as is always the case. They prepared their final rain
medicines, not for the current year but for the one to come. The door was
closed unceremoniously and all departed for their respective villages. It
is at this point that the male rainmaker 'gives the knife' (*kũpegwa lupyu*)
to villagers – that is to say, gives villagers permission to begin the harvest. People say that cutting sorghum before being 'given the knife'
risks angering the spirits, who may consequently withhold rain in the
future. 'Giving the knife' is the final rainmaking rite of the season.

Theopraxy, Gender, and Transformation

In the previous chapter we considered some of the constituent elements of Ihanzu transformative processes, including the ideas that

male precedes female and hot precedes cold, and that the life cycle –
itself inherently gendered – moves from parent to child, east to west,
and back again. These principles similarly underpin the annual rain
rites just described. They manifest themselves, however, less as a
coherent symbolic system than as a series of shifting associations and
combinations that emerge in these rites' practical, spatio-temporal
unfolding.

The first rite conducted during annual rainmaking ceremonies, the
night cutting of the sod, involves uniting fire and a fresh *mūlama*
branch. Both are everyday items. Both bear a host of characteristics,
meanings, and associations. Fire, men and women often remark, is red,
hot, and dry. This is why, at least in certain contexts, many link fire
closely with blood and lightning and say it is masculine. The *mūlama*,
on the other hand, is one among several 'cool' or 'gentle' trees (*mītī nī
mīpolo*). Cool trees – the only kind used for rainmaking activities – are
generally large, deciduous shade trees that grow in cool, wet spots like
riverbeds. People routinely opine not only that such trees are fertile
and good for rain, but also that they are feminine. The ritual logic of
combining fire with the *mūlama* gradually reveals itself: to combine fire
and a *mūlama* branch during the nocturnal sod cutting is to combine as
equals male and female, hot and cool, in an attempt to bring about
transformation. It is the practical combination of these differently gendered but complementary elements that makes this happen. For transformations to occur, a careful balance is required: too much heat or
male, just like too much coolness or female, will do nothing. Transformations demand hot and cold, heating and cooling, male and female,
at just the right moments, in just the right ways. To get the balance
right, these things must be positively harnessed and managed – in a
very practical sense – through specific ritual activities.

Yet fire, here and elsewhere, also embodies another set of principles.
For even while fire shares properties of heat, blood, dryness, and masculinity, it is at the same time taken as evidence of the successful combination of male and female principles. For instance, male and female
firesticks, when combined as equals, are said to 'give birth' (*kūtuga*) to
fire, just as male and female bodies and fertilizing fluids, when appropriately combined, can give birth to children. Such combinations generate heat. They have transformative potential. This is why the fire at the
night cutting of the sod can be seen on the one hand as male and on the
other as evidence of the productive combination of male and female.
The ostensible contradiction between these two positions is more

apparent than real and only appears so when the two are considered atemporally. However, once we allow the temporal, context-dependent local sense to emerge in these rites' unfolding, contradiction vanishes. This is because 'practical sense "selects" certain objects or actions, and consequently certain of their aspects, in relation to "the matter in hand," an implicit and practical principle of pertinence; and, by fixing on those with which there is something to be done or those that determine what is to be done in the given situation, or by treating different objects or situations as equivalent, it distinguishes properties that are pertinent from those that are not' (Bourdieu 1990, 89–90). When temporally contextualized, fire is first male and then, once combined with the *mūlama* branch, is taken as evidence of the genders' generative union. Male precedes female; hot precedes cool; the genders unite as equals.

This theopraxy of transformation underpins other aspects of Ihanzu annual rain rites, sometimes in rather striking ways. The rainshrine, for example, is made entirely of cool, female *mīlama* trees; and male rainmaking assistants, while preparing medicine, constantly move in and out of the shrine: naked. Inside the shrine, the men grind medicine on a grinding stone, a quintessentially female object, one that no man, nor even a boy, would use under any other circumstances. Moreover, the rainmaking pots – a central, permanent feature of the rainshrine – are small, ordinary, and undecorated, the type women use for cooking. This prompted one rainmaking assistant spontaneously to proffer that 'these are female pots.' The fact that male rainstones are kept in these female pots is no accident, either. Nor is the fact that their ritual combination – when they are cleaned, rubbed with oil, and mixed with special medicinal 'waters'– causes the water to 'boil' without fire, which is evidence once again of the genders' (re)productive, transformative combination. In the 1993–4 season, a severe drought year, rainmaking assistants returned to the shrine repeatedly to remix the medicinal waters and to recombine the rainstones and pots. The repeated grinding and remixing of medicines, and joining and rejoining of male stones and female pots, is akin to coitus, at least to the extent that achieving transformation – be it producing children or rain – is rarely a straightforward, one-time event. The genders must be managed and combined as equals, frequently several times, in order to produce the desired outcome. But these gender combinations for rainmaking cannot be reduced to sexual intercourse, nor can they be adequately explained as derivative of it. It is rather that both sexual intercourse and rainmaking are premised on the same theopraxic principles.

It is worth adding that certain Ihanzu understandings of transformative potentiality have long held sway. In the 1920s, a District Officer posted in Ihanzu was told that during annual rain rites, a number of twigs were put 'into a big jar full of cold water, which then "boils without heat," and is a powerful "medicine."' Taking this statement at face value, the DO concluded that 'there must be some chemical properties in the twigs to cause effervescence, or "boiling," but so far no-one has been able to discover what twigs are used.'[4] What he failed to realize was that the significance of this reported boiling lies not in any yet-to-be-discovered arboreal chemical compound but in Ihanzu knowledge of complementary gender combinations and their generative potentialy. 'Boiling' evinces successful gender combinations and potential transformations.

The periodic slaughter of 'the brawling goat' evinces the same principles of transformation, and aims practically to re-establish a complementary and therefore productive relationship between male and female, hot and cool. Discord among the living leads to discord among the dead, and thus to potential dearth of co-operation, rain, and fertility. This, people say, is because blood spilt during conflict is hot and thus destructive of cool rain. It is 'male' heat that comes at the wrong time, as it were, in the ritual sequence, long after the land should have been rendered 'cool.' This particular out-of-sync heating can only be eliminated by slaughtering a pregnant goat and mixing the fetal matter into the rain pots. Normally sheep, not goats, are the preferred sacrificial animal, given their gentle and cool dispositions. Yet when it comes to bloodshed and heating the land, only goats will do, since these ruminants are said to be hot, unruly, and troublesome (mbankalūku). Thus, if conflict blood heats the land, fetal matter cools it. Slaughtering the hot, vexatious goat brings to an end social disorder by reducing the source of heat, while placing the fetal parts into the rain pots cools the spilled blood and returns fertility – in a most literal sense – to the land. In this way the appropriate balance between hot and cool, male and female, and their temporal sequencing, is practically re-established.

Of course, movements in time also imply movements in space. The east–west axis, in particular, deserves close attention, since ritual participants, when asked, say that this axis is highly significant in these and other rain rites. This is because it conjures and alludes to the divinity figure Mūnyankalī.

When the rainshrine was opened at the start of the season, the grandson took great care to orient the sacrificial sheep with its head to the west, tail to the east. At all rain rites I attended, these included, ritual participants invariably ensured proper east–west alignment of their ritual implements, sacrificial animals, and practices in the same way. This spatial concern, often implicit, always evident, aims to evoke the most patent of all east–west movements: Mũnyankalĩ's daily movements across the sky between his two wives, and his ongoing sexual encounters with each. These spatial and temporal movements are, as we saw in the previous chapter, at once personal and cosmic: movement from east to west, from birth to death, from beginning to end and back again. While spatial concerns practically conjure these links, addresses made to Mũnyankalĩ make such references explicit.

Addresses to Mũnyankalĩ commonly draw on themes of prosperity and fertility (that villagers have plenty of children, rain and grain, etc.) and frequently request that disease, witchcraft, and hunger cease (cf. Obst 1912a, 116). They do this by evoking the gendered nature of Mũnyankalĩ's being and activity, noting that he is moving from one wife's house in the east to another wife's house in the west (Adam 1963b, 11–12, 22; Kohl-Larsen 1943, 303–5). Such addresses evoke life processes and the notion of gender complementarity that keeps these processes moving along. Male and female reside and act harmoniously together. Following a similar logic, the rainshrine was opened at sunrise in October and closed, some six months later, at dusk. I was told this is always the case. As with all east–west referents, people explicitly link this seasonal opening and closing to Mũnyankalĩ and his movements between his two wives.

One final aspect of Ihanzu annual rain rites takes on great importance. This is the royal blessing of the seeds: a practice that has proved pervasive, its practical logic persuasive, for well over a century (Reche 1914, 85; Werther 1898, 99). Prior to the onset of the rains each year, each household gives a small amount of grain to its local rainmaking assistant. He, in turn, takes this to the two royal rainmakers in Kirumi with the aid of children and an elderly women. The rainmaking assistant, as male, leads the way; the elderly woman, as female, follows. Once in Kirumi they divide the grain between the male and female rainmakers. The rainmakers then remix and bless the grain, and the assistants return it to their respective villages. A month or so later, the rains arrive. And when they do, people say, the rains emanate from Kirumi, home of the rainmakers. There they begin, in the spiritual centre of Ihanzu, and expand outwards in all directions until they envelop the whole of Ihanzu. One elderly woman's account, very like others I heard, went this way:

> Rainmaking assistants collect seeds from villagers, bring them to the royals in Kirumi and then return home [with the blessed seeds]. They walk slowly. And they don't talk to anyone. [They are] silent. They don't look back either. They don't look back towards Kirumi. They just keep walking, looking straight ahead. The rains follow them as they walk, you know, but they don't touch them. They [the rains] follow behind them and wash away their footprints as they walk. But they never get wet. Never! When they arrive home, the rainmaking assistants go inside their houses. The rains pour down everywhere. It rains, it rains, it rains! The rainmaking assistants get the rains from Kirumi and bring them home.

In short, the rains – which, remember, are 'male' and 'female'– radiate outwards from Kirumi, from and through the male and female rainmakers who own them and who, together, produce them. Gendered rains and blessed grains reach the furthermost corners of Ihanzu. In this way, each year, royal rainmakers give life to villagers just as parents give life to offspring. Both duos combine in equal amounts and give their gendered seeds and waters. If husband and wife bear children by combining as equals, then male and female rainmakers, by doing the same, give birth to all Ihanzu. Parallels extend from life's beginning to its end.

At the onset of each new farming season, when all await and desire rains and the possibility of renewed life, villagers return as tribute their own lifeless seeds to the royals, just as children return their seeds to their parents on death. Both transactions acknowledge and enact, in identical ways, the generative potential of differently gendered pairs. Both the human life cycle and annual rainmaking rites are premised on the same generative principles. Both proceed on the assumption that, when male and female combine as equals, the powers that that combination unleashes can transform the world. By dividing, blessing, and returning gendered grains and rains to villages, royal rulers position themselves as the principle actors in a cosmic drama on the regeneration of life.

Because the male and female rainmaker are (currently) brother and sister, never husband and wife, such royal reproductive 'cooperation' implies that royal incest is central to rainmaking. The Ihanzu are not alone in this idea, of course, as incest and rainmaking are commonly linked across much of sub-Saharan Africa. There is a well-known Ihanzu saying that, though somewhat cryptic to outsiders, makes perfect sense in context: 'Rain is more important than the child you have borne' (*Mbula ĩũwai kũlĩko ng'wana nũtugile*). One elderly man, who lives in Kirumi village, explained it to me this way:

> It [rainmaking] had its own taboos. Yes, it is said that 'rain is more important than the child you have borne' [...] Those chiefs, those two. There were really taboos! But it's normal. Isn't it normal, eh, to build or to make [something]? That is, they had their own secrets all to themselves ... That's the reason people say: 'rain is more important than the child you have borne.' The sense is that you can ... [pause], go to ... [pause], eh, go to ..., go and get together with your mother or sister. You do it [sex] slowly. That water [fertilizing fluids], well, you take it over there [...] and put it there [pointing towards the rainshrine]. That is the sense [in the saying], 'rain is more important than the child you have borne.' Isn't it true? So that was the secret. You get together with your sister or mother [...]; she puts something like this [signifying setting something on the ground]. Their waters enter. You [then] take it over to the rain[shrine]. Indeed, *that* is what pulls everything!

Circuitous though this elder's explanation may be, his point is unmistakable: royal incest is *the* secret to bringing the rain to Ihanzu. Only when the two differently gendered rainmakers combine sexually are the most powerful forces of the Ihanzu universe unleashed. Naturally enough, the true significance of this saying lies not in any ethnographic or historical facts it may contain. It seems most unlikely, after all, that rainmaking royals actually engage in secretive sexual activities, collect their gendered fertilizing fluids, and use them as rain medicines in the rainshrine to bring male and female rains. More instructive is that many people say it is so, and furthermore, that royals' supposed actions are informed by specific notions of transformation that make it entirely plausible, necessary, even desirable. Royal waters – fertilizing fluids – when equally combined, bring more royal waters: male and female rains. The saying, then, refers to the relationship between commoners and royals. It is a commoner quip, directed at royal rainmakers, suggesting that royal fertility can and should be used to create rain rather than offspring for themselves. To the extent the royals channel their own reproductive waters into rain, then, they fail to produce progeny of their own. Yet by investing their 'waters' in the production of rain and not children, royals consequently give birth to and, in that sense, become the parents of all Ihanzu.

Concluding Remarks

The Ihanzu share a particular understanding of transformation, one that is predicated on the notion of gender complementarity. In Ihanzu eyes, the fact that the genders possess transformative powers makes sense. It is natural. It is how the world works. And it is largely through rituals such as annual rain rites that such understandings emerge and are practically put to work, and through which the Ihanzu cultural, social, and moral orders are continually forged and fashioned, made and remade, enlivened and transformed. The local logic of these rites, such as it is, emerges not as an overarching conceptual schema. Such understandings do not exist – at least for the women and men of Ihanzu – as a coherent, all-embracing 'African system of thought' or 'folk model' aimed at systematizing and symbolizing the world around them. Far from it. Rather, annual rain rites, like all Ihanzu rain rites, are theopraxic in nature and locally meaningful because they have the potential to bring rain. It is, above all, their underlying gen(d)erative spatio-temporal logic that gives them this potential. Such principles need not be formulated discursively to do what they purportedly do, even if on occasion people can and do discuss such things. To discuss sex, after all, will not bring a child any more than discussing sexually laden rain rites will bring rain. In both cases, actions speak louder than words. By carrying out the rites they do – by conjoining masculine and feminine as equals in the form of fire and trees, stones and pots, men and their shrine, male and female leaders and their seeds – ritual participants aim, time and again and in varied ways, to set the world in motion.

Chapter 5

(Wo)men Behaving Badly:
Genders within Bodies

The most important of these [rain] rites among the Zulu required obscene behaviour by the women and girls ... At various stages of the ceremonies women and girls went naked, and sang lewd songs. Men and boys hid and might not go near ...

[This] is my first example of a ritual of rebellion, an instituted protest demanded by sacred tradition, which is seemingly against the established order, yet which aims to bless that order to achieve prosperity.

(Gluckman 1963, 113–14)

Some months had passed since the annual rain rites had taken place. Yet no real rain had fallen. When this happens, as it sometimes does, villagers take other measures to ensure the onset of the rains. These include ferreting out rain-witches (chapter 7), ancestral offerings (chapter 6), and holding women's rain dances, the topic of this chapter. Thus for the second time on one unseasonably hot January day in Kirumi, the women danced naked and sang their way through the village, bellowing and gesticulating obscenities as they went. Men hurriedly removed themselves from their path, for fear of being caught, unceremoniously stripped of their clothing, and 'played with' by the unruly mob. One hapless middle-aged man, apparently too slow to outrun the wild women, had already been captured. He managed to avoid further incident by quickly agreeing to pay a fine.

Such a fate, I was fairly hopeful, would not befall me. This was due to the hours of negotiation a few days previous between me and the women. If I provided the dancers with a goat or, preferably, a 20-litre bucket of beer, 'it would please the ancestral spirits,' the women reassured me. I could thus attend the dance without myself suffering undue ridicule or abuse. Of much greater importance, from their per-spective anyway, with such a gift my presence would not undermine the ritual's principle objective: to bring the rain to this parched land.

At a distance I sat, hastily jotting down notes about the women's rain dance, and being mildly enchanted by the realization that I was witnessing my first ever 'ritual of rebellion.' I was familiar with Max Gluckman's (1963) landmark lecture on the topic, which suggested that all such women's rites, in spite of their manifest differences, could be explained as women's reaction to the prevailing patriarchal gender order. Such rites ultimately reinforced rather than undermined the gender *status quo*. This seemed as good an explanation as any for the rites that unfolded before me. After all, men and women from across Ihanzu had repeatedly told me that 'men are the important ones' (*Ago-haa nī akūlū*). What is more, local men's and women's everyday control, or lack of control, over vital political and economic resources seemed to bear this notion out. Thus the idea that these rites were women's rit-ual response to men's everyday dominance seemed perfectly sensible. Indeed, as I later discovered, a number of contemporary scholars con-tinue to find 'rituals of rebellion' a useful way to think about such rites, and Gluckman's original formulation a useful way to explain them (e.g., Spencer 1988; Creider and Creider 1997; Weil 1976).

But that was my first year in Ihanzu. The longer I remained, the more difficult it became to see this particular women's 'ritual of rebel-lion' as such. Nor, after some time, was it possible to see everyday life in Ihanzu as being wholly about 'patriarchy.' It became increasingly clear, for example, that in certain everyday contexts women exercised more power than men, and gained prestige in the process. This was certainly so, we will recall from chapter 1, with women's control over grain and beer. Moreover, in many ritual contexts – including when discussing these particular rain rites – my interlocutors insisted that male and female were and must be equal. Thus, as my understanding of subtleties of gender in Ihanzu grew, the seeming elegance of my pre-vious understanding of this so-called ritual of rebellion was gradually and irreversibly undone. This led, quite inevitably, to interrogating how anthropologists think and theorize about 'rituals of rebellion' and 'patriarchy.'

This chapter offers an alternative reading of a so-called ritual of rebellion, one that pays close attention to the complexities of Ihanzu notions of gender and transformative processes. The first of these is the idea that women are naturally wetter than men, thus making them in some contexts better suited than men, physiologically speaking, to attract rain. The second idea we have seen before, and holds that rain rites succeed only when the cultural categories 'male' and 'female' conjoin as equals. The palpable contradiction between these two propositions is overcome in these rites when women embody both genders simultaneously. This they do by playing up their wet, fertile femininity while at the same time co-opting what are considered more typical male characteristics of aggression, abusive behaviour, and obscenity. By combining and collapsing masculinity and femininity within themselves, women dancers create the ultimate gendered combination to bring the ultimate communal good: rain. As in all Ihanzu rain rites, participants seek not to symbolize or represent the productive union of male and female, but rather practically to unleash that productivity. The point, recall, is to bring rain. It is thus Ihanzu men's and women's experiences with gendered transformative processes – not their reactions to alleged patriarchal structures – that give both shape and meaning to these particular rain rites.

Some years ago, in his highly influential paper, Max Gluckman (1963) coined the term 'rites of rebellion.' He gave two examples of such rites, both from southern Africa: the Zulu Heavenly Princes Cult (*Nomkubulwana*) and the Swazi *ncwala* ceremony. My principle concern in this chapter is with the former type of rite, since it most resembles the Ihanzu women's rites to be described, and since it bears most directly on the issue of gender in Africa.[1]

As is now well known, Gluckman argued that Zulu women, by acting out certain rain rites surrounding the Heavenly Princes Cult, were able to reverse temporarily the gender status quo, thus allowing them to become men's equals if not their superiors. During such rites 'a dominant rôle was ascribed to the women, and a subordinate rôle to the men' (1963, 114). Furthermore, 'this temporary dominant rôle of the women – a dominant rôle that was publicly instituted, indeed approved, and not exercised tactfully in the background – contrasted strongly with the mores of these patriarchal peoples' (Gluckman 1963, 114). For at all other times women were characterized by their 'subordination and modesty' and 'were in every respect formally under the tutelage of men' (Gluckman 1963, 115).

Thus, if Zulu society can be characterized as 'patriarchial,' then Zulu women's rituals of rebellion are about redressing the gender balance of power by inverting it. In other words, if everyday life is wholly about gendered hierarchies and male dominance, then ritual life is largely about gender symmetry or female dominance.[2] Such ritual inversions, Gluckman argued, functioned to release underlying psychosocial tensions over men's and women's relative powers in Zulu society. In no way did these rites challenge, let alone undermine, the social structure. They actually reinforced it.

Zulu rain rites may have served as Gluckman's ethnographic anchoring point. Yet his argument led him – and many others since – well beyond the Zulu case. For Gluckman implied that all such 'rites of rebellion' found across Africa and beyond could be similarly explained as women's reaction to the prevailing patriarchal gender order. What is more, many contemporary scholars continue to make more or less the same argument.

Take Paul Spencer's exemplary monograph on the Kenyan Matapato Maasai (Spencer 1988). Spencer devotes an entire chapter to women's fertility 'rituals of rebellion,' noting, like Gluckman, that these rites must 'be viewed against the backcloth of this [male-dominant] regime to which they are subjected by older men' (1988, 200). During women's collective fertility gatherings, in which women persecute certain men guilty of abusing their 'daughters' and wives, Spencer explains, 'the normal social order is upturned and women take over a domain that lies outside the normal bounds of village existence' (1988, 202). Although his argument adds subtlety to Gluckman's by incorporating Peter Rigby's (1968) more culturalist approach, Spencer follows Gluckman to the letter in suggesting that such gatherings have a brief reality of their own 'which readjusts the balance of power between the sexes' (1988, 204) in a society where 'women are dominated by men' (1988, 7; cf. Llewelyn-Davies 1981).

For others, this argument has become such an obvious anthropological platitude that to evoke Max Gluckman by name is apparently no longer necessary. Writing on girls' initiation rituals among the Nandi of Kenya, Jane and Chet Creider (1997) call into question Langley's (1979) earlier suggestion that these rites are primarily about gender inversion through transvestism. Evoking Mauss, they argue the contrary – that it is the act of giving clothing from boys to girl initiates that is of central importance (Creider and Creider 1997, 55–6): 'The apparel is given by the boyfriend to the girls as part of themselves, as something precious to them, to show the girls that they care for them, and to encourage the girls to bring honour to them (the warriors) by their brave behaviour during initiation' (1997, 56). They conclude by noting that 'The real reason for Nandi girls' initiation ... is that *it is women's way of achieving equality with men*. By undergoing an experience requiring an amount of bravery equivalent to that experienced by boys during circumcision, Nandi women are saying to the men, "Look! We are just as good, i.e., brave, as you are!"' (Creider and Creider 1997, 58; my emphasis).

Female rites of reversal or rebellion are once again said to be about turning the mundane, male-dominant gendered world back to front (see also Weil 1976, 191–3).

Gluckman's argument and the recent reincarnations of it are not without their difficulties.[3] First of all, to speak of 'patriarchy' or 'male dominance' without further qualification ignores the distinction between gender representations and practices, and thus threatens to impose an ill-fitted analytic straightjacket on an empirically untidy world (Ortner and Whitehead 1981a, 10ff; H.L. Moore 1994; Ortner 1996). Experience tells us that people's ideas about gender do not directly reflect on-the-ground gender practices; that gender practices and people's images of those practices often chart quite independent courses (Tsing 1990; Rogers 1990; Keeler 1990; Stølen 1996; Peletz 1994). To insist on monolithic notions like 'patriarchy' to characterize whole societies, as Gluckman did and others still do, is to insist on presenting an unnuanced, unitary picture that glosses over the complexities of people's experiences with and ideas about gender.

A second and related difficulty with this argument results from inattention to the potentially conflictual and contradictory nature of gender representations themselves (Bloch 1987; Caplan 1989; Hatley 1990; Archetti 1996; Meigs 1990, 15; Melhuus 1996). To be sure, speaking of 'patriarchy' and 'rebellion' does allow for two (and only two) contradictory notions of gender: the first links male dominance with everyday 'patriarchal' practices; while the second links female dominance with the ritual 'rebellion' realm. But this does not go far enough. For if there are contradictory notions of gender between mundane and ritual domains, as there frequently are, then such contradictions must equally be found *within* these domains.

In Ihanzu and elsewhere, ideas and practices surrounding gender relations in everyday and ritual realms are multiple and multifaceted. As we have seen, both women and men hold that female can be superior, or inferior, or equal to male, depending on the context. This makes wholly untenable the still common assertion that 'rites of rebellion' are simply a reversal of *the* everyday gender system, discussed in singular and monolithic terms, since no such 'system' exists. Once we admit to the possibility of multiple and conflicting ideas and practices of gender relations in people's daily lives, it is no longer clear what a ritual reversal of these ideas and practices could possibly mean. What is required instead is closer attention to the specific ethnographic contexts in which such rites unfold, and to exercise the anthropolgical imagination more creatively in how we 'explain' these.

Ihanzu Women's 'Rites of Rebellion'

When the annual rites discussed in the previous chapter fail, as evidenced by no rain for extended periods, then the two royal rainmakers discuss holding a women's rain dance (*isīmpūlya*). In both structure and content, these rites present themselves as a classic 'ritual of rebellion.' The ceremony is always performed in Kirumi, normally either in January or February, though only in those years when the rains have failed completely. Once begun, the rain dance usually lasts two days. It may, however, carry on for several, depending on whether the rain has begun to fall. As soon as the rain begins, or it seems likely that it may, the women may return to their homes confident that the royal ancestors have heard their prayers. The ritual's aim, participants and others say, is to bring rain to Ihanzu.

The female rainmaker is in charge of organizing and orchestrating these rain rites. Her name is Ng'welu; she lives in Kirumi. Throughout the rain dance, participants are based at her home, where they eat, sleep and gossip. Side by side with the male rainmaker's assistants runs a parallel structure of female rainmaking assistants, a group of women who fall under the ritual authority of the female rainmaker. They, too, are called *ataata*. The female assistants, each from a different Ihanzu village, spread the word that a rain dance is to take place in Kirumi on a specific day.

Apart from Ng'welu and her assistants, certain other women take part in the dance. Any woman who has borne at least one child may participate. Extraordinarily fertile women, those who have given birth to twins, have special roles to play that I will discuss presently. Infertile women (*agumba*; sing. *mūgumba*), in contrast, are normally prohibited from taking part. Finally, under no circumstances may menstruating women participate in these dances. This would threaten the well-being of all participants and would likely destroy the dance by causing lightning strikes, given the commonplace associations between blood, heat and lightning.[4]

The women divide themselves into four groups, based mainly on seniority. The oldest women (*akombi nīakūlū*) will have attended the dance many times and are thus regarded as experts. They are responsible for preparing certain medicines and for singing and playing a ritually significant buffalo-horn drum called *mbīlū*, which they strike with a *mūlama* (*Combretum molle*) branch. They must also prepare castor-seed oil (*mono*) and a sorghum mix, which all dancers will consume. The next group (*akombi nīakete īntepe*) generally organizes the labour of the younger women. These women are fairly senior and are said to understand the 'correct' ritual procedure reasonably well. The third group is called *adamu*. These are the primary dancers, though in practice all participants dance. All these women have attended the dance previously and are responsible for instructing those who have never before attended. They also do most of the hard work, including fetching water and cutting firewood. The final and youngest group is made up of novices, those young women (*iyombwe*) who are attending the dance for the first time. Each novice brings with her a small amount of sorghum, which will be cooked and eaten by all as boiled sorghum (*mpeke ya ilo*).

Of consequence, certain men may also take part in these ceremonies – namely, those who have fathered twins. No men participated in the rites during the years I was there, but I met two who said they had done so on previous occasions. Several people also mentioned that the male rainmaker, if he wished, could participate. While men's actual participation in these rites is rare, the fact that some may, in theory, participate is significant, for reasons we return to below.

The rain dance to be described took place in January 1994,[5] nearly a month after rainmaker Omari and his assistants had prepared their rain medicines at the rainshrine but to no avail. People had begun seriously to worry, and not without good cause: if the rains do not arrive by late January or early February, the opportunity to plant sorghum – or almost anything else, for that matter – is irretrievably lost. It will be a famine year. As the situation worsened, a number of villagers were publicly accused of bewitching the rain in Kirumi, a topic we take up in chapter 7. Several of the accused were fined. Some were expelled from Ihanzu. Other villagers, worried about the lack of rain, began to leave the area in search of wage labour in other parts of Tanzania. It was against this backdrop that in the beginning of January the female rainmaker, Ng'welu, suggested to her brother that the women began their rain dance. He agreed.

The First Day

Anti-Witchcraft Medicines

Women began arriving in Kirumi, some from as far as fifteen miles away, in preparation for the dance. All slept at the female rainmaker's homestead. Men avoided the area.

The following morning, ten elderly women dressed in black danced and sang their way to rainmaker Omari's homestead, where Ng'welu was given some anti-witchcraft medicine (*makota*) by her brother. Unlike the men at the rainshrine, the women use no rain medicine per se during their dance.

The women then spiritedly sang and danced their way out of his homestead, down the path to a clearing on the outskirts of Kirumi. The few men who happened to be wandering about quickly went indoors. Some younger women, mainly *adamu*, soon joined the elderly women, bringing their numbers to about thirty. The aim of this first trip into the bush is to prepare the area – their main dance ground for the duration of these rites – against possible witchcraft attacks that might damage the participants and threaten the efficacy of the dance.

I was told that the mothers of twins, using the tips of buffalo-horn drums (*mbīlū*), began digging small holes about a foot apart around the perimeter of the dance ground. They dropped small amounts of the medicine into these holes, and refilled them with earth. The *adamu*, after disrobing, seated themselves naked atop each hole and, while singing, bounced over the holes to pack down the earth. Other *adamu* removed their clothes and danced naked around the dance ground. When the entire grounds had been ringed with medicines, the women clothed themselves and danced and sang in their characteristic single file back to Ng'welu's homestead (plate 5.1). At each cross-path (*mīnsambwa anzīla*) along the way the women stopped and buried some medicine. Members of the *adamu* group then packed down the earth, as on the dance ground, with the aid of their naked backsides. This, I was told at the time, protects all paths leading to the house against witches who, given their perversely evil dispositions, might follow. Once back on the homestead, individual dancers were dabbed with medicine to protect them against witchcraft. The women also dabbed those infants

Plate 5.1. Senior women returning to Ng'welu's homestead after preparing the dance ground (photo by T. Sanders)

which some women carried on their backs with medicines, since infants are thought exceptionally vulnerable to witchcraft attacks.

Anointing Drums and Snakes

Now afternoon, the women set off for their witch-proof dance ground. On this trip they carried castor-oil seeds (*mono*), sorghum brought by the novices, two ritually significant, water-filled, long-necked gourds (*mūmbū*), two half-gourds (*lúkulu*), two small earthen pots (*shūngū*), a pestle (*mūtoangīlo*) and mortar (*itūlī*) and a few small baskets (*itoto;* sing. *kītoto*) from which to eat the sorghum mixture. Along the path they beat their buffalo-horn drum and praised the ancestors in song and dance, as they did for the duration of the ceremony. They also sang many lewd songs. One man, seeing the women approaching, dropped his hoe in the path and dashed for cover in a nearby house.

At the dance ground the senior women continued beating their buf-falo-horn drums and singing. Others, including all first-time partici-pants, removed their black cloth wraps and danced naked. Still other women went to fetch water and cut firewood. The elderly women then began a rather lengthy process of preparing castor-seed oil: roasting, grinding with the pestle and mortar, and then boiling the seeds until the oil could be skimmed off and put into the long-necked gourds. While this was going on, other senior women boiled the sorghum. When all had eaten the sorghum mix and the oil was ready, they all departed for Mount Ng'waūngu.

Ng'waūngu, besides being the tallest boulder-strewn hill in Kirumi, is perhaps the most sacred place for the royal clan members: this is where their ancestral spirits meet. There are two royal clan caves on the hill – Mūmbau and Nkonzele – and it is at these sites that the royal clan section normally holds its ancestral offerings (*mapolyo*) when clan-section members or their animals become ill, or during drought (see chapter 6).

Both caves, I was later informed, the women entered naked. At the first they addressed the royal spirits and anointed some ancient drums with castor oil.[6] At the second cave, there are no drums but there is another notable attraction that is never missing from people's accounts: an enormous ancestral snake, usually described as a python, a rare snake in Ihanzu and the only auspicious one. This and in fact all pythons are closely associated with ancestral spirits. As a man, I was not allowed to attend these particular rites; but I was told that at the cave, the women entered and anointed the snake, or rather, the ancestral spirits. I had heard such comments many times before, and they require some elaboration.

Late one afternoon, I was walking along a path in the bush with an elderly man who was trying to explain this to me, how an animal can be a spirit, and how one animal/spirit can be one and many at the same time. 'Do you see this tree?' he asked. 'Let's say this tree is the tree of the *Anyampanda wa Kirumi*.' Then, pointing to the tree's flowers and leaves he asked if I saw them, which I readily affirmed. 'Those leaves and flowers are like individual people,' he continued, 'each one an Ihanzu, each one a member of the *Anyampanda wa Kirumi*. And let's say that one of these leaves has a problem. Where does it go? Of course it goes there,' he said, gesticulating theatrically at the base of the tree. 'All the leaves and all the flowers are individuals but they all come from one base, one seed, just there at the bottom. That is your snake in the cave.'

Many such ancestral snakes are said to live in ancestral caves around Ihanzu, not only this royal one. They are anointed at ancestral offerings for personal illnesses. I have myself attended dozens of such offerings, and entered many ancestral caves during them where snakes (always pythons) are said to live. To date, I have seen none. Even so, extraordinary stories routinely spread across Ihanzu after these same offerings concerning our fearless encounters with implausibly large reptilian creatures. This is not so puzzling. I once asked a young man who had been with me at an offering about these stories. He replied: 'The snakes in the caves that everyone talks about, well, they're there, but they're not there. You see, it's sort of like Jesus for Christians. Now who has seen Jesus? No one. But no Christian with a brain would claim he isn't there.'

The python in this case is a physical manifestation of the royal *Anyampanda* spirits. And since everyone knows that spirits meet in these caves, the snake must also live there, or at least make an occasional appearance. Whether the python is there at any particular time is, for all practical purposes, irrelevant.

When the women left the cave, they began collecting firewood on the mountain, something that is at other times forbidden. This prohibition holds for all sacred ancestral sites – no trees may be cut in the area until there is an ancestral offering, at which time it is required. Just before sundown, the women danced and sang their way back to Ng'welu's homestead, carrying on their heads the firewood they would burn that night.

There, women ate, stoked the fires, and rested for several hours. Later that evening, after disrobing once again, the women began dancing, first at the house and later in the bush. No men were to be seen. The dancers made their way to the rainshrine, where they danced just outside, asking the chiefly ancestral spirits for rain once again. Until about four in the morning the women danced naked around Kirumi, into the bush and back again, up and down almost every path, singing their songs and beating their buffalo-horn drum.

Songs, Dances, and Ritual Violence

Many of the women's songs are blatantly sexual and, as men and women themselves point out, obscene (*matusi*).[7] These songs are also sung during female fertility rites (*mīlīmū*) and twin life-cycle rituals. Some of the more conspicuously sexual lyrics feature super-powerful clitorises, implausibly sized penises, and copulating monkeys. One song that dancers sang repeatedly, for example, consists of only one line, which is repeated: 'The penis is dried up and worthless; it stops the rain from shitting down' (*Ilūga ikalamūku lagiiye īmbula kūnia*). Other songs contain more oblique references to male and female genitalia, fornication and giving birth. Some songs appear simply to be about farming, praising the spirits or asking former rainmakers for rain. All songs, though – even the ostensibly respectable ones – are peppered with loud and spontaneous outbursts from the dancers – 'Penis!' 'Vagina!' 'Fuck!' – a fact I discovered when later listening to my tapes to recheck my transcriptions. These taunts, women say, are not directed against men, spirits, or the dead rainmakers about whom they are singing. They simply fit neatly with the spirit of the dance. Such gratuitous public use of obscenities is far from normal behaviour for Ihanzu women or men, though most seem to agree that such heated outbursts are more a male pastime than a female one.

If many locals see these rainmaking songs as obscene, they share similar views about the dances. Several women told me that under the cover of night, novices are made to dance lewdly around the rainshrine, each gripping one of its sizable outer posts, 'like huge penises.' A few women also pointed out – in no uncertain terms – that the desired effect of their nocturnal dancing was to work female dancers up into an orgasmic frenzy. Virginia Adam reported similar things in the 1960s, when dancers 'took all their clothes off, or else rolled them up around their waists. They imitated copulation, and danced around imitating sexual acts.'[8] The significance of such dancing will become apparent below.

Throughout their dance, women act in a generally aggressive and violent manner, sometimes towards women but especially towards men. Dance participants revel in stories of the atrocities they supposedly commit, or have committed on previous occasions. One popular story tells of a Kirumi man named Kingu, who in 1992 was seized, stripped of his clothes, and paraded naked around the village late into the night. Everyone I spoke with, women and men alike, made much of the fact that the unruly female mob 'played with' Kingu, much against his will, pulling mercilessly on his penis and hurling him about high over their heads like a beach ball. Later he was fined a goat. Such incidents of violence, while pointedly recalled and perhaps greatly exaggerated, are in reality few in number. Nor are they as extreme as many suggest: all Ihanzu women I know can wield a machete as well as any man, and could therefore inflict serious harm if they wished. But they do not. Participants' 'violent' behaviour is more ritualized than damaging.

Days Two and Three

On the second day, women from the outlying areas continued to arrive at Kirumi. Men at this point stayed well away from Ng'welu's homestead, now full of women, perhaps sixty or seventy, from all across Ihanzu.

Since dancers had danced on and off until around 4 a.m., most slept for much of the day. Later that day some of the women emerged from the compound, dropped their clothes, and began to sing their obscene songs boisterously as they paraded around the area, making lewd gestures and yelling obscenities throughout the village (plate 5.2). Men vanished. One particularly hapless man was not fast enough, however, and was caught by the women: he quickly agreed to pay a goat so he could leave unharmed.

Just before sundown, the women danced naked and sang their way into the bush for the last time, where they carried on for much of the night. After returning to Mount Ng'waŭngu, where they again addressed the ancestral spirits and anointed the drums and snake, the women returned to Ng'welu's house, donned their clothes, and slept.

The following morning, the women rose and prepared for their return journeys home. The weather had changed for the better: clouds

Plate 5.2. Women doing the rain dance (photo by T. Sanders)

were forming and there were some light showers. The royal spirits had apparently heard and taken to heart their requests. Their 'rite of rebellion' – if we wish to call it that – had proved, to participants and others, a resounding success. To see why, we must return to our discussion of gender and transformative processes.

Bodies, Substances, and Gender Thermodynamics

All Ihanzu seem to agree that men's and women's bodies are 'naturally' different. Men's and women's bodies are thought to possess different elements that can be drawn from, when necessary, to achieve particular outcomes. Even so, those elements, while sometimes imagined as characteristic of either men or women, are not confined, strictly speaking, to male or female bodies. (Remember that a male or female body always already contains both genders within it in the form of seeds, blood, and milk.)

One gender distinction the Ihanzu commonly make is that female is wet (-totu) while male is dry (-kalamūku) (cf. Beidelman 1993, 39). These qualities are said to be observable in any man or woman: the former is often said to be lean while the latter allegedly has more soft fat. People often instance women's vaginas as evidence of their watery composition, men's lack of vaginas as evidence of their dryness. Women are also thought to possess additional vaginal and birthing waters that men, for fairly obvious reasons, do not.

Having a watery body, as women allegedly do, is a good thing. Water equals fertility – a proposition that is unremarkable in this arid region where, without water, life in all forms rapidly grinds to a halt. Water is said to be cooling, a life force, and something without which women could not give birth. In the form of rain, water allows crops to grow. As fertilizing fluid, it produces children. In conversations, people often underscored the life-giving properties of water by reminding me that, when taken to the local mission hospital, critically ill patients are always given water intravenously as a matter of urgency.

Conversely, having dry bodies – as men allegedly do – is not necessarily a good thing at all. This point comes into sharp focus when we recall that 'dry' (kalamūku) penises, mentioned above in song, impede the rain from falling. The term -kalamūku implies a certain waterless (and often lifeless or useless) quality and frequently has negative connotations. It may be used to describe barren or parched land (ihī nkalamūku), or a phenomenally filthy person (mūntū nūmūkalamūku), one who never bathes, one who remains at a distance from water. When applied to the entire male universe, it is always negative – or at least it implies a water deficiency, a lack of a certain life-giving quality, somehow falling short of women's God-given moist make-up. If women are cool and thus fertile for the water they contain, then men are comparatively hot and infertile for their relative lack of water. Female is to wet as male is to dry.

As part of a wet/cool/female–dry/hot/male dichotomy, people sometimes also evoke blood. As we saw in chapter 1, blood is thought to pass through the patriline and is associated with masculinity. For this reason, many with whom I spoke suggested that men possess more blood, or perhaps hotter blood, than women. This is why, many agree, men tend to be more aggressive – verbally and physically – than women. In Ihanzu eyes, blood is inimical to water and is commonly associated with red, heat, disorder, lightning, brawling, and warfare. Thus, as if male bodies were not already dry enough from their relative lack of water, they are made even more so by having excessive or over-heated blood. Female bodies, for their part, are doubly cool both for their excess waters and for their relative lack of blood. People say this leads women to be naturally relaxed, passive, and followers.

Crucial, however, is that male and female characteristics do not map themselves neatly onto male and female bodies, as such generalized statements might imply; and villagers recognize that men and women do not always behave in accordance with their supposed bodily dispositions. No one I knew, for example, would claim that men are categorically drier than women, or that men, as men, have no 'wet,' fertile abilities. Both men and women contain within themselves semen, water or fertilizing fluids which they give to their offspring in equal amounts (see chapter 3). Thus men have water, even if, on balance, they tend to be slightly drier than (most) women. Then there are those extraordinarily 'wet' men – namely, the male rainmaker and those who have sired twins. Such men may in fact be 'cooler' than women. To complicate matters further, women heat up and cool down on a regular basis: menstruating women are always 'hot' and can in fact be hotter than ordinary men.

The point to grasp here, above all, is that the Ihanzu draw specific thermodynamic distinctions between male and female. These distinctions sometimes correspond to male and female bodies, but not always. States of dry and wet, hot and cold, male and female operate within and across differently sexed bodies. These ideas take on particular significance in light of the transformative processes underpinning these rain rites.

Ritual Principles

Two epistemological principles inform all Ihanzu rain rites. The first of these, which we have seen before, suggests that the joining of genders transforms the world by bringing children, rain, or most anything else. In this respect male and female together can make things happen. To join the genders is to generate, to create and transform by activating the cosmic and divine powers of the Ihanzu social and natural worlds. Just as men and women conjoin and bear offspring, male and female rainmakers reputedly engage in royal incest to give birth to the people of Ihanzu and bring rain. All power derives from the appropriate combination of differently gendered pairs. This is gender complementarity.

The second governing principle found in Ihanzu rituals of transformation, which has been widely reported across Africa, is that 'like attracts like' (Wilson 1957, 10; Herbert 1993, 85–6; Klima 1970, 47; Ten Raa 1969, 50–1).

In Ihanzu, black (-dwalu) is ritually auspicious. It is the preferred colour for clothing worn during rain rites as well as for sacrificial animals. The reason for this, all seem to agree, is that rain clouds are also black. Black is cool and brings life-giving waters that cool the land. One black thing invites another.

The colour red (-kaūku), on the other hand, is ritually inauspicious. It threatens to attract other undesirable hot (-pyu) and fierce (-taki) things, such as lightning, which is also said to be red. Wearing red during an ancestral offering, or menstruating during a female rain dance would, people say, cause lightning to destroy people and livestock, crops and homes. On several occasions I saw men and women either sent away or fined for attending rain rites wearing such colours. By the same token red animals are wholly unacceptable as sacrificial ones. Heat summons more heat.

Other ritual items follow the like-attracts-like logic. For example, trees are sorted into two mutually exclusive categories that might be glossed as 'cool,' 'gentle' trees (mītī nī mīpolo) and 'hot,' 'sharp' trees (mītī mitaki) (cf. Jellicoe 1978, 80; Rigby 1966, 9; Spencer 1988, 205; Ten Raa 1969, 41). The former are desirable for rainmaking and for appeasing the ancestral spirits. The latter are not. The noteworthy point, once

again, is that 'cool' trees attract cool rains while 'hot' trees do not and
are more likely to attract 'hot' lightning.

Thus, in ritual contexts, black clothes and animals bring black rain
clouds; red clothes, menstrual blood, and other types of blood bring
lightning and destructive weather. Gentle, cool trees bring like qualities in rains. In all ritual instances, for good or for bad, similar things
attract one another.

From these two fundamental principles, the operative logic of this
particular 'rite of rebellion' emerges. In Ihanzu eyes, women are physiologically better suited to carry out these rain rites. They are wetter
than men. Their bodies make this so. Since like things attract one
another, women's wet bodies attract wet rains. Men's dry bodies do
not; in fact, they threaten to attract more heat. One elderly man from
Ilongo village made these connections much more concisely than I
have:

> Asūngū atotu anga mbula. ĩAgohaa akalamūku. Ĩyĩ itĩ itotu kūtambula. Asūngū
> inio yao shanga yumaa, mazĩ mazĩ du. Ũsese kĩūmū hata mĩaka ihĩ. Hata
> kūtombe inino da lūhikū lūlū, lūng'wĩ, kĩkūūma lūkūlū. Ila ūmūsūngū shanga
> wũmaa. ĩMazĩ ĩpūma kila mala aze atotu ūdu. Kūlūlo kūlūnga ĩasūngū ĩmpya nĩ
> mbula.
>
> Wakati wa masĩmpūlya akũina kimpūnyu hata ūmūng'wĩ! Ĩyĩ kũ mahala ane
> ĩonesha, ĩonesha kũwa akete mazĩ dū n'ĩmakuta. ĩAlūngū ĩkalowa n'ĩmbula ĩkaza.
> Wai-ne ataata akūgenda kĩmpūnyu kūnzi? Agĩla anga kĩntū kĩhi nĩka mazĩ mazĩ.

Women are wet like rain. Men are barren, dry. This is easy to explain.
Women, their vaginas, never dry out; they are always wet. We [men] can
be dry for years on end. Even if we have sex only a few times in one day,
we become really dry. A woman, however, never dries out. Water comes
out of them all the time that keeps them wet. For this reason you can say
women are like rain.

During the women's rain dances they dance naked, even in the middle
of the afternoon! This is because they are displaying themselves, showing
that they have lots of water and fat. The ancestral spirits rejoice and the
rains come. You don't see those [male] rainmaking assistants wandering
about outside naked, do you? They don't have anything wet [to show].[9]

On balance, women's bodies are superior vessels to men's for such
rites, given their wetness. This is why the women require no rain medicine per se for their dance, only anti-witchcraft medicine to protect

themselves. Their 'wet' bodies are quite enough to get the job done. Women, not men, are therefore the main actors in these rites. Tellingly, lest we forget, certain men may participate too: those who themselves evince excesses of wetness and fertility, those who bring rain or sire twins. What is more, dry, hot women – those who are menstruating – cannot. Thus by allowing only those wet men and women who have given birth to participate, and by disallowing menstruating and barren women, dancers present female wetness and fertility in a dramatically exaggerated fashion.[10] In this way, dancers become 'hyperfeminine.'

But how, exactly, do these rites combine masculine and feminine elements as equals to (re)produce rain? How is it that men and women can insist that these rites are *not* about conflict between the genders? It is here that the violence, obscenity, and sexuality come to the fore. If women's bodies are marginally superior vessels to house wetness and hence fertility, then they are also better equipped to house *both* genders at once (cf., Broch-Due 1993; Jacobson-Widding 1985, 10–11). Men, no matter what they do, are physiologically impoverished. Their bodies are dry – at least, compared to (most) women's. It is thus impossible for most of them to attract fertile wet rains. Yet women – or at least fertile, non-menstruating women – have a decided advantage on this score: first, they are wet; and second, they have no difficulties co-opting characteristically male capacities through ritual action. By becoming aggressive, violent, and generally obscene – all traits that Ihanzu villagers commonly associate with male and heat – women dancers successfully embody some of the more stereotypical features of Ihanzu masculinity. But as before, these co-opted gender traits become a positive if not perverse exaggeration of the gender they embody. In this way, dancers come to embody and display, in a highly ritualized and exaggerated form, some of the more typical characteristics of both male and female as they know them, and furthermore, push them to their logical conclusions. Through ritual action, certain female and male dancers come to embody hyperfeminine *and* hypermasculine characteristics. Single bodies become composite, androgynous beings containing and combining two distinct genders within them.

This accounts for participants' preoccupations with sex and sexuality during these rites. By embodying both genders simultaneously, dancers aim to bring male and female into a perfect and equal union within themselves. Embodying both genders in this ways implies an internal generative gendered intercourse, a sort of auto-reproduction unleashed *within* individual dancers' bodies. Small wonder, then, that participants in these rites devote so much time to dancing (*kucheza*) – a term used interchangeably with sexual intercourse (*kitoma*) – during which they professedly seek a heightened state of sexual arousal. In times of dire need, as a method of last resort, what better way to bring rain than for dancers to combine sexually, en masse, 'hyperfemininity' with 'hypermasculinity' within themselves? The ultimate combination of masculine and feminine principles brings the ultimate communal good: rain. Only by dislodging the genders from singular anatomical moorings, and by allowing them to combine productively within singular bodies, can these rites do what they do.

Rebellions, Transformations, and Anthropological Explanations

It is worth noting that Max Gluckman's popular thesis could be used to explain the Ihanzu women's rain rites. Almost. That is, if we were prepared to take dominant discourses about male dominance at face value, to ignore the power and prestige some women hold, and to dismiss local ideas about gender complementarity and transformative processes, then it would take little imagination to argue that rituals such as the one described portray daily gender relations back to front. Many scholars, wittingly or unwittingly following Gluckman, have done just this.

But these Ihanzu women's rain rites take the shape they do, not because they are responding in ritual and inverted form to everyday gender relations, but rather due to people's ideas about gendered transformative processes. Explanations that dwell on 'gender rebellion' are self-referential and perhaps 'explain' within a Euro-American episteme. Beyond this, they mean little.

The above ethnographic material is particular to the Ihanzu case. The theoretical implications are not, however, and suggest that we reconsider whether other African societies have been uncritically (mis)represented as 'male dominant' or 'patriarchal,' and women's rites of rebellion as being solely about 'women's power.'[11] On this score it is interesting to note, as Gluckman does in a less frequently cited essay, that Zulu women's 'rites of rebellion' contain elements that are both male *and* female. The former he explains as women's reversal of everyday gender roles; the latter, he explains (away) as those tasks that women dancers would carry out later in life (Gluckman 1956, 121). Yet this is analytically shaky ground. Gluckman's apparent need to explain away the feminine in what should be – at least by his own theoretical reckoning – masculine rites overrides alternative considerations and explanations. Is it possible, as in the Ihanzu case, that specific transformative practices similarly underpin and inform Zulu ritual participants' actions? Or that Zulu women, like Ihanzu dancers, succeed ritually in productively combining two genders into single-sexed bodies to bring rain? Pursuing these questions would be worthwhile, though I do not intend to do so here. I wish instead to turn to another Ihanzu rainmaking rite, one in which the genders operate not within, but without men's and women's bodies.

Ancestral Rain Offerings: Genders without Bodies

In January 1994, a few weeks after the women's rain dance and still with no significant rainfall, a rainmaking assistant and diviner from the northern village of Ikolo paid a visit to another diviner in Ihanzu's eastern village of Mkiko.[1] Some rain-witchcraft–related paraphernalia (a mixture of seeds, a gourd, and a burnt tree branch) had been discovered in their village, and they hoped to discover the identity of the rain-witch(es) in order to neutralize their powers. Although no rain-witch was in the end named – they rarely are in divination sessions – the ancestral spirits made it clear through the diviner's oracle that a small, anti-witchcraft ceremony was required in order 'to cool' the suspected rain-witchcraft. To this humble request the spirits appended a more consequential and time-consuming task: the rainmaking royals in Kirumi must formally offer the spirits a black sheep born at night, as well as three vats of beer.

This was not the first time this season that the spirits had requested a beast and beer. The month previous, they had done the same, also through the chicken oracle, when Omari, the male rainmaker, decided to 'divine the state of the land' (*kūlīngūla ihī*); and again the month before that, at a royal ancestral offering for cattle illness. In mid-February, as severe drought and famine loomed near, a large, ancestral rain offering thus took place in the village of Kirumi. These rites, which will be detailed momentarily, have direct bearing on a series of Euro-American debates on gender.

Over the past two decades, feminist and/or poststructuralist scholars have had a good deal to say about gender performance.[2] Collectively and individually, these writings suggest that women and men are what they are because of what they do. These scholars thus take issue with the propositions that women and men are 'natural' categories of being, anchored firmly and forever in their distinctive biological make-ups; that their different behaviours and psychological characteristics can be deduced directly from their reproductive functions; that biological differences produce social consequences, but never the reverse. In short, these social theorists stand naive biological determinist views on end, insisting that gender is neither natural nor given. Instead, 'a person's gender is not simply an aspect of what one is, but, more fundamentally, it is something that one does, and does recurrently, in interaction with others' (West and Zimmerman 1987, 140). Differences between men and women, then, while made to appear natural and ontologically given, are in fact the product of everyday gender performance.

Writings on gender performance vary greatly, but they also share certain concerns. One is the desire to de-essentialize woman and men by delinking sexed bodies from gendered constructions of them. Bodies, qua bodies, tell us nothing meaningful about how gender is constituted. Rather, one's gender is fixed – that is, made to seem biological and thus natural – through 'an enactment that performatively constitutes the appearance of its own fixity' (Butler 1990, 70). A second common concern, closely linked to the first, has been with individual social identities or, more to the point, gendered subject formation. Scholars have thus explored, for instance, the culturally specific ways that boys are produced as men, and girls as women, and how gendered identities and subjectivities are defined, redefined, and negotiated through ritual and everyday practices (Kratz 1994; Kulick 1997; Power and Watts 1997; Blystad 1999; Busby 2000). Their manifest differences notwithstanding, we might say that such studies are about 'performing with gender.'

This chapter aims to build on the first of these concerns while moving beyond the second. In this respect, it continues the long-standing feminist project of decoupling sexed bodies from gendered constructions of them. It does this, however, not by highlighting the malleability of sexed bodies or their sociocultural construction, but by severing the link between sex and gender entirely. The aim, then, is not to demonstrate how people perform *with* gender – how actors, through particular actions, come to embody particular gender visions or subjectivities – but instead, to show how gender is performed irrespective of men's and women's bodies. I call this a performance *of* gender. Through ancestral rain offerings, we shall see, the Ihanzu perform disembodied gender categories; moreover, these performances are concerned not with forging and fashioning personal gender identities, but rather with a broader cosmic project of the regeneration of life. Performances *of* gender are, above all, about harnessing and actively managing gendered forces inherent in the Ihanzu social and natural worlds.

Ancestral Offerings for Rain

Ancestral offerings for rain (*mapolyo a mbula*) take place only when the rain has utterly failed and it has been divined that the royal *Anyampanda* clan spirits have demanded such an offering.[3] These offerings take place over two days, but the entire ritual sequence may last for a month, sometimes longer. It is only the two royal rainmakers who can bring such rain offerings to fruition.

Within hours of the January 1994 oracular pronouncement, the message was relayed to the royal rainmakers in Kirumi, and proceedings to initiate an ancestral rain offering began. To initiate the offering (*kūkūmbīka*), the male rainmaker, Omari, summoned three grandchildren to his homestead. These were classificatory grandchildren vis-à-vis the royal clan-section – that is, one of their own grandmothers or grandfathers is or was a member of the *Anyampanda wa Kirumi* clan-section. 'Grandchildren,' in this sense, can be full-grown adults. And for these offerings, they always are. On this occasion the two grandsons were men in their fifties, the granddaughter a woman in her forties.[4]

Grandchildren feature centrally in all such ancestral offerings, whether for rain or for personal illness (see Sanders 1999). While the two royal rainmakers play important roles in these rites, as do others, it is the grandchildren who must initiate each and every activity in the process. They can only do this, informants stress, if at least one grandson and one granddaughter participate, even though three or four grandchildren sometimes assist during ancestral offerings. In all cases and at all times, both genders must labour jointly and equally.

That evening, the grandchildren placed white sorghum flour, water and ritually significant leaves into a special long-necked calabash (*mūmbū*). While addressing the royal clan spirits, they placed the calabash in Omari's homestead's doorway. Each grandchild addressed the spirits. The grandsons' addresses preceded the granddaughter's, as is typically the case. Their addresses were brief and to the point: 'We have begun an offering for rain,' 'we are preparing your beer,' and so on. Grandchildren made similarly brief addresses to the spirits throughout the offering to initiate each new task.

A few days later, a grandson and granddaughter began brewing ancestral beer. (The other grandson lived farther away and did not participate on this occasion.) While virtually any Ihanzu man, woman, or child can explain the complex process of brewing sorghum beer, it is largely women, as we saw in chapter 1, who ordinarily brew beer. With ancestral offerings, however, things are different. On these occasions, granddaughter and grandson must brew beer together. At each stage in the brewing process, a grandson and granddaughter must cooperate (*kiunga*) and 'reside together harmoniously' (*wikĩ ũza palũng'wĩ*). And cooperate they did. At this offering and at all others I attended,[5] they jointly carried out the tasks ordinarily left to women: together they dug the beer brewing trench, collected firewood, fetched water, and mixed the beer.

Ordinarily, beer brewing is subject to delays, particularly in years when there is lots of rain. This, however, was not so this year. The grandchildren finished the beer in just under three weeks. The final day of brewing marked the eve of the offering proper. Villagers from across Ihanzu, many of whom had an avid interest in such matters, began arriving at the male rainmaker's homestead in Kirumi. All wore black or similarly dark colours, the only auspicious colours for rainmaking. Bright colours – especially red – are strictly prohibited, since such 'hot' colours are said to anger the spirits and can attract destructive lightning.

Just before sundown, the two grandchildren took a small amount of ritually significant beer (*kĩnyaũlũngũ*) to a royal clan cave on nearby Mt. Ng'waũngu, and to the graves of three former rainmakers of renown (two male, one female). At each location, they briefly addressed the royal spirits and left a gourd of beer. The grandchildren then returned to the male rainmaker's homestead, where, now assisted by another grandson, they spent several hours laboriously running the remaining beer through reed filters, removing the solid dregs, preparing it for the next day's events. The men and women, young and old, who had come for the offering slept at the male rainmaker's homestead, many dancing and singing until the small hours of the morning.

The morning of the offering, a few jokers or *anyisoi* (sing. *mũnyisoi*) made their first appearance, acting outlandishly, as ever. They taunted guests and made crude and insulting jokes about the royal clan. They soon set off for the cave and graves where the grandson and granddaughter had, the previous night, left the *kĩnyaũlũngũ* beer-filled calabashes. Unceremoniously and with no formal addresses, the jokers sat down at each site and swigged down the beer. At one grave, a joker spouted some impromptu abuse at several royal clan members, living and dead, and accused all of being rain witches. He also told the royal spirits that, much to his delight, he had now filled himself with ancestral beer and was drunk at their expense. Mildly inebriated, the jokers boisterously stumbled their way back to the homestead.

They arrived around eight a.m. When they did, the crowd – about eighty men and women in all – began leaving for the royal offering site at Mount Ng'waũngu. Omari the male rainmaker led the way; everyone else followed in single file, walking slowly, speaking either in quiet tones or not at all (plate 6.1). Most followed him up the mountain to a designated clearing.

The female rainmaker, who had followed up the line, remained at another clearing at the bottom of the mountain with several elderly women (many of whom had also participated in the women's rain dance). It was their job to prepare castor-seed oil (*mono*) to be used later in the offering. Throughout the offering these women sang songs, the same songs commonly sung at the birth of twins (*ipaha*) and during the women's rain dance and girl's initiation rites (*mũlĩmũ*). Many of these songs contain sexually explicit content.

On the mountain, people seated themselves in distinct groups, where they remained throughout the offering. Diviners, together with the male rainmaker and a few elderly men, sat at the highest point in the clearing, while most elderly men sat just below them. Women sat farther down the clearing and in the path. Those who had never before attended an offering, young men and women, sat in the lowest position (see figure 6.1). These particular seating arrangements were not accidental, but followed a specific cultural logic I will explore below.[6]

One grandson and a rainmaking assistant continued up the path to the first cave, both removing their shirts when they got there. Sucking in a mouthful of beer, the grandson sprayed it over the cave's entrance and briefly addressed the royal spirits; the two then descended to join the group in the clearing. This grandson then collected some branches from 'cool' trees, which he placed in the centre of the clearing, cut ends to the east, leaves to the west. Another grandson now assisted, bringing the total to three grandsons and one granddaughter. Together, the grandchildren forced the sacrificial animal – a black sheep, born at night, as dictated by the spirits – to the ground with its head to the west, atop the leafy branches. They smothered the sheep until it passed out, at which time a Muslim slit its throat.[7]

Plate 6.1. People going to rain offering at Mt Ng'aũngu, Kirumi (photo by T. Sanders)

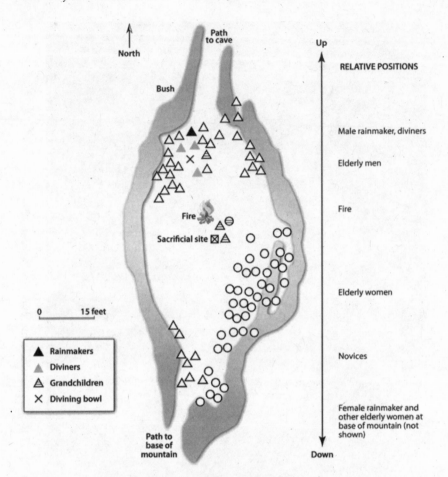

Figure 6.1. Seating arrangements during entrails reading

A grandson and the granddaughter began starting a fire with a fire-drill, the method people say is 'traditional' (*jadi*), and one of the most important rites of the offering. If, at any ancestral offering I attended, I had a momentary lapse of attention, people invariably made sure I noticed and noted in my notebook the fact that the grandson and granddaughter were starting a fire and that they were using firesticks to do it. For all other purposes, people today start fires with matches.

The grandson began by twirling a long, slender firedrill (*kīlīndī*) in the hole of a smaller, stationary hearth (*kiziga*), while the granddaughter held the hearth in place (plate 6.2). In a loud tenor, as a faint smoke rose from the point where the sticks met, he addressed the spirits:

Ūewe Mūnyankalī nūpūmile kū mūtala wako nūkūlū n'ūinzū kū mūtala wako nūnino, wakīla mūnū m'Ihanzu wahanga kūkete ipolyo, ipolyo la m'ikulungu. Kūkete ipolyo la mbula. Kūipoelia ntūlī n'īnkolo naitugilwe ūtikū. Ūko n'ūninzū ūtwale ninzà aya ni mabī ūmagūmīle mū lūzī mū Nyanza.

You, Mūnyankalī, who come from your senior house and are going to your junior one, you have passed through Ihanzu and have seen we are carrying out an ancestral offering, an offering in the cave. We have an offering for rain. We are offering water [re: beer], and a sheep that was born at night. Take good news to the place you are going; and the bad [witchcraft], toss it into the waters of Lake Victoria.

The grandchildren then switched positions. While twirling the stick, the granddaughter made a similar address to the spirits. The grandson held the hearth (plate 6.3). After they had switched several more times and addressed the spirits for several minutes, the fire eventually ignited. Soon, it was blazing strongly. The grandchildren now began the first of the offering's three most significant addresses: giving meat to the spirits.

Meat for the Spirits

'Giving meat to the spirits' (*kūtagangīla*) is one of three significant addresses made during Ihanzu ancestral offerings. It is the first named address and is often a lengthy one. As with the ritual fire starting, people rarely omit this address from their accounts of these offerings.

After roasting several pieces of the sacrificial sheep on the fire, the granddaughter and a grandson each took a handful of cooked meat. The grandson stood in the clearing's centre. The crowd fell silent. Theatrically, he threw a piece of meat to the east, paused briefly, and launched into a highly impassioned address to Mūnyankalī and the spirits in that direction. To the west, north, and then south, he did likewise, each time tossing a morsel of meat before making his speech. Between each address, the women ululated.

When he finished, the granddaughter took centre stage. Again, the crowd remained silent. All eyes and ears focused on the granddaugh-

Plate 6.2. Grandson starting fire with firedrill, while granddaughter holds the base (photo by T. Sanders)

Plate 6.3. Granddaughter starting fire with firedrill, while grandson holds the base (photo by T. Sanders)

ter's deeds and words. She, too, zealously addressed the spirits in all four directions – east, west, north, and south, in that order – tossing, before each address, a piece of roasted meat. The women again ululated after each address.

These addresses are composed on the spot and delivered at high speed, and they are never identical. Nevertheless, they draw on the same thematic repertoire. They invariably address Mŭnyankalĭ, the name used for the sun in ritual contexts, and refer in particular to his movement between his two wives' houses. Such addresses also routinely speak to royal spirits directly, male and female alike, asking them for rain, twins, abundant harvests, fertility, and prosperity most generally (see Sanders 1999, 56–60).

Following their addresses, the grandchildren placed the sacrificial animal's entrails in an oblong divining bowl (ntua) so that the diviners could determine whether or not the spirits had accepted the meat offering. The bowl, like other ritual items, was carefully oriented on an east–west axis. The entrails told, as they always seem to, of the spirits' gratitude for the offering, of plentiful rains to come, and of general health, fertility, and prosperity for all Ihanzu (Adam 1963b; Obst 1923, 221–2). (See plate 6.4).

The women who had remained at the base of the mountain then danced and sang their way up the path, through the main clearing, to the first cave. The grandchildren took a handful of chyme from the sacrificial sheep and joined them. At the cave, one at a time, the grandchildren addressed the spirits and tossed the chyme around the entrance to 'cool' the spirits. The grandson then descended to the clearing. The female rainmaker, the granddaughter, and a few other elderly women of the royal clan removed their clothes and, carrying the half-gourd of castor-seed oil, entered the cave. The granddaughter addressed the spirits, and the women anointed some ancient cave drums with oil. They then visited a second, nearby cave (the one they visited during the women's rain dance), where (I was later told) they anointed an enormous ancestor-snake that is said to live there. Donning their clothes, the women joined the other women in the clearing below.

The grandchildren then roasted and doled out meat from the sacrificial animal. Most ate in their respective groups, while a few small ad hoc groups visited and feasted on the royal graves that the grandchildren had visited the previous day. The loin, which people explicitly associate with giving birth, was eaten on a female rainmaker's grave, while others ate the front leg on a male rainmaker's grave. One of the

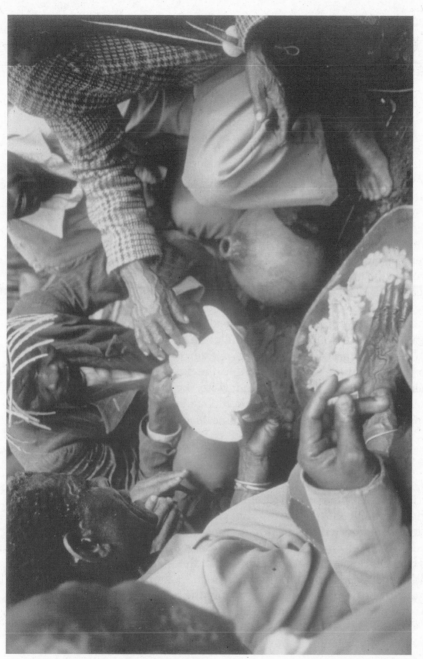

Plate 6.4. Diviner reading sacrificial animal's lungs (photo by T. Sanders)

jesters snatched the sacrificial sheep's liver and darted off into the bush, where he cooked and ate it alone. When all had eaten, they returned en masse to the male rainmaker's homestead, where people sang and danced briefly (plate 6.5).

Beer for the Spirits

The second major address of the offering, 'giving beer to the spirits' (*kūlonga shalo*), always takes place on the male rainmaker's homestead. On this occasion, in preparation, the male rainmaker sat in the doorway to his house. Others seated themselves around the courtyard and cattle pen expectantly.

As always, the grandson initiated the address. He stood in the centre of the courtyard, holding a ritual whisk (*nsing'wanda*). At his feet sat a divining bowl (again, placed east-west) filled with ancestral beer and water. Dipping the whisk into the bowl and splashing it to the east, he began his theatrically intoned address to the spirits, repeating this procedure to the west, south and then north. When he finished, the granddaughter moved to the centre of the courtyard. She, too, offered beer and water to the spirits in all four directions, and addressed the spirits in each. This was followed by a similar address from the royal rainmakers' classificatory father. Finally, a jester, the source of minor mayhem throughout the offering, brought the day's events to a close. He similarly addressed the spirits and, with the whisk, splashed water and beer in all directions. People drank late into the night. Most spent the night on the male rainmaker's homestead.

Final offerings

The next morning, the final day of the offering, the crowd rose before sunrise.[8] While people milled about and talked quietly outside, the granddaughter cooked stiff sorghum porridge inside. On the same fire, the grandson roasted the meat remaining from the previous day's sacrifice. The grandson and granddaughter then divided the stiff porridge into two, placing each portion into a separate calabash bowl. They also divided the roasted meat in this way. Each took one bowl of stiff porridge and one of meat and emerged from the house.

As the sun rose, the grandson stood in the centre of the courtyard, ready to begin the third and final noteworthy address of the offering. The crowd fell silent. He hurled a piece of roasted meat to the east,

Plate 6.5. Men and women dancing at rain offering (photo by T. Sanders)

immediately followed by a piece of stiff porridge. He then addressed Mūnyankalī, the rising sun: 'You Mūnyankalī who come from your wife in the east and are going to your wife in the west ...' He repeated the sequence to the west, then to the north and south. The grand-daughter followed the grandson, throwing meat and then porridge. She also addressed the spirits in each direction.

The grandchildren fed a few small pieces of roasted meat and stiff porridge to the male rainmaker, who was sitting idle throughout. They then fed a few other royal clan members, as well as a group of senior men and diviners, who sat near the house. From inside the house the grandchildren brought out more bowls of roasted meat and stiff por- ridge – two each – which they served to the group of younger men, and finally to the women. Following the meal the grandchildren dis- tributed the remaining ancestral beer likewise: clan elders, younger men, and finally women.

In the last major rite of this ancestral offering, a few elderly men and women, including the male and female rainmakers, entered and drank beer inside the house. The grandchildren served the beer from two rit- ually significant long-necked, beaded calabashes or *mũmbũ* (plate 6.6). The white beads worn by the calabashes are closely associated with the ancestors, who formerly wore them in abundance (See plates 2.1, 2.2, 2.3 in chapter 2). These beads are today associated both with the Ihanzu of bygone times, and with the powers of fertility those ances- tors now control. Outside, for the last time, the grandchildren briefly addressed the spirits before covering over the trench they had used to brew beer. With this, the ancestral rain offering was brought to a close.

Discussion

While the rain offering itself lasted only two days, the entire ritual sequence is a more lengthy and complicated affair. Throughout these offerings, ritual participants play, sometimes in rather striking ways, on themes of fertility, sexuality, gender difference, and complementar- ity. These concerns derive from the desire to manage constructively the gendered forces in the Ihanzu universe in order to bring rain.

As with annual rain rites (discussed in chapter 4), the divinity figure Mūnyankalī features centrally throughout ancestral offerings. The masculine Mūnyankalī moves each day from the house of one wife to that of his other wife. Male is active, female is passive. And in these daily movements, he 'cooperates' – that is to say, has sex – with each.

Plate 6.6. Grandson and granddaughter inside house displaying beer-filled calabashes or 'wombs' (photo by T. Sanders)

This is the idealized gender order in which, because masculine and feminine reside together harmoniously, they successfully reproduce. Thus, as in other Ihanzu rain rites, ancestral addresses aim to establish an idealized gender order and by that means, to change the world. Mūnyankalī, with his wives, neatly captures and encapsulates the fundamentals of the Ihanzu cosmos and its gendered operation.

Such evocations, while most apparent in ancestral addresses, are not limited to addresses alone. They are also reiterated through the spatial concerns that ritual participants share, all of which evoke Mūnyankalī's daily movements. Recall, for instance, the careful attention that ritual participants accord to the east–west axis: specifically, to the orientation of the sacrificial animal, the divining bowl, and meat and beer offerings. These concerns ordinarily go unmentioned, though men and women, if asked, willingly elaborate. Paying attention to spatial orientation during these rites 'makes sense,' one young woman from Kirumi told me, 'because Mūnyankalī moves from east to west.' All spatial references in ancestral offerings serve to evoke Mūnyankalī, his two wives, and the specific nature of their gendered cooperation and transformative power.

Gender complementarity similarly evinces itself with the ritual fire, the one the grandchildren lit using a firedrill and hearth. These fire-starting implements drew great attention at this offering and at others like it, since the men and women of Ihanzu see them as transformative agents. The firedrill and hearth are considered differently gendered and, together, capable of having sex and (re)producing. Matutu, an elderly man from Kirumi, explained it like this: 'The long, slender stick, that's the male. And the short, fat stick with the hole in it, that's the female ... The male is active, the female passive. Still, can either do anything alone? No, of course not. But if they cooperate, if they have sex, fire is born.'

The firedrill that is twirled round is active, determined, and male; the shorter, stationary piece of wood with a hole in it, the hearth, is passive and female. Such understandings are not unique to the Ihanzu and are found right across sub-Saharan Africa (Århem 1985, 13; Jacobson-Widding 1990, 68; Beidelman 1997, 205).[9]

Another way the Ihanzu actively manage male and female as complementary elements in these rites is through grandchildren. Grandchildren participate centrally in these rites, as in others. But what makes granddaughters and grandsons appropriate, above all others, as ritual officiants on such occasions? The answer, in brief, is that grandchildren are appropriately placed to fill these ritual roles, due to the equality and sexuality that inheres in their structural position.

In Ihanzu, grandparents commonly look after their grandchildren. Children may reside for short or long periods with their grandparents when, for example, parents carry out migrant labour in other parts of the country. In some cases children are raised by their grandparents, especially when the latter require regular assistance with domestic chores. In general, grandparents do not discipline their grandchildren. Instead, in Ihanzu today, as in the past, the grandparent–grandchild relationship is characterized by easiness and mild teasing (*maheko*), 'affection and equality' (Adam 1963b, 23). This equality is manifest structurally in several ways. First, grandchildren are frequently named after their grandparents. When young children cry excessively, people say this is due to a grandparent's troubled spirit. Naming a grandchild after a grandparent – this can be done weeks, months, or even years after birth – placates the vexed spirit and also connects and collapses the generations. Second, further evincing this generational equality, grandparents and grandchildren often refer to each other as siblings (*aheu* or *ng'waitu*). For these reasons, the grandparent–grandchild relationship is marked by a notion of equality that is never found or expected, for instance, in parent-child relationships (cf. Turner 1955).

A corollary of this structural equality, odd though it may seem to some Westerners, is that grandchildren may woo their cross-sexed grandparents and vice versa. And they often do, albeit jokingly. Sexual joking between Ihanzu grandparents and grandchildren is commonplace, even (or perhaps especially) in public. Such joking, common elsewhere in Africa (Beidelman 1997, 63), often revolves around the idea that a grandson is scheming to steal 'his' rightful wife (i.e., his own grandmother) away from his 'brother' (i.e., his grandfather).

With such a heavy ideological emphasis on both equality and sexuality, it is no wonder that the Ihanzu grandparent–grandchild relationship presents itself as an ideal one for rain offerings. This relationship is equal in ways that others simply are not. It is also the most blatantly 'sexual' and thus potentially (re)productive relationship, albeit in a joking manner.

During ancestral offerings, grandchildren play a central role throughout. And they always do so as a grandson and granddaughter, lest the rites fail to do what they should. Here, in these rites, grandson and granddaughter made all addresses jointly, but never simultaneously. The grandson went first, the granddaughter followed. This particular sequencing, the same throughout the ritual, evoked in practice a transformative logic of gender complementarity. The genders work together. Male precedes female. Each fulfils his or her half of the gender bargain. However, while the roles that grandson and granddaughter play in rites such as these are at face value about male and female bodies cooperating in particular ways to reproduce and transform, their ritual actions are far more complicated and, in practice, extend well beyond their differently sexed bodies.

Performances of Gender

In these rites, sexed bodies are sometimes purposively managed as part of a gendered process of transformation, as with male and female grandchildren. This is also true for ritual participants themselves, whose relative spatial positions during these rites form part of a larger cosmic drama of gender complementarity and transformation writ small. At the offering site men sat above women (see figure 6.1). The male ritual leader sat in one of the highest positions, while the female ritual leader remained for most of the offering in the lowest position. Between the men and the women was the fire, a ritually transformative agent often equated with sexual intercourse, grinding, and other transformative processes.

Such seating arrangements were not happenstance, nor was their significance a figment of my imagination. At different offerings, they recurred time and again. At one offering I attended in 1995, a few young women who had not previously attended an offering mistakenly sat above the elderly men. Almost immediately, several more-seasoned ritual attendants, both men and women, reprimanded the women and told them to relocate to their proper position 'below,' which they promptly did. Otherwise, quipped one elderly woman, the offering would fail. Remember that 'above' and 'below' are ideally considered 'male' and 'female' respectively and that no gender hierarchy is in this context implied. These particular seating arrangements, and people's attention to them, demonstrate ritual participants' concern with strategically placing male and female practically to bring about transformation.

Even so, such practical concerns about proper and productive gender combinations are not limited to the manipulation of men's and women's bodies, not in the least. Consider the attention given to Mūnyankalī, his wives, and his repeated movements between and combi-

nations with them. Or the intense focus on the ritual fire and firesticks
and their transformative potential. Neither can the grandchildren's differently sexed bodies be linked directly or unproblematically to this
particular transformative process. The grandson made the first
address, holding and spinning the male firedrill as he did so, while the
granddaughter held the female hearth. They then switched positions,
the granddaughter spinning the male firedrill, the grandson securing
the female hearth. Here, a man, the grandson, performed male *and*
female; a woman, the granddaughter, performed female *and* male. In
short, two embodied genders performed two disembodied genders.

[margin handwriting: grandchildren w/ firedrill & hearth. both perform both roles]

It is the grandchildren, and the rites they conduct, who demonstrate
perhaps most blatantly the disregard people have in this context for
establishing a relation between male and female bodies and gender.
Together, throughout these rites, grandchildren engage in what I call a
performance of gender. Over the course of the offering, the grandchildren made numerous addresses. Usually brief, these addresses did little more than state the obvious: 'We are making an offering'; 'We are
brewing beer'; 'We are digging a beer trench'; and so on. There were a
few important exceptions, though. People point to three addresses in
particular they find highly significant. In order of appearance these
were giving meat to the spirits (*kūtagangīla*); giving beer to the spirits
(*kūlonga shalo*); and on the final day, giving meat and stiff porridge
simultaneously to the spirits. The importance of these addresses and
offerings and their temporal sequencing becomes clearer when placed
in the context of everyday gender arrangements (see chapter 1).

There we saw that the Ihanzu draw everyday associations between
female and grain on the one hand, and male and livestock on the other,
a gender dichotomy that is inscribed in and through a host of everyday
practices. On this occasion, the royal spirits' demand that they be given
beer and a sheep was, in essence, a request they be given the two most
fundamental features of the Ihanzu living world: feminine and masculine, in the form of beer and meat. Indeed, I have never heard of an
offering where demands for grain and livestock were not made, and
Ihanzu spirits have, for many years, demanded both for such offerings
(Kohl-Larsen 1943, 305).

The grandchildren variously appeased these demands throughout
the offering, but most crucially, in their three principle addresses.
Grandchildren made the first address by tossing meat, a male element
of the Ihanzu cultural world. If meat is rendered practically masculine
in part due to its associations with men's livestock interests and activi-

ties, it was on this occasion rendered even more so through ritual roasting, a process that removes the soft, watery, fatty, and 'feminine' bits while simultaneously creating a hard, dry, and lean male meat. 'Natural' male flesh, in short, was transformed into 'cultural' male meat.

The grandchildren made the second significant address with sorghum beer. Given the everyday associations women and men draw between grain, beer, and women (and because, during the offering, 'natural' female grain is transformed into 'cultural' female beer) this second address and offering provides the feminine elements of the cosmos. Taken together, when considered temporally, these two addresses realize the idealized transformative gender order, once again, in which male precedes female.

The final address and offering made on the final day is a blatant assertion of gender equality. Here, the grandson and granddaughter combine masculine and feminine elements as equals by tossing meat and stiff porridge in the same address. Even here, though, within each address, male meat is tossed prior to female stiff porridge. Thus, embedded in the temporal, practical flow of ancestral addresses and varied offerings lies their ritual logic: through specific ritual actions, participants call into existence, through performance, a specific set of gender combinations and transformations.

What is particularly striking about these addresses, and the point worth noting, is this: it is *not* the case that the grandson makes 'male' addresses while the granddaughter makes 'female' ones. Non-human gender categories need not neatly coincide with sexed bodies. Instead, what we find are two opposite-sexed grandchildren, cooperating and working together to give the spirits each gender separately. The first major address, throwing meat, although made by a man and woman, is a masculine address. The second address, made with beer, is again made by both male and female, and is feminine. In the final address the grandson and granddaughter each make addresses that encapsulate both genders. It is in this sense that ritual participants enact particular types of gender combinations to bring rain, quite irrespective of their own sexed bodies. Gender can and does operate independent of physiological sex.

Conclusion

In many ways during ancestral offerings, ritual participants perform gender. But these performances are not about 'doing gender,' if by this

we mean forging, fashioning, and embodying particular gender identities or subjectivities. These, rather, are performances not *with*, but *of*
gender. Through specific actions, ritual participants act out and conjoin
in a complementary fashion masculine and feminine elements and
forces of a thoroughly gendered cultural universe. And they do this
independent of their own sexed bodies. In so doing, their aim is not to
'fix' gender within their own bodies. It is, rather, to unleash the genders' joint generative powers. For when masculine and feminine cooperate and reside harmoniously together, fertility flows in abundance.

Using the power of the gender within them what i) called for

Chapter 7

Witchcraft, Gender, and Inversion

A discussion of making rain requires a discussion of thwarting it. That means witchcraft. Witchcraft, it has often been remarked, is about inversion. Africanist anthropologists and the peoples we study have long portrayed witchcraft as 'the darker side of kinship' (Geschiere 1997), as 'kinship reflected in a dark, distorted mirror' (Crehan 1997, 222–3). Where local notions of kinship and community collectively represent 'the good society,' witchcraft provides a terrifying counterimage by playing that image back to front (Beidelman 1963b; Middleton 1963). From this perspective, witchcraft reverses the normal and desirable, rendering it perverse and morally repugnant. Seeing witchcraft as inversion has thus proved important for anthropologists to the extent that it provides privileged insights into local understandings of morality, kinship, and community.

By the same token, images of the African witch or sorcerer often emerge as the thoroughly inverted moral person (Buxton 1963, 104). Beidelman's comments on the Kaguru of Tanzania can stand in for the views of many others:

> The character of the witch is physically and morally inverted from what the ideal, proper human being should be ... Witches are inverted: nocturnal, ash-white, and traveling upside down without ordinary impediments. They treat kin like non-kin, having sexual relations with them. They treat humans like animals, killing and eating them. They treat wild animals like people, cooperating to gain and share food ... A witch's nakedness is a further inversion, since Kaguru are prudish regarding exposure, and public nakedness suggests incest. (Beidelman 1993, 138–43)

Anthropological observations such as these, often based on local understandings of witches, are important insofar as they allow us better to problematize local notions of moral personhood. However, taken at face value, such ideas about inversion can also be problematic, leading analysts to overlook various other ethnographic nuances and complications. For the supposition that 'the witch' is, and must be, the imagined inverse of 'the moral person' rests on two questionable assumptions. The first is that witches and witchcraft in any particular society must be singular and monolithic. The second is that each society has only one type of moral person. If these were not the logical implications of the inversion argument, then there would be no particular reason to link witchcraft directly, if inversely, to moral personhood in the first place.

While it might be true that some people in some places share singular visions of witchcraft and/or moral personhood, it is important to bear in mind that this is an empirical question, not a theoretical one. It must be demonstrated, not assumed. The Ihanzu, for instance, have at least two understandings of moral personhood – one male, the other female – each of which comes with its own idealized attributes, expectations, and potentialities. And each in its own unique way is considered 'natural,' even while it operates within, between, and without differently sexed bodies. In this context, to speak of an inversion of moral personhood in the singular makes little sense. What is more, these twin Ihanzu notions of moral personhood articulate in specific ways with not one, but two distinctive notions of gendered witchcraft.

This chapter suggests that Ihanzu images of male and female witches and witchcrafts are locally meaningful because they are premised on, and draw their powers from, a notion of gender complementarity and transformation. More specifically, it is the complementary combination of male and female witches and witchcrafts that enables Ihanzu witches to mobilize their diabolical powers to maximum effect. This chapter thus highlights the extent to which Ihanzu witchcraft forms part of a broader moral imagination (Beidelman 1993) and provides villagers with an imaginative framework within which to speculate about the world as it is and the powers that move it. However, in these imaginings, the conceptual inversions that male and female witches and witchcrafts evince go well beyond any simple inversion of a supposed monolithic morality. Witchcrafts and moralities must be seen in the plural, with all the complexity that implies.

Ihanzu Witches and Witchcraft

Witchcraft (*ũlogi*) forms a central part of the Ihanzu day-to-day world. It can affect anyone and most anything at any time. Witches can be held responsible for virtually any usual or unusual misfortune: when people fall ill and die, crops spoil, businesses and motorized transport fail, petrol-powered grinding machines and water pumps jam, and rains refuse to fall. Also, I was often told, wealth and political power can be gained, maintained, and destroyed through witchcraft (Sanders 2001a, 2003a). As is true across the continent, Ihanzu witches' diabolical doings are routinely attributed to envy, jealousy, and greed.

Given the sheer breadth of everyday domains in which witchcraft purportedly operates, most Ihanzu I know have either been affected personally by witchcraft or have relatives, neighbours, or friends who have been. On these grounds, one might be tempted to label Ihanzu, as others have of nearby places, a 'witch-ridden society' (Gray 1963). This, however, would be misleading, since such labels too easily risk exoticization, besides conjuring images of irrational natives obsessed with fictional phantasms.

Evans-Pritchard (1937) long ago showed that the Azande reasoned no differently from their European counterparts yet also knew that witchcraft featured centrally to their world. This is because witchcraft addresses itself more to the 'why' than to the 'how' questions. To recall one of Evans-Pritchard's oft-cited examples, when a free-standing granary collapsed and killed a man sitting under it, the Azande knew perfectly well that termites were responsible for eating and weakening the granary's legs, thus causing the unfortunate event. This is the 'how' question. But Azande witchcraft goes further: Why was *that* particular man sitting under *that* granary at *that* specific moment? These are questions not adequately answered by other ways of knowing, such as 'science': What does 'coincidence,' 'chance,' or 'probability' really explain anyway? In this sense, witchcraft provides answers to questions of a different order than the narrow answers that 'science' can provide. Witchcraft must therefore be seen not as a marker of mistaken or muddled thinking but as a way to order and make sense of an otherwise chaotic world (see Moore and Sanders 2001).

Seen in this light, it would be entirely wrong-headed to see witchcraft beliefs as something that the Ihanzu and other Africans have and that Westerners have somehow outgrown. Peoples everywhere have specific ways of making sense of their world. Rather than insisting on witchcraft's singular character, we would do well to consider it as on equal footing with more familiar find-them-at-home folk understandings that similarly order and give meaning to our world: say, world religions of all sorts, New Age spiritualities, neo-paganism, and conspiracy theories, as well as common Western notions like 'development,' 'progress,' and 'modernity.' All of these notions, and others, impose a neat conceptual order on an empirically messy world. They tell us how the world is and what makes it tick.

From an Ihanzu perspective, witches and witchcraft are omnipresent and not in the least exotic. As for many in Africa, 'there is nothing remarkable about a witch ... nor is there anything awe-inspiring about witchcraft' (Evans-Pritchard 1937, 19). Rather, such matters are entirely prosaic, taken-for-granted features of people's daily lives. That said, even though the consequences of witchcraft can be dire, the men and women of Ihanzu do not live their lives obsessively dreading them. On balance, villagers' fears of being struck down by witchcraft are no greater than is the average Westerner's fear of being struck by an automobile. In either case, people can take certain precautions to avoid misfortune, and they spend much of their time worrying about altogether different matters.

Local theory has it that both men and women can be, or can become, witches. Witchcraft is thought to pass through the matrilineage from a mother to her sons and daughters. However, this 'genetic' transmission of witchcraft, or its manifestation, is erratic and unpredictable. Witchcraft may be evident in an entire household or homestead, or it may be absent for generations. Thus, even if someone is a member of a lineage that has a reputation for witchcraft, it is not at all certain that that person will be a witch. Belonging to a 'witch lineage' is more indicative than demonstrative. This is further complicated by the fact that alleged witches may choose not to use their powers, even if they have them, and also because witchcraft can be bought, sold, and learned.

The Ihanzu do not distinguish linguistically between inherited and acquired witchcraft – a distinction that anthropologists, following Evans-Pritchard, often gloss as 'witchcraft' versus 'sorcery.' Anyone, my informants claim, can choose to become a witch. This usually involves a witch-to-be apprenticing him- or herself to a practising witch, or acquiring witchcraft medicine and knowledge from a skilled diviner.

On balance, the Ihanzu care little about whether any particular suspected witch inherited his or her powers or learned them, and I have never heard anyone raise such hair-splitting concerns. This is because, in either case, witchcraft is thought to occasion the same lamentable outcomes: whether they inherit their craft or learn it, witches are mystical spoilers.

Not all witches can spoil equally. Some are alleged to have greater powers of destruction than others. And some excel at particular sorts of witchcraft while failing utterly at others. It is these particular power differentials, especially the diabolical division of labour, that we must consider here. We thus begin with commonplace Ihanzu images of what are considered 'female' forms of witchcraft, before turning to 'male' witchcraft. Each of these differently gendered witchcrafts is accompanied by its own inversions. In the final section I consider how Ihanzu imaginings of differently gendered witches and witchcrafts are simultaneously imaginings of gender complementarity: a locally inflected meditation on the operation of gendered forces in their world.

Female Witchcraft and Witches

Some witches, people say, are particularly adept at killing their own kin: a feat they accomplish with the help of their hyena familiars, which they mount and ride at fantastic speeds through the bush at night. On these 'witch-motorcycles,' as one woman from Ikolo called them, witches visit their victims – sometimes as far away as Arusha, Dar es Salaam, or even Europe – and bewitch them with special 'medicine.' Witches can enter their victims' homes as small animals like lizards, bats, or owls, or they can simply shrink to fit underneath the door or through the cracks in windows. I was told that others need not enter the house at all, but instead dance naked on the doorstep, knock at the door, and smear medicine on it with their exposed buttocks.

Once betwitched, a person will allegedly die, sometimes within months or years, sometimes within weeks or even days. The witch then proceeds to the grave and, by placing a finger on it, medicinally exhumes the corpse. These corpses, together with others that have likewise been fiendishly revived, are then exploited as zombie labourers (*atumbūka*), their tongues removed by the witch so that they remain silent, their soul-less bodies made invisible with the witch's medicine. Zombies are forced to toil nocturnally on the witch's fields and homestead, hoeing and harvesting, grinding grain, cooking, and brewing sorghum beer. Witches, thanks to their zombies, thus reap monumental if ill-gotten harvests and enjoy inordinate amounts of stiff porridge and beer. The witch, all the while, does nothing whatsoever except eat – literally and figuratively speaking – the fruits of zombie labour.

Witches who kill people in this way are said to form part of a coven. At night, witch covens ride their hyenas to locations near and far where, often under large fig trees, they dance naked and boast of their wicked deeds. People say that to become a full member of such a coven, a prospective witch must sacrifice a close family member, perhaps a brother, sister, or child. Striking at the heart of social life in this way is meant to prove irrefutably novice witches' predilections for evil while simultaneously 'hardening their hearts' (*kukomaa roho*) against any feelings of humanity or sympathy for their victims that they might otherwise feel.

This type of witchcraft, concerned as it is with killing close kin and with illicit domestic production, reproduction, and consumption, is considered female witchcraft and is most commonly associated with female witches. It is personal. Men, too, can practise personal witchcraft – I know many who have been suspected – but it is the female witch who stands out in people's minds as the personal witch par excellence. This is because, I was told, women are more intimately acquainted than are men with clan happenings and gossip. Such knowledge therefore strategically situates women to undermine lineage and familial relations in ways not always possible for male witches. Moreover, because women are more closely linked, ideally and in practice, to the domestic sphere – cooking, beer brewing, and childrearing – it is little wonder that the stereotypical female witch should both reproduce and invert these images by illicitly creating a zombie 'family' that ensures the ongoing production and reproduction of her household. On the one hand, ordinary-women-turned-witches do what women always do by running their households and managing the relationship between household production and consumption. On the other, they invert normal processes of reproduction. Instead of feeding others, they feed *on* others. Ordinary women and female witches both control grain. But where the former ideally exchanges with and gives to needy others, the latter does not, and instead perversely reroutes all profits back to herself. In this respect, female witches invert the very essence of moral womanhood: by killing their own relatives, those with whom they share matriclan, matrilineage, and 'womb' relations, female witches undermine the meaning of 'moral woman.' By undermining the social relations they are supposed to nurture and maintain, female witches invert local understandings of femininity.

Many times, in many contexts, different villagers told me that such one-on-one witchcraft is rife throughout Ihanzu. That it is a problem is something every Ihanzu knows. Yet personal witchcraft is, by nature, a secretive matter, something that happens within families and clans and that therefore remains mostly hidden from view. 'Mud homes all look alike' (*ĩnyumba ĩmpyani ĩmatembe*), goes one Ihanzu saying, suggesting that anything can go on inside a house, witchcraft included, with outsiders none the wiser. When it comes to personal witchcraft, appearances can be deceiving.

But ordinary villagers, and even anthropologists, sometimes catch occasional tip-of-the-iceberg glimpses into this hidden realm of witchcraft. These partial glimpses come through rumours and ongoing speculations about certain villagers doing one another medicinal harm. Such rumours are frequently heard in the context of day-to-day activities. Tasks such as cutting firewood, fetching water, shelling peanuts, threshing grain, hoeing fields, and drinking beer provide suitably offstage milieux for discussing which witch is doing what to whom, and why. I have heard many such stories over the years, one of which to my surprise involved me:

> In early 1995, towards the end of my initial two-year stay in Ihanzu, I had left home in central Ihanzu to conduct a large-scale household survey in the western Ihanzu plains villages. To that point I had spent less time in those outlying areas than I had in the central villages. My research assistant and I pitched our tent and began work.
>
> A few weeks later, a man sought me out and pleaded that I take his ill brother, Marko, to the Lutheran mission hospital, a three-hour drive across Ihanzu, and bad roads, to Mbulu Distict in the east. Since I had one of only four vehicles in the whole of Ihanzu, such requests were not uncommon. It was also one of the few ways I could return something useful to the people there.
>
> We arrived at the hospital that evening, and the man was admitted. Since I was there and staying for the night anyway, I decided to have their standard battery of tests run on myself since I had been feeling mildly under the weather. To my surprise, I tested positive for malaria, typhoid, brucellosis and giardia, and was hastily admitted. A month later, I had fully recovered, as had the man I had brought.

When I returned home to my village, neighbours and kin greeted me with delight. They also castigated me for being so foolish as to accept milk from a strange, elderly woman in the west. The woman, I learnt, had bewitched me with milk, which was why I had caught all those diseases and nearly died. Or at least that was the talk of the village. The male rainmaker implored me not to return to the west, but gave me some anti-witchcraft medicine in case my work demanded it. The fact that I did not feel near death, nor that no one had given me milk, old woman or otherwise, fell on deaf ears. Everyone knew I had been bewitched by a certain evil old woman – I will call her Nya Kali – jealous that my village, Kirumi, had 'their white man' while her village had none.

I knew Nya Kali, the alleged witch, though I had met her just once, the previous year, and even then only in passing. To my knowledge, Nya Kali was never confronted about her alleged offence. For our purposes, the noteworthy point is that in this case of personal witchcraft, and in many others, women are commonly suspected. And rumours circulate far and wide about their alleged doings. This association between woman and personal witchcraft becomes especially clear at funerals, where people routinely argue – always in hushed tones and in slightly off-stage settings – about who is responsible for the death and why.

I have attended dozens of Ihanzu funerals, but never one where the issue of who bewitched and killed the deceased was not raised and passionately debated in private. For the Ihanzu, dying a 'natural' death is a tantalizing but ultimately untenable possibility. In practice, everyone dies from witchcraft, no matter what the age or circumstances. Even long after the funeral, witchcraft speculations can endure. Consider the following illustrative story, which fired the collective imagination for months during my stay:

In the early 1990s, a man in his 30s named Martin was allegedly killed with witchcraft in Mpambala village, western Ihanzu. It all began at a party, where Martin was drinking beer with two male friends. One of these men, a Christian named Marko, had given Martin a pair of police boots months earlier for which he expected a goat in return at some future date. At nightfall, Martin and Marko left the party to return home to the next village. Inexplicably, however, when they reached the Sibiti River, Marko suddenly demanded he be given either his goat or his boots immediately. Martin, of course, had neither with him. The two returned to the village from which they had just come to retrieve the boots from another friend's house. A minor scuffle ensued that many witnessed, and Marko hit Martin in the stomach. Marko retrieved his boots, and left for his home. Martin stayed with a friend that night. Quite unexpectedly, he died. The following morning Marko was arrested for murder and later imprisoned. The rumours began.

Several members of local vigilante groups (nkīlī) in western Ihanzu, at the time and thereafter, had astonishing things to say. On their routine, nightly patrols around villages, vigilante guards claimed to spot the dead man, Martin, wandering about on many separate occasions. Several guards claimed they were too frightened to continue their patrols. With lightning speed, questions circulated around western Ihanzu. Why, after months of silence, had Marko suddenly demanded his boots or a goat? Why had the fight occurred? How could someone be killed by a single blow, and without a weapon? The common consensus: Martin's death was due to witchcraft; Marko was simply the instrument the witch used to hide this fact.

Men and women speculated wildly about the clan squabbles, misunderstandings and tensions that might provide insights into the killer's identity. Martin, I often heard, had strained relations with both his mother and his mother's sister. Their names were regularly mentioned around the beer houses as the potential witches responsible. Villagers also told how even the government recognised Martin was the victim of witchcraft – since the dead man had been repeatedly sighted in zombified form, they were forced to release Marko after only a year. From others I heard different stories. One young man I spoke with said that some time after the burial, mule-cart tire tracks and crushed sorghum stalks were found meandering from Martin's grave to the front door of his mother's house: a sure sign she had medicinally removed Martin's corpse at night to be used as a zombie labourer.

Because personal witchcraft is largely confined to the realms of rumour and gossip, and because public accusations and denunciations are extremely rare, such witchcraft remains more a matter of 'permanent suspicion' (Lienhardt 1951) than anything else. For all the rumours and suspicions that surrounded Martin's untimely death, no one was ever publicly accused or denounced. Under such circumstances, where anyone and everyone can be a witch and definitive answers are rarely forthcoming, it is easy to hold that the female witch is the prototypical personal witch, even if men are, on occasion, suspected of such activi-

ties. With male witchcraft and witches, on the other hand, the consequences of non-action are much greater and widespread. Public
accusations against practitioners of this sort of mystical malevolence
are commonplace, and firmly establish in the popular imagination a
link between male witchcraft and the public realm.

Male Witchcraft and Witches

Male witchcraft is different from female witchcraft. It does not target
individuals but public goods: it dries up water holes, and it ruins grain
and rain over vast distances, sometimes over the whole of Ihanzu.
Unlike female witchcraft, this type of witchcraft is untargeted and is
therefore considered an indiscriminate mystical assault on everyone.
While women can theoretically employ such witchcraft – there are
some infamous ones who allegedly have – it is men who are most frequently implicated in such nefarious activities and who feature most
prominently in popular imaginings of them.

People say that waterhole, grain, and rain witches are motivated not
simply by evil and their joy of destruction – though that is part of the
answer – but, more calculatingly, by their desire to acquire these things
for themselves. A man who bewitches a waterhole may do so to spoil it
for others, but also to cause water to appear on his own land; an attack
on the rain aims to attract it from his neighbours' plots to his own; and
a man who ruins others' grain is thought to pull it medicinally from
others' plots to his own. As with other forms of witchcraft, including
the female witchcraft already discussed, witchcraft directed against
public goods hinges on a certain zero sum logic. Just as the female
witch reputedly destroys her clanmates to harness their (re)productive
powers to her own ends, so the male witch destroys others' rains and
grains to acquire them for himself. The witch's gain, in short, is the
moral man's bane (Sanders 2003a).

Ihanzu images of rain witches are much less vivid, and much less
spectacular, than those of personal witches: these witches in all likelihood do not have nocturnal jaunts on hyena familiars, nor do they go
in much for naked dancing or boasting of their evil ways among their
cohorts. The prototypical rain witch, rather, is a man like any man, but
one who works alone. Unlike the female personal witch, who is shame-
lessly (if secretively) social – to the point of dancing naked, and boasting excessively, with other witches about their evil deeds – the
stereotypical male rain-witch is the quintessential loner. (This state-

ment requires immediate qualification, since his wife provides an important counterpoint to his loner status, as we shall see momentarily.) The male witch inverts not only everyday sociality, but also popular images of maleness, in that he attacks all things public. Because in everyday life men are conceptually and practically associated with the public realm, including herding, public meetings and politics, and many other things (see chapter 1), male witches are thought best capable of undermining all things public. The assumption, as with all types of witchcraft, is that some understanding is a logical prerequisite for destruction. If female witches understand kin and can thus destroy them, male witches are better positioned to understand and destroy public goods.

Rain and grain witches are accused publicly in ways that personal witches never are. During the two years and farming seasons I lived in Ihanzu, rain-witchcraft accusations were routine. I recorded details of twenty-one cases during that period (see Sanders 1997, 220–44), most of which took place at large, public 'rain meetings' (*shalo ka mbula*). Such meetings occur during droughts, ostensibly to discuss the reasons for the drought, though they invariably end in accusations of rain-witchcraft and just as quickly lead to lengthy, public trials of those accused (see Sanders 2003b).

The same patterns of suspicion and accusation developed each year. From what I could tell from discussions about past rain-witchcraft cases, they resembled those of other drought years. Early in the season, from late December to early January, accusations were made against specific and non-specific people, though none were take very seriously. No one was fined, expelled from Ihanzu, or threatened with expulsion during that period. This is because, while it was unfortunate that the rains had not yet begun, it did not at this point make or break the harvest.

Around mid-January the situation changed dramatically. This is a crucial period in the farming cycle because it determines, like nothing else, the state of the year's harvest. If the rains fail until the end of January and into the beginning of February, there is little hope of obtaining any reasonable harvest. Another famine year is virtually guaranteed. It is from this point onwards that rain witches were sought and brought to justice in earnest. Fines were doled out liberally; the accused were threatened, and sometimes expelled from their villages.

Rain-witchcraft accusations are gendered in specific ways. Early in the season, when it was less pressing that the rain falls immediately, many nameless women and some men were divined to have played a role in thwarting the rain. This information was noted during public meetings, though rarely acted on. As the season progressed, and the worsening drought increasingly threatened everyone's livelihood, villagers' attention turned to men alone, who were publicly denounced, fined, threatened, and sometimes expelled from Ihanzu. In the precolonial past, I was told, they were sometimes tortured or killed.

On the whole, then, rain-witchcraft accusations made against men were taken much more seriously than those made against women. Women tended to be suspected or accused at the season's beginning, when rains are not yet critical; women were not always identified by name, were rarely tried and, even if they were, often went unpunished. Men's lot was different. Men tended to be accused of rain-witchcraft late in the game, when drought signals a pending disaster. Men were nearly always identified by name and dragged through public trials, and they were often punished, sometimes severely.

These patterns of accusation suggest many things, but one of their effects is to reinscribe in the popular imagination a practical and conceptual link between men and rain-witchcraft and, by implication, to reinforce the imagined connection between women and more personal forms of witchcraft. Male witches destroy rain, while female witches destroy people: a diabolical division of labour that is far from accidental. For if female and male witches can inflict different sorts of mystical harm as individuals, then the two acting in concert, as a husband-and-wife team, provide the Ihanzu with their true 'institutionalized nightmare,' in Monica Wilson's (1970) terms.

Gendered Reproduction, Destruction, and Inversion

Many Ihanzu have it that male and female witches do their work jointly. Together, male and female witches complement each other. The imagery of this complementary cooperation as it presented itself in discussions could hardly be more striking. A wife-witch kills her kinfolk, transforming them into zombies so that they can labour in her fields, prepare meals, and brew beer on the homestead. Such witchcraft guarantees an ongoing immoral link between processes of production and consumption. Yet toil as they might, zombies cannot produce grain without rain. And without grain, zombies cannot cook food. Or brew beer. Thus, a woman's witchcraft, while clearly self-serving and damaging to others, is fundamentally incomplete;

through her actions alone, she cannot ensure her own or her household's reproduction from one season to the next. For this she needs male witchcraft.

A witch-husband, for his part, mystically steals rain from elsewhere and attracts it to his own fields. This allows his witch-wife's zombies to do their work. Illicit production and consumption within the household can therefore take place. But it is important to note that the witch-husband alone, like his witch-wife, is ill-equipped to ensure his own long-term reproduction, since men often consider themselves – and are seen by many – as domestically incompetent. Attracting or ruining rain is one thing. Successfully running a household is quite another. Processes of domestic production and consumption lie ultimately beyond men's control, whether in moral or immoral contexts. Thus, just as the witch-wife needs a witch-husband, so, too, does the witch-husband need a witch-wife. Together, and only together, the disastrous duo ensure their own continued reproductive success by inflicting maximum ruinous results on the rest (cf. Nadel 1952, 19).

Villagers are often explicit on this point, emphasizing how husband–wife witch teams work together. Moreover, this gendered cooperation is sometimes made manifest during public accusations. At one rain-witchcraft trial I attended in 1994, the accused man, under some duress, confessed: 'It is in our clan. My father really knows how to bewitch the rain. My mother really knows how to bewitch people.' When asked why they would possibly do such things, he responded: 'To get lots of rain, grain, and to get [zombie] workers to farm at night.' Such confessions are not unusual, from what people tell me.

Ihanzu images of male and female witches fit neatly with understandings of gender complementarity, whereby the genders jointly harness and control the most powerful forces in the universe. But unlike ordinary moral gendered beings who jointly labour to generate wealth, offspring, and other things, gendered witch duos use these forces to their own perverse, antisocial ends – and ensure maximum mystical damage in the bargain. In this sense the male–female witch team provides an imaginative, diabolical inversion of the male–female rain-maker pair. If male and female rainmakers combine efforts and powers to provide the ultimate societal good, then male and female witches join forces for society's ultimate ruin. In either case, for good or for evil, the underlying assumption is that masculine and feminine forces must combine in a complementary fashion in order to achieve full effect. Gender complementarity and transformation undergird both imaginings. And so it goes with the entire Ihanzu universe.

what drives
ppl to
confession?

How, exactly, the genders unite in these cases varies, and we find some interesting inversions in the imagery of those unions. One such inversion emerges from the temporal flow of witchcraft activities.

Male rain witches do the brunt of their work roughly between December and May, during the wet season. This is the time (in drought years anyway) during which public rain-witchcraft accusations and trials are in full swing. No rain-witch, no matter how malicious, wicked, or silly, would attempt to bewitch the rain in the dry months, since there is no rain to bewitch.

Conversely, people say that female witches are most active the other half of the year, during the dry season. Just as the threat of rain-witchcraft diminishes, the threat of personal witchcraft begins. It is common knowledge in Ihanzu that the dry season, between June and November, sees far more deaths than any other time of the year – and remember, all deaths are attributed to witchcraft. Whether or not there are really more deaths just then is unclear, but what is certain is that villagers spend far more time in the dry season at funerals and elsewhere socializing, gossiping, and drinking beer than at any other time of the year. Such intense sociality provides the necessary preconditions for the sometimes anxious deliberations and speculations over who is killing whom through witchcraft, and why. During this time of dramatically intensified social interaction with kin and others, it is nearly expected that the darker side of kinship – personal witchcraft – will rear its unsightly head. Which it does. Wet-season witchcraft is to male as dry-season witchcraft is to female; together, they form a locally recognized annual cycle of differently gendered 'witch seasons.'

The temporal sequencing of gender that motors this cycle along its path of destruction provides another form of inversion. For here, female precedes male, rather than the usual reverse. The male witch could never go first since, with his rain alone, there would be no zombies to farm, cook, brew beer, and all the rest. No witch, male or female, could survive. Yet if a female witch begins in the dry season by killing kin, then her witch husband can follow with rain in the wet season. Only in so doing – by inverting the normal modus operandi of gendered cooperation – can differently gendered witches and witchcrafts succeed.

When it comes to witchcraft, the genders and their reproductive powers are sometimes inverted in other ways, as in the following well-known and much discussed case.

There is a middle-aged couple who live in Matongo village. This couple, it is rumoured, are witches. Msa, as I will call him, is a reasonably well-to-do Christian man. He and his wife Maria, also a Christian, own and farm unusually large tracts of land: three acres near their home, one acre in Maria's father's village and another thirteen acres at a third village. In their house they have three large grain stores that provide ample grain for them and their two adopted children even in the worst famine years. This, together with nineteen cows, twenty-six goats, five sheep and thirty some chickens, makes them one of the wealthiest families in the area.

The fact that their children are adopted is not, people claim, incidental. Maria is infertile. Their children in reality are those of Msa's sister, a fact everyone (except Msa and Maria) was eager to make clear to me. But most are unsympathetic, for Msa has allegedly made a pact with the diviner, willingly exchanging his wife's child-bearing capabilities for a guarantee of copious quantities of livestock and grain. As such, it is said that the couple will be wealthy for life in terms of livestock and grain, though irrevocably impoverished when it comes to children.

There is more to the story than this. First, several villagers told me that, due to Msa's illicit pact, Maria's breasts fluctuate in size inversely with the amount of grain in their grain stores. Before the harvest, when grain stores are at their lowest levels, Maria's breasts are said to swell to near monumental proportions. Conversely, when stores are filled to the top, just after the harvest, her breasts are virtually non-existent. This annual waxing and waning of breasts and crops points up in a somewhat conspicuous manner the direct trade-off imagined between different types of wealth and fertility, in this case, crops versus child-bearing capabilities. It also suggests that Maria's gender vacillates with the seasons, as her wet, feminine features and potentialities are diverted from her own body and into crops.

At the same time, while Maria becomes, in a sense, more male, her husband Msa is said to become 'female.' It is common knowledge, several villagers told me, that Msa now has a monthly menstrual cycle and menstruates as his wife once did. In short, he has become 'female.'

Much could be said about this case and others like it. I wish simply to point out that, even as male and female witches' bodies mutate between male and female forms, witch pairs become both inversions of moral males and females, as well as gendered inversions of each other. The genders and their productive combinations remain central to people's explanations and understandings of witchcraft's operation. To put it differently, male witches may become female in bodily form, female ones male, but they continue to combine and work together equally as differently gendered entities to achieve maximum destruction.

Conclusions

For the men and women of Ihanzu, as for many peoples in many places, witchcraft serves as a way to make sense of the world around them. It provides an imaginative framework through which people actively consider and converse about the powers, good and bad, that move their world.

In Ihanzu, as across the continent, witchcraft is about inversion – or perhaps more correctly, inversions in the plural. In addition to ideologically inverting legitimate processes of production and reproduction, and the rainmakers who control those processes, the male–female witch pair invert and pervert two particular forms of moral personhood: one male, one female. Female witches undermine kin and clan relations, those things women supposedly know best and nurture. Male witches do much the same in the public realm, undermining the public basis of social life for all villagers, denying all villagers the right to reproduce themselves. Then there are male and female witches who switch from male to female or the reverse, but still join forces to do their job as differently gendered pairs. Such imagery bespeaks a far more subtle and complex equation than any simple inversion of *the* moral order or person might imply. Yet in all cases, Ihanzu witchcraft and the powers associated with it are premised on a notion of gender complementarity and transformation, and hence particular understandings of gendered (re)production and, in this case, destruction. As with all things in life, male and female must cooperate to unleash the powers they jointly control.

In closing, it is worth noting that many contemporary anthropologists have argued that African witchcraft should be seen as a critical commentary on the world at large – as a critique of such things as the free market, structural adjustment, and globalization most generally (Comaroff and Comaroff 1993; Masquelier 2002; Bastian 2003). The foregoing suggests, on the contrary, that not all 'African witchcraft' is the same – that witchcraft need not always be 'about' politics, economics, or rapid social change. The Ihanzu, like many, do have certain types of witchcraft that comment fairly directly and critically on today's neoliberal project (see Sanders 2001a, 2003a). It is just that rain-witchcraft is not one of them. In Ihanzu, rain-witchcraft has endured for many, many years – as far back, in fact, as anyone can remember. And it waxes and wanes not with the economic and political climate, but with the rain and its absence.

Conclusion

This book has aimed to provide a multifaceted picture of Ihanzu rain-making. To this end, we have explored a variety of Ihanzu rainmaking rites and events – annual rites at the rainshrine; 'rituals of rebellion;' ancestral offerings; rain-witchcraft – as well as the locally inflected 'logics' that underpin them. Rainmaking is of the utmost importance to the women and men of Ihanzu. It sits central to their history. It forms a crucial part of who they imagine themselves to be. And its gendering is key to Ihanzu knowledge of transformative powers and processes in the world. But most of all, rainmaking is crucial to the women and men of Ihanzu because it brings rain.

To say as much is not simply to state the obvious. It is meant rather to point to the inevitable gap between anthropological and Others' projects of sense making. For these two projects are never the same thing, even if some anthropologists, by writing about 'local models,' 'emic perspectives,' and the like, have pretended they are. Ihanzu rain-making and its gendering are not a model of, or for, reality. They do not form a coherent, conceptual whole just waiting for anthropologists to decode, give meaning to, or 'explain.' Neither do they symbolize anything. In Ihanzu eyes, rainmaking makes sense not because it *symbolizes* or *means* things but because it *does* them. Rainmaking is a complex set of practices that is informed by and gives rise to a particular epistemology or set of knowledges about the world and its workings.

Such knowledges of the world – those things we just 'know' – do not spring mechanically from the world-as-it-is. Known worlds, ours and others,' make sense to their inhabitants because they are characterized by particular sociohistorical understandings. Such understandings create and are created by societal concerns of the moment: by what people talk about; particular 'problems' and their 'solutions'; and what 'the really interesting questions' happen to be. In Ihanzu, rainmaking with its gendering forms one such domain of knowledge, understanding, and engagement.

Within a Euro-American epistemology, on the other hand, 'the body' has become a central preoccupation. It forms the basis of knowledge of all sorts. Little wonder, perhaps, in our neoliberal world, where 'the individual' in so many ways reigns supreme. Within anthropology and feminist and gender studies – all part of this world – 'body-talk' is equally evident and prevalent. Here, thinking through 'the body' has enabled scholars to address long-standing questions in the human sciences: the relationship between the individual and society; agency and structure; knowledge and its location; the locus of historical change; and others. Within anthropology, thinking through 'the body' has allowed scholars to reinsert real actors and actions into our analytic frameworks, which in the not so distant past were dogged by structural-determinist arguments of the structural-functional, ecological, Marxist, and high-structuralist kind. But what does it matter? So what if the body has become, for so many reasons, a Euro-American fixation?

For one thing, the way we imagine the world both inside and outside the academy shapes the scientific enterprise and the knowledges we produce about ourselves. In this case, our pretheoretical commitments and metaphors surrounding the body frame certain types of 'problems,' which in turn elicit specific 'solutions.' It is no accident, for instance, that the human genome project has received such massive financial, political, and intellectual support just now, aiming and claiming to uncover the very essence of our humanity deep within ourselves, deep within our bodies. By mapping our genes, 'the problem' of who we are as human beings will finally be 'solved,' or so some advocates would have us believe. On a similar note, 'transgendered' individuals are today rendered both a conceptual problem and a clinical condition, treatable though surgery, psychotherapy, and pharmaceutical interventions. These and many other Euro-American 'problems' and their 'solutions,' the questions and answers they elicit, are framed – indeed given life – by very specific ideas about bodies. We could as a thought experiment ask what such projects might look like, or if they could exist at all, if the body were not considered central and all-important.

The way we imagine the world not only shapes the scientific and everyday knowledges we produce about ourselves. It also shapes the knowledges we produce about others. As I hope to have demonstrated in this book, Euro-American understandings of the body have under-pinned and fundamentally (mis)shaped the things we as social scien-tists think we know about male and female in other places: about non-human gender forms, 'gender symbolism,' and how we 'explain' them. Social scientists need to recognize the fundamental point – as some of course have – that the Euro-American metaphors and analytic fictions that underpin the scientific enterprise are not 'true' knowledge-of-the-world; which is to say, they are not *themselves* the world, but rather attempts to represent and explain it. Insofar as we mistake our models of the world for the world itself, we fail adequately to entertain alter-native ways of knowing and hence explaining.

The Ihanzu epistemology discussed in this book posits particular objects, relations, ways of seeing, and ways of being in a thoroughly gendered world. Such understandings are interesting not because peo-ple in other places, in other cultures, in other societies, hold weird and wonderful beliefs about the world that are different to our own. To say as much would be to imply that Others 'believe' whereas We 'know'; that faraway peoples in faraway places have 'cultural beliefs' – which are wrong – and that only we Westerners possess true, objective knowledge. Such implausible conceits do not serve the social sciences well. Since no one, academic or otherwise, has a flip-top head into which 'raw facts' can simply be dumped, the more pertinent question is which analytic metaphors, lexicons, or fictions best capture some-thing we wish to know about the world and hence most adequately 'explain' it.

By exploring Ihanzu rainmaking and its inherent gendering, this book has aimed to develop an alternative set of conceptual tools – gender complementarity, embodied capacity, and performance of gen-der – that do not begin and end with bodies. While these tools spring from a particular ethnographic encounter, this need not render them 'local,' if by this we mean that they remain forever fixed to an-Other people in an-Other place. And this, in a way, is the point: it is not only necessary that social scientists recognise Others' sensibilities about the world. Much more than this, those sensibilities must march in analytic step with commonplace Euro-American ones, and in some cases simply replace them. Such a levelling of the epistemological playing field would mean that Other knowledges are not subordi-nated and relegated to 'the local.' Nor would they be merely 'cultural.' They would instead be rendered global and relevant to comparative projects of sense making in the social sciences and beyond, which of course includes anthropology. Proceeding in this manner may, in turn, serve to shape our own academic and everyday relations with and sensibilities about our own world: what we 'know,' in a word, to be true.

Notes

Preface

1 I would particularly recommend Steven Feierman's (1990) excellent work on the politics and history of rainmaking in Shambaa, northern Tanzania; and Randal Packard's (1981) work on similar topics in Zaire.

2 This preliminary survey was supplemented by a 194-household random survey I conducted in 1994 in four villages (23 subvillages), with the help of four locally based assistants. It aimed to gather basic background data on household composition and economics. As a sampling frame I used funeral logbooks, which record in each village who has paid what at various funerals, and who has not. Villagers maintain these records meticulously, making them far more useful than official government records for such purposes. Statistics in this book derive from these survey data.

3 Although Shabani and I both lived in Kirumi, we spent considerable time camped in most of the other eighteen Ihanzu villages throughout the period, usually for a week or two at a time. During those periods we participated in anything and everything from funerals to farming, from herding to healing rites. Besides speaking to anyone who was interested, we made efforts to target specific individuals for their expertise on particular topics, always ensuring an adequate purposive mix of informants stratified according to salient social categories.

Introduction

1 See for example, Schapera (1971); Zimon (1974); Packard (1981); Petermann (1985); and Feierman (1990). For a detailed overview of twentieth century anthropological literature on African rainmaking, see Sanders 1997, ch. 1.

2 The Ihanzu have been known by many names. Early on Germans called them Issánsu, Issansu, Issanssu, Wa-Issansu, and Waissansu. Later, British administrators used the terms Anisanzu, Wanisanzu, Isanzu, Ishanzu, and Anizanzu. More recently, they have been called the Isansu (Tomikawa 1970), the Izansu (Koponen 1988, 234n), Izanzu (Odner 1971, 152), Ihanbu (Thornton 1980, 216, 234), Inhanzu (ibid., 231) and Ehansu (Douglas 1969, 124). Swahili speakers call them the Wanyisanzu, and this is the name that government officials commonly use. The last anthropologist to work there called them the Ihanzu or Isanzu, depending on the context (Adam 1961, 1962, 1963a, 1963b). The only thing that seems not to have occurred to anyone is to call them by the name they call themselves, the Anyĩhanzu (This should actually be Anya-Ihanzu, yet it is always heard as Anyĩhanzu). I call them 'the Ihanzu,' omitting the prefix *Anya*, which means simply 'the people of.' Locals refer to their language as 'Kĩnyihanzu,' and to their land as 'Ihanzu.' While anthropologists have, for good reason, increasingly castigated one another for collapsing peoples, cultures, and places under a single banner (Gupta and Ferguson 1992), many peoples around the globe – 'the Ihanzu' among them – find such conflations useful. Mappings in this book of 'the Ihanzu,' the people, onto 'Ihanzu,' the land, are purposive and reflect local usage.

3 I did know that rainmaking had been important in the past, thanks to Adam's excellent conference paper on the subject (Adam 1963b), but I had no idea whether it was the case in the 1990s.

4 Of course Hastrup (1993, 176) is correct that anthropological projects have their own internal dynamics and sets of concerns and that their validity cannot ultimately be judged by whether they 'please the natives.'

5 Others asked whether rainmaking was best understood as 'religion' or 'magic,' with the twin issues of rationality and irrationality invariably looming close at hand. See, for instance, Spire (1905, 19); Eiselen (1928); Carnell (1955); Feddema (1966, 192); and Ten Raa (1969).

6 Thus Packard (1981) has shown how indigenous notions of rainmaking, chiefship, and history among the Bashu of eastern Zaire are inextricably linked; Lan (1985) has demonstrated the crucial role that *mhondoro* spirit mediums – themselves bringers of rain – played in mediating between past and present, ancestors and the living, in Zimbabwe's struggle for independence; and Feierman (1990) has explored how the Tanzanian Shambaa have employed concepts of 'healing the land' (when rainmaking is politically centralized) and 'harming the land' (when rainmakers compete) to discuss the dramatic political, economic, social, and cultural upheavals in which they have participated for centuries.

7 In practice these two approaches are not always easily separable, and some
   writers attend to all of these issues at once, albeit to varying degrees. It is
   often a question of emphasis rather than either/or.
8 On differently gendered rainstones, see Rogers (1927); Hartnoll (1932, 738;
   1942, 59); Cooke and Beaton (1939, 182); Middleton (1971, 196); James (1972,
   38); and Packard (1981, 69). On gendered rain pots, see Cory (1951, 51n);
   and Hauenstein (1967b, 13). On male and female rain drums, see Weatherby (1979). On male and female rain statuettes, see Ntudu (1939, 85); and
   Johnson (1948, 41, 96 [plate]). On sexual relations and prohibitions, see
   Schapera (1971, 123). On gendered and sex-laden rain rituals, songs, and
   ancestral addresses, see Hauenstein (1967a, 1967b); Hoernlé (1922); Jellicoe,
   Sima, and Sombi (1968); Lindström (1987, 77); Murray (1980); Schoeman
   (1935); Ten Raa (1969); Vijfhuizen (1997); Håkansson (1998, 276); Evans-Pritchard (1929); Jacobson-Widding (1990); Krige (1968); and Leakey (1977,
   203). On male and female seasons, see Feierman (1990). On male and
   female rains, see Bleek (1933, 308); Ginindza (1997, 152); Holas (1949); Marshall (1957); and Sanders (1998).
9 Among recent attempts, arguably the most influential example – unques-
   tionably the most ambitious – comes from the social historian Eugenia Herbert. Herbert's *Iron, Gender and Power* (1993) is a tour de force on the
   interrelationship between metallurgy, sexuality, and other social practices
   across the whole of sub-Saharan Africa. More specifically, Herbert attends
   to the prominence of 'gynecomorphic' furnaces across the region, many of
   which come (or came) equipped with breasts, female scarification, and
   beaded belts, vaginas, and wombs. Male smiths operate these female furnaces to produce iron, and the process of iron production is itself replete
   with sexual symbolism. Herbert argues that while metallurgic practices
   vary considerably across the continent, underlying them is a common cosmology or set of beliefs. These beliefs spring from people's everyday lived
   experiences, especially bodily experiences, including the fundamental facts
   of human reproduction. That men and women can together produce children is well known, and this fact has occasioned a regional 'procreative
   paradigm,' which is then mapped onto other transformative activities.
   Human reproduction thus serves as the base metaphor for African metallurgy; or, put another way, African metallurgy 'makes sense' because it
   mimics procreation. Through analogy, metaphor, metonym, or equivalence,
   metallurgic practices and other 'African transformative processes invoke
   the human model as the measure of all things' (Herbert 1993, 5).
10 For a particularly interesting non-Africanist example of this approach, see
   Delaney (1991).

11 I am not suggesting that anyone in Ihanzu (or myself) holds a simplistic, mechanical view that rain rites should immediately produce rain. I am simply suggesting that such utterances should not always and immediately be treated as symbolic of something else. This is a point about anthropological explanation and not about 'belief,' which is in any case a highly problematic concept that is not used in this book (see Needham 1972).

12 Steinmetz's (2005) interesting discussion of the social science's underlying 'epistemological unconscious' has obvious relevance here. However, his understanding of the unconscious – 'a deep structure encompassing processes and forms of knowledge that are not accessible to conscious awareness but that are nonetheless capable of patterning conscious thought and manifest practice' (2005, 46) – frames matters in a different light. It is no doubt true that the social science's underlying sensibilities remain mostly submerged, and that they inform both theorizing and practice. However, I find it more compelling to imagine these guiding (in)sensibilities as 'pretheoretical commitments,' since they are not irretrievably lost: they can be brought to the surface, discursively articulated, and sometimes even changed. Arguably this project of revelation is and long has been central to anthropology and other social sciences.

13 This invention, inextricably linked to the Western 'gendered gaze,' was a multifaceted project. It made itself felt through the academic production of Yoruba history, which read gender where it was absent; through colonial policies, practices, and ideologies and their differential impact on males and females; and through perpetual mistranslation of the terms 'male' and 'female,' which sit central to the Yoruba language and culture. Bastian (2000) makes a similar argument for Igbo-speaking Nigerians, though she does not go so far as to suggest that gender was 'invented' outright by colonialists.

14 For overviews of earlier material along these lines, see Strobel (1982); and Potash (1989). For more recent literatures and trends, see Ampofo et al. (2004).

15 Alexander Butchart's (1998) study argues along similarly Foucauldian lines and shows how Europeans discursively constructed and produced the African body. In it, he aims to demonstrate how 'the African body has been created and transformed as an object of knowledge, how its attributes and capacities are contingent upon the methods applied to know it, and therefore how strategies of the state and industry, along with the various sociomedical sciences that assume its existence, are possible' (1998, 2). Although a fascinating read, the book is curious in that it scarcely mentions gender, which one would have thought might feature centrally in any construction

of the body, European or otherwise. Additionally, like many Foucauldian works, this one recognizes that it both reproduces and is the product of a particular configuration of power/knowledge. Though by no means inevitable – there are many readings of Foucault – this leads Butchart to take the unfortunate position that the book 'can make no claims about being more correct than alternative explorations' (1998, 184).

16 Fractal geometry is a central element of chaos theory and hinges on the notion of self-similarity. Though chaos and fractals are relatively recent ways of thinking and theorizing in the natural sciences, social and cultural anthropologists have arguably been thinking 'fractally' (albeit, admittedly, in less systematic ways) since the nineteenth century. See Mosko (2005) for an excellent overview of the relation between chaos theory and social anthropology.

Chapter 1: Ihanzu Everyday Worlds

1 This is true of the Tanganyikan mainland. Zanzibar, the other part of today's United Republic of Tanzania, became an independent sultanate in December 1963; the sultan was deposed in January 1964 by the African nationalist Afro Shirazi Party (ASP), and in April of that year the Zanzibari government united with Tanganyika to form the United Republic.

2 The African Development Bank has recently noted as much: 'Although both the IMF and World Bank insist that major gains were achieved in many African countries [owing to structural adjustment], the recent refocusing of their operation suggests that while valuable lessons were learned, actual performance, especially in respect to growth and poverty reduction, was disappointing' (Africa Development Bank 2000, 15). Even enthusiastic supporters of recent reforms have been forced to recognise that 'the major failure of reform, as it has developed to date, lies in the apparent lack of tangible benefits for many of the poorest sections of Tanzanian society' (Temu and Due 2000, 710).

3 John A. Corrie, Co-President of ACP/EU Joint Assembly, 'Focus on the Plight of the Poor, EU Tells Tanzania,' *East African* (Nairobi), 4 January 2001.

4 Kirumi Division is divided into four wards (*kata*) – Mwangeza, Nkinto, Ibaga and Mpambala – which are further subdivided into eighteen *ujamaa* villages.

5 This is not to imply that the Ihanzu are a homogenous group that can be mapped directly onto a particular parcel of land. Some have religion, education, political position, and economic advantage, while others do not; there are self-defined 'Ihanzu' urbanites living in Tanzania's towns and

cities, some of them second or third generation. And a few live, work, and study in Europe. Such heterogeneity would render 'the Ihanzu' a meaningless term, were it not for the fact that the Ihanzu routinely use it to essentialize themselves, albeit in different ways in different contexts. This book focuses on 'the Ihanzu' as commonly imagined in the villages, images that hinge inexorably on living and farming in the rural 'homeland.' On this score it is important to note that anthropological projects that essentialize Others are not the same thing as anthropological projects like this one that aim to write about and through Others' projects of essentialization.

6 Acting District Officer A.W. Wyatt (c. 1928), 'Mkalama: The Back of Beyond,' Rhodes House, Oxford (hereafter RH), File MSS Afr. s. 272.

7 'Mkalama Annual Report 1919/1920 (16 April 1920),' pp. 2, 22; Tanzania National Archives (hereafter TNA), File 1733/1.

8 The one and only early attempt of which I am aware – a rubber plantation set up by Herr Bell near Mkalama village – failed miserably immediately after the First World War. See 'Mkalama Annual Report 1919–1920,' p. 21, TNA, File 1733/1.

9 Administrative Officer in Charge, J.F. Kenny-Dillon, 'Mkalama Annual Report, 1924,' p. 2, TNA, File 1733/14, 91; Assistant Probation Officer, 'Local Courts, Iramba Division,' 1957, TNA, File 68/L4/2.

10 Since there are no secondary schools in Ihanzu, students who go on go elsewhere.

11 The Ihanzu do not know the artists of the many rock paintings scattered about the region (see Culwick 1931; Kohl-Larsen and Kohl-Larsen 1938, 1958; Masao 1979); the rock paintings, it is worth noting, hold no cosmological significance for the Ihanzu, nor do they play any role in rainmaking rites (cf. Lewis-Williams 1977). Many say that the massive and weighty cave drums found in the caves (Hunter 1953) were made and played by giant savages (*washenzi warefu*) who allegedly lived in the area prior to the Ihanzu themselves. (A few claim they were called Wareno and came from the west). Living off a patently odd diet of wild animals and trees, these savages reputedly had the good sense to hide their drums in the caves in times of war. The drums, like the paintings, are said to have been there when the Ihanzu first arrived.

12 Meat relishes are the most desirable but are also the least frequently eaten. The largest portion of an Ihanzu's diet actually comes from cultivated sorghum and wild greens.

13 I have never heard of any Ihanzu making sunflower oil from their crop, as some people apparently do in other parts of Iramba to the south.

14 These data, and others throughout the book, come from a 194-household

random survey I conducted in 1994 in twenty-three sub-villages. See note 2 of the Preface.

15 Men even have a preferred 'pig arrow' (*mpando*), a colossal, double-edged anti-swine weapon that, when shot, more closely resembles a flying knife.

16 There are dozens of wild greens that are regularly picked, prepared, and eaten, even (and especially) during famine years. *Ndalu* is the most common relish and is made of a combination of several leaves found in the rainy season (the combination of leaves changes with the rains). The most hardy type of leaf used to prepare *ndalu* – it is available even in the worst years of hunger – is called *ikūluga*, of which there are two locally identified varieties: *ikūluga la mbata* (*Ceratotheca sesamoides*) and *ikūluga la lume* (*Sesamum calycina ssp. angustifalia*). To make *ndalu* relish, one of these *ikūluga* species is mixed with other leaves like *alimbī* or *gogoo* (*Cucumis sp.*), *mūkombi tagata* (*Asystasia schimperi*), *moga* (*Amaranthus sp.*) or, in times of sheer desperation due to its less than palatable taste, *kumbūkumbū* (*Crotalaria sp.*). *Ndalu* is popular and, most years, plentiful. Other leaves commonly prepared as relishes, when available, are *mūshisha* (*Amaranthus hybridus*), *mūshisha a ng'ombe* (*Amaranthus hybridus*), *nsonga* (*Crotalaria sp.*), *nsansa* (*Phaseolus vulgaris*), *nsogolo* (*Tribulus cistoides*), and the ever bitter though undeniably delectable *mūng'ang'ī* (*Gynandropsis gynandra*).

17 *Shama* in Kirumi village, for instance, has (from top to bottom) a chair, chair's assistant, four *agizi*, and thirty-four other members who represent a large block of homesteads in southern Kirumi. The chair gives orders to his assistant, who in turn informs the *agizi* to visit each household to tell villagers what day they must show up. Organizers take careful note on the day of who is and is not present, and those absent are usually fined and excluded from future work parties (though eventually all are allowed to rejoin). Although men and women may sponsor such work parties, it is more common for the former. In 1993–4, four men in Kirumi sponsored *shama* work parties.

18 For each person added to the group the amount of beer given increases by one gallon up to around ten people. When workers exceed this number, which is rare, they and the sponsor negotiate how many earthen vats of beer they will receive. In such cases the total invariably comes to less than a gallon per person.

19 The literal translation: 'At whose place is beer being drunk today?' The term *magai* is used in this context even though technically, *magai* is a nonalcoholic sorghum drink; *ntūlī* is its alcoholic counterpart.

20 This figure (49 per cent) is based on my survey material from Matongo *ujamaa* village. Figures vary slightly from village to village, with higher

proportions of home brewing in central areas. Of those which brewed beer in the Matongo area in 1994, 51 per cent brewed once, 27 per cent twice, and 22 per cent three times or more during the year.

21 Ihanzu men were once known as keen hunters, but this, for a number of reasons, has changed. First, the government prohibits such activities for all Ihanzu bow-and-arrow users and for gun owners without a hunting licence. Also, wildlife populations in the area have declined sharply since the turn of the last century, having been greatly deprived of their habitat through anti-tsetse fly bush-clearing campaigns (Johnson 1948, 87–91). (For a fascinating and readable historical account of wildlife policy in East Africa from the German colonial period up to the mid-1960s, see Ofcansky (1981, esp. 112–63). Large game animals are virtually absent from Ihanzu today; one must go farther north into the bush and Hadza country to find them. Leopards and hyenas sometimes visit and steal villagers' sheep, goats, and dogs (my dog, Tusker, was stolen by a leopard), and small game such as wild pigs, hyraxes, porcupines, dik-dik, and countless types of birds are fairly common. Baboons are numerous and often steal crops; snakes, too, are many, most of them poisonous: black cobras, green mambas, and puff adders. Apart from dik-dik, which are rare, none of these animals are eaten except during the most extreme famines.

22 There are several fishing techniques. Net fishing (*nyavu*) is the most common. Nets are often imported from outside Tanzania. Their use normally requires five or more boys or men working together: two holding the net on either side of a narrow part of the river, another in the water ensuring that fish do not slip under the net. *Ngwaku* or 'hook stick' fishing is also very popular; this involves sweeping a long stick with a hook across the water to snag big catfish. Line and hook fishing is sometimes used; a hook is baited, the line tied to a tree. Less common are spear fishing (*nsomeke*), which is time- and labour-consuming and not terribly productive; and large fish traps (*mŭgono*) – loosely woven sticks in the shape of an enormous funnel – which are placed at a narrow point in the river.

23 It is becoming more common to make smaller bricks and to bake them, though it is only a small minority of people who are competent with this technique. Baked bricks last much longer than unbaked ones, though it takes more work and know-how to produce them.

24 Sponsors must give different amounts of beer depending on the house-building group to which they belong (see below), the most senior giving the most beer.

25 In order of seniority, these are *Anyampala, Anyamŭgongo, Anyandaa* and

Anyakikua. Anyampala, or 'elders,' consists of those who have built several houses throughout their lives and who have therefore given a significant amount of beer to fellow villagers in the process. *Anyamũgongo*, 'people of the back,' build on the back of the house; *Anyandaa* are 'those of the womb/ stomach,' and refers to the space just inside the door at the house's centre; and, finally, *Anyakikua* are those with little or no experience building houses and who have not yet built their own. These groups are organized on the basis of neighbourhood or village residence rather than, say, by kinship.

26 V. Adam 1963. 'Draft of Report on Isanzu for Community Development Department of Tanzania,' p. 72, British Library of Political and Economic Science (hereafter BLPES).

27 All animals have a monetary value, though for non-monetary transactions with, say, bridewealth payments and fines, these values typically are lower than market value and are negotiable. For fines and bridewealth payments in the early 1990s, for example, a cow was the equivalent of five goats (or sheep), or 5,000 Tanzanian shillings (TSh), or 25 chickens, or five 20-litre buckets (*ndoo*) of beer. The monetary value changes in practice. A man with a bridewealth debt of five cows, for example, might be able to reduce the value of the cows to TSh 3,000 per head if he were to pay cash, which is not seen as a reduction of the bridewealth amount. The market value of a cow was at the time well above TSh 5,000.

28 Much of Mbulu District, unlike other neighbouring areas, is at a higher altitude and has a cooler, more lush climate.

29 The percentage of population in each of the twelve Ihanzu matriclans is as follows: *Anyampanda* (30.5 per cent), *Anyambilu* (16.2), *Anyankalĩ* (13.3), *Anyansuli* (8.4), *Anyambeũ* (7.8), *Anyang'walu* (6.9), *Anyambwaa* (4.5), *Anyisungu* (4.0), *Anyambala* (2.3), *Asambaa* (2.3), *Anyakumi* (2.0), *Anyikĩli* (1.5). Though clans are not localized, some clans tend to have greater concentrations in particular villages according to whether they were originally Iramba or Ihanzu clans.

30 V. Adam 1963. 'Land Tenure in Kirumi,' unpublished ms at BLPES, ch. III, p. 15.

31 These shilling figures and exchange rates are at 1995 rates.

32 These again are at 1995 rates and cost considerably more today.

33 All of these men are middle-aged or elders; about half are Muslims, the other half self-identified 'pagans.' The reason men and women commonly give for the decline in plural marriages is that it is simply too expensive to maintain two or more households and that extramarital relations offer a more affordable alternative.

Chapter 2: The Making and Unmaking of Rains and Reigns

1 This conversation, as Werther records it, took place in the Sukuma language between one of his assistants and a local.

2 The earliest version of this story I have found was recorded by a British administrator in 1920. Hichens, 'Mkalama Annual Report 1919/1920 (16 April 1920),' p. 4, TNA 1733/1.

3 A thorough examination of the regional and Ukerewe literature would be necessary to establish whether this migration actually occurred. From a cursory examination of the literature on Ukerewe, I have found no more linguistic or cultural similarities than one might find with many other East African Bantu-speaking agricultural peoples.

4 Hichens, 'Mkalama Annual Report 1919/1920 (16 April 1920),' p. 4, TNA 1733/1. An unsigned entry in the Mkalama District Book made around 1926 notes: 'Tradition states unanimously that the tribe formerly inhabited Ukerewe Island, whence it migrated under stress of famine to the shores of Lake Eyassi [sic]. After a short stay there, it moved to its present location around Mkalama, which was found uninhabited' (p. 18). Adam reported in the 1960s that the migrants arrived to Ihanzu 'about 8 generations ago, after their journey from Ukerewe in Lake Victoria' (Virginia Adam 1961. 'Land Ownership and Local Descent Groups in Kirumi,' unpublished manuscript at the British Library of Political and Economic Science), p. 4a, doc. 1/15. Jellicoe noted in 1961 that, according to the Ihanzu chief, the Ihanzu arrived 'probably only about 100 years ago' (1961, 'Interim report on Isanzu,' p. 45, Rhodes House [hereafter RH], MSS. Afr. s. 2038 (4)). I would have thought that they lived in their present location much earlier than the 1860s.

5 Unlike some peoples in the region (e.g., Hartwig 1976, 18–24), the Ihanzu have no elaborate, memorized historical texts, nor any locally recognized 'professional historians' whose job it is to remember lengthy political and social narratives about the past. It is nevertheless possible to reconstruct a skeletal picture of the era immediately preceding colonial contact, for several reasons. First, elders have plenty to say about their past(s) through life histories, songs and stories, memories and myths. Second, there are plenty of colonial documents that can be critically read. The earliest of these comes from C.W. Werther (1894, 237–47; 1898). In 1911, a German scholar named Erich Obst spent four months in Ihanzu, and from this produced the most valuable early data available (Obst 1912a, 1912b, 1915, 1923; Reche 1914, 1915). I have examined German and British colonial records in the Tanzania National Archives, Dar es Salaam; and other colonial records at Rhodes House, Oxford, and the Public Record Office, London, including the

Mkalama and Singida District Books compiled by early British administrators. Missionary activities in the area were never vast, but there are a few useful works from the German Leipzig Lutheran Mission in Iramba (Ittameier 1912, 1922, 1922–3) which in 1928 became the American Augustana Lutheran Mission (Danielson 1957, 1977; Johnson 1923–6, 1931, 1934, 1948, 1951–2, 1954; Kidamala and Danielson 1961). Finally, the British social anthropologist Virginia Adam spent much of 1961 and 1962 in Ihanzu. Adam's study was broad ranging, the scholarship of the highest calibre. See Adam 1961, 1962, 1963a, 1963b, and her extensive collection of unpublished field notes and papers archived at the British Library of Political and Economic Science, London.

6 Wyatt, n.d., p. 6, 'Mkalama District Book,' School of Oriental and African Studies (hereafter SOAS); Hichens, 'Mkalama Annual Report 1919/1920 (16 April 1920),' TNA 1733/1; V. Adam 1963. 'Draft Report on Isanzu for Community Development Department of Tanzania,' p. 9, BLPES. The Maasai were troublesome not only for the Ihanzu, but for their southern and western Bantu-speaking neighbours as well: the Iramba (Danielson 1977, 18; Kidamala and Danielson 1961, 74–5; Peters 1891, 508–9), Turu (Jellicoe 1978, 92–3; Sick 1915, 29), Gogo (Obst 1923, 304), and Sukuma (Ashe 1883, in Millroth 1965, 15n; Itandala 1980, 9–13). See also Waller (1978). Informants claim that women and children were hidden in caves during raids, which explains why, when Werther visited Ihanzu in 1897, he never saw a woman (Werther 1898, 72).

7 M. Jellicoe 1961, 'Interim Report on Isanzu,' p. 45, RH MSS. Afr. s. 2038 (4); Wyatt, n.d., p. 6, 'Mkalama District Book,' SOAS.

8 M. Jellicoe 1961, 'Interim Report on Isanzu,' p. 45, RH MSS. Afr. s. 2038 (4); Wyatt, n.d., p. 6, 'Mkalama District Book,' SOAS.

9 Woodburn (1988a) downplays the significance of Ihanzu–Hadza traffic, especially denying the likelihood of any trade in ivory, which might imply dependence of the latter on the former (1988a, 52–3). Regardless of the relative importance – or lack of importance – of these trading links, their existence tells us little about possible dependency relations between trading partners.

10 These claims are well-established for the Turu, Iambi, and Iramba. The claim that Sukuma visited Kirumi in the 1890s is based on what informants told me and the nature of Sukuma society at the time. The fact that multiple, small-scale Sukuma communities had by the late nineteenth century developed across Sukumaland in which people relied heavily on ritual leaders (*ntemi*) to provide rain, coupled with the fact that these same leaders were increasingly being deposed, their ritual powers increasingly being

called into question, makes it plausible that some eastern Sukuma would have visited Kirumi in an effort to seek out legitimate rainmakers (see Holmes and Austen 1972, 386; Tanner 1957, 201; Sanders 2001b). Informants also say that Hadza visited the Kirumi rainshrine long ago, and it is certain that two Hadza men named Majui and Tawashi regularly visited Chief Omari in the 1950s (Woodburn 1979, 262n). Intriguingly, the Ihanzu claim that *all* Hadza are members of the royal *Anyampanda wa Kirumi* clan section, and James Woodburn (pers. comm.) informs me that, when asked by Ihanzu, they admit this is true, though relevant only for their occasional dealings with Ihanzu. Woodburn also claims that Hadza have no rainmaking institutions. Ihanzu men and women see the Hadza, like their own rainmakers, as 'owners of the land,' a status that would seem to derive from their hunting and gathering way of life.

11 Marguerite Jellicoe (1961) states that the Ihanzu 'took the leading part in driving Masai out of the District' ('Interim Report' p. 45, RH MSS. Afr. s. 2038 (4)). Werther noted that during his battle with the Ihanzu in 1893, medicine (*dawa*) was prepared and used against them to stop their bullets, though he does not provide any more precise information on the source of this protective medicine (Werther 1894, 241).

12 The role of the Ihanzu rainshrine and rainmakers is similar to the role played by other rainshrines and rainmakers in other parts of precolonial Africa (see Iliffe 1979, 28–30; Kimambo 1991, 30, 34; Lan 1985; O'Brien 1983; Swantz 1974, 75–82; Young and Fosbrooke 1960, 41–2).

13 Hichens, 'Mkalama Annual Report 1919/1920 (16 April 1920),' pp. 13–16, TNA 1733/1.

14 They hunted using bows and poisoned arrows, often in large groups. With the use of dogs, and by setting the bush ablaze, men flushed out animals, which they then killed. Elderly men often snared antelope, zebra, and small birds (Reche 1914, 71). Elders' stories make clear that Ihanzu hunters regularly ventured into surrounding areas, such as Iramba and Hadza country.

15 One early source reported that Ihanzu smiths, in addition to smithing, carried out a limited amount of smelting (Werther 1894, 238).

16 Virginia Adam 1961, 'Land Ownership and Local Descent Groups in Kirumi,' BLPES 1/15.

17 For a man killed, the guilty man's clan reportedly paid fifteen cows and thirty goats; for a woman killed, the bloodwealth was thirty cows and thirty goats, sometimes more (Reche 1914, 85).

18 Wyatt, n.d., p. 9, 'Mkalama District Book,' SOAS; Hichens, 'Mkalama Annual Report 1919/1920 (16 April 1920),' p. 7, TNA 1733/1; Bagshawe,

'Kondoa-Irangi Annual Report 1920/1921,' pp. 14–15, TNA 1733: 5; V. Adam 1963. 'Draft Report,' p. 9, BLPES.

19 The latter name is from oral sources.

20 If male leaders initiated boys' circumcisions, it was the male elders who were responsible for carrying them out. In some years several hundred boys attended. Circumcision took place just prior to the harvest, in May or June, and involved spending up to two months in the bush under the tutelage of elders (Reche 1914, 76). In the past, life histories make evident, Iramba and Iambi boys often participated in these Ihanzu circumcision rites (cf. Adam 1961, 2).

21 Hunting was sometimes done communally, by burning the bush (Reche 1914, 71). It appears that Semu had his own gun-wielding elephant hunters, the only men in Ihanzu to own guns (Werther 1894, 238, 242).

22 The Ihanzu salt trade was at one time considerable (cf. Kjekshus 1977, 94–6). Semu is said to have supplied protective medicines for salt fetching; together with Nya Matalū, he was also responsible for preparing medicines to ensure a large salt harvest each year. Salt fetching pilgrimages (*mūhīnzo wa buda*) followed the harvest in July each year. Led by a ritual guide (*mūkūlū a mūhīnzo*) whose job it was to ensure the group's welfare, stopping periodically to rest, and preparing special medicines to placate ancestral and other spirits, the salt pilgrims took a leisurely pace – anywhere from four to five days to arrive, fetch their salt, and return (see Senior 1938). Semu and Nya Matalū were always given some of the salt from each trip, though it appears from informants' statements that it was never much and was meant mainly for household consumption.

23 Wyatt wrote in the 1920s of precolonial Ihanzu 'chiefs': 'They appear to have derived their authority solely from their supposed powers as "rain makers."' Wyatt, n.d., p. 7, 'Mkalama District Book,' SOAS. While Wyatt is referring here to male 'chiefs,' the same was so for the female ones, too.

24 V. Adam 1963. 'Draft Report,' p. 9, BLPES.

25 This is not the place to re-examine early German colonial history in East Africa. Others have done this successfully and at great length. For a thorough and meticulously documented overview of local conflicts with German colonial forces, see Iliffe (1969, esp. 9–29; 1979, 88–122). Dundas (RH MSS Afr. s. 948) and Rodemann (1961, 33–70) offer some fascinating nuts-and-bolts details of encounters – including number of troops, artillery, locations, and so forth – though the former, regrettably, dispenses with all references to his primary source materials. Finally, Kjekshus's work deserves mention for its helpful list of eighty-four German–'native' conflicts between 1889 and 1905 (1977, 148–9). Details of battles between 1889 and

1896 are given, including dates and locations of battles, sometimes tribal leaders, destruction caused, and body counts (ibid., 186–90).

26 Dundas, 1914, 'History of Germans in East Africa, 1884–1910' (m.s.), pp. 34–5, RH MSS. Af. s. 948; I have seen what I presume is the same document cited in several places (e.g., Iliffe 1969, 215; Jellicoe 1978, 375) as a book published in 1923, though I have not managed to get my hands on a copy.

27 The Rangi of Kondoa rioted in 1895 and 1896 (Admiralty 1916, 82–3; Kesby 1981, 54); the Gorowa rebelled in 1896 (Admiralty 1916, 82–3). And as we shall see, the Ihanzu too, along with their immediate neighbours the Iramba and Iambi, proved unruly in the face of German military advances. Aggression against German forces was not always immediate. The Turu, for example, who had long been expecting the arrival of their legendary 'red men without toes,' offered no initial resistance to colonial forces whatever, as the German troops were said to fulfil their prophecy. The Germans were indeed red men, and with their boots on, as far as anyone could tell, had no toes (Jellicoe 1969). It was only with the realization that the Germans had come to stay – and to collect taxes, and remove and sometimes kill local leaders – that Turu began to cause problems for the colonial regime. The Germans soon appointed local Turu leaders (*jumbe*), whose responsibility it was to collect taxes. These leaders had little, if any, real authority and were often chased off by irate villagers who refused to pay taxes (Sick 1915, 60).

28 The most famous of these movements was the Maji-Maji rebellion (see Gwassa 1970; Iliffe 1967, 1969, 9–29).

29 Dundas, 1914, 'History,' pp. 34–5, RH MSS. Af. s. 948. One of the better-known leaders and rainmakers in Iramba, Kingo, apparently survived German rule by refusing to have anything to do with them. 'Kingo himself states that his attitude in this respect was one of divine instruction from the sungod Munankali' (Hichens, 'Mkalama Annual Report 1919/1920 [16 April 1920],' pp. 7–8, TNA 1733/1). It probably helped that, somewhat inexplicably, no German patrols were sent against him.

30 *Jumbe*, a term that is variously translated as 'chief' or 'headman,' were political agents employed under the German regime all across German East Africa.

31 Wyatt, n.d., p. 6, 'Mkalama District Book,' SOAS. I have found no additional written records on this *jumbe*, Mũgunda, who he was or why he was appointed in the first place. One of my best informants, without my asking, named Mũgunda as the first German-appointed leader of Ihanzu and claimed he was a local man from Tumbili village. He also noted adamantly that this man was not even of the royal rainmaking lineage. He could thus

never have been expected to command the respect and authority necessary 'to rule' Ihanzu as the Germans had hoped.

32 Wyatt, n.d., p. 6, 'Mkalama District Book,' SOAS.

33 Dundas, 1914, 'History,' p. 34, RH MSS. Af. s. 948.

34 Ibid., Hichens, 'Mkalama Annual Report 1919/1920,' p. 4, TNA 1733/1.

35 See note 33.

36 Lyons, n.d., Iramba (Kiomboi) 'District Book,' vol. I, RH Micro. Afr. 472, reel 22; Wyatt, n.d., pp. 6–7, 'Mkalama District Book,' SOAS. Lyons (n.d., p. 3, 'Mkalama District Book,' SOAS) says that one of his informants witnessed Kitentemi's hanging. One of my informants claimed that Kitentemi's two principal seers (*amanga*; sing., *mūmanga*), named Masilia and Mkiï, were taken to Kilimatinde with him (cf. Maddox 1988, 757–8).

37 Oberleutnant Ruff, 24 March 1910, 'Einsiedler Adolf Siedentopf,' TNA G55/27.

38 Resistance in the context of political action and nationalism has long played a pivotal role in historical studies of Tanzanian societies. Dar es Salaam historians first took up this topic in earnest in the 1960s (e.g. Gwassa 1969; 1970; Iliffe 1967; Ranger 1968a, 1968b).

39 Oberleutnant Ruff, 24 March 1910, 'Einsiedler Adolf Siedentopf,' TNA G55/27.

40 Erich Obst, a German geographer with a knack for ethnography, travelled through the region in 1911. He came across a large camp in Hadza country made up of about half Hadza, and half Ihanzu people, the latter living there 'to escape from the military station at Mkalama' (Obst 1915, 28; also 1912b, 5–6).

41 Hichens, 'Mkalama Annual Report 1919/1920 (16 April 1920),' p. 7, TNA 1733/1. See also Wyatt, n.d., p. 6, 'Mkalama District Book,' SOAS. Another early British administrator, Bagshawe, reported that the 'Germans recognised none of them [tribal leaders] and their influence, which remained nevertheless at full strength amongst the tribesmen, was a potential source of mischief' (Bagshawe, 'Kondoa-Irangi Annual Report 1920/1921,' pp. 14–15, TNA 1733, 5).

42 Bagshawe, 'Kondoa-Irangi Annual Report 1919/1920 (14 April 1920),' pp. 15–16, TNA 1733/1.

43 Bagshawe, 'Kondoa-Irangi Annual Report 1919/1920 (14 April 1920),' pp. 13–14, TNA 1733/1.

44 *Ndege* means 'bird' in Swahili, but not in the Ihanzu language.

45 Hichens, 'Mkalama Annual Report 1919/1920 (16 April 1920),' p. 8, TNA 1733/1. Nor, it appears, were these arrests arbitrary or for good measure alone: 'On the arrest of one of these jumbes above mentioned, more than

two hundred people presented charges of extortion against him; although his tribe was starving, he was found to have more than three thousand kilos of foodstuffs stored in his own house' (Hichens, 'Mkalama Annual Report 1919/1920 [16 April 1920],' p. 10, TNA 1733/1).

46 Ibid., pp. 8–9, TNA 1733/1.
47 F.J. Bagshawe, 'Annual Report, Kondoa Irangi, 1920/1921,' pp. 14–15, TNA 1733, 5.
48 Finding chiefs and establishing chiefdoms does not necessarily mean inventing them from thin air, though the debate is sometimes framed in this way (e.g., Graham 1976; Iliffe 1979, 318; Beidelman 1978; Cohen and Odhiambo 1989, 25ff; Jackson and Maddox 1993; Lonsdale 1977; Ranger 1983; Vail 1989). In many instances, precolonial identities, including 'chiefs,' were already there (Atkinson 1994; Bank 1995; Greene 1996; Ranger 1993; Roosens 1994; Willis 1992). The Ihanzu case falls somewhere in between, in that the (male) rainmaker provided a plausible local model for the 'invention' of a chiefship. Such inventions are a matter of degree, not kind, and must be based on empirical demonstration, not theoretical presupposition.
49 Hichens, 'Mkalama Annual Report 1919/1920 (16 April 1920),' p. 10, TNA 1733/1.
50 Singida District Officer, 'Singida Annual Report 1927,' pp. 8–10, TNA 967, 823.
51 Ibid., p. 12. Chief Sagilŭ is also occasionally referred to as Mpĭlolo.
52 Administrators had seen the alleged benefits that a 'progressive' chief could bring to his 'tribe' – education, religion, effective legal courts, civilization – as Chief Mgeni of the Turu had aptly demonstrated during his reign (1924–39) as Paramount Chief of Turu. In fact, Chief Mgeni was reckoned by the District Commissioner to 'rank amongst the best chiefs in Tanganyika' (Jellicoe 1978, 103–4; also Iliffe 1979, 327). It was in the face of Mgeni's chiefly model that administrators were filled with lofty aspirations for Sagilŭ's progressive potential as the deliverer of his people from a supposed primitive past and into the 'modern' world.
53 See note 51, p. 12.
54 Ibid.
55 Lyons, March 1928, 'Iramba (Kiomboi) District Book,' vol. I, RH Micro. Afr. 472, reel 22.
56 Virginia Adam, 'Field notes' (July 1963), pp. 19–21, BLPES 1/10.
57 As for the rest, around 18 per cent self-identify as Christian (1 per cent Catholic and 17 per cent Lutheran), and 2 per cent as Muslim.
58 Although this was an unusual transfer of power, it remained within the royal matrilineage. From the information I have, there are no indications

that this transfer caused any problems beyond some initial confusion, after which time people readily agreed that if a chief were to carry out administrative duties, as well as rainmaking ones, he must be competent in both.

59 Nkili was Omari's mother's sister, as the royal kinship diagram shows, though in Ihanzu kinship reckoning, she is his 'mother.' I follow local convention here and speak, as do locals, of Nkili as Omari's mother.

60 M. Jellicoe, 'Field notes' (April/May 1961). Archived with Virginia Adam's documents at BLPES.

61 For a compelling account of the advent and eventual victory of TANU, see Iliffe (1979, 485–576).

62 Abrahams (1981) provides an analysis of this transition period focusing on the Nyamwezi.

63 Many today also recall that Americans donated bright yellow maize that, when ground and cooked, made bizarre-looking stiff porridge; and that President Kennedy, under whom this aid was dispensed, was a great man.

64 For some excellent overviews of Tanzania's *ujamaa* policy, see Abrahams (1981, 54–89; 1985), and Coulson (1982, 235–62).

65 Two additional *ujamaa* villages came into existence in the late 1970s.

66 Lwoga (1985) discusses similar disputes that took place in the 1970s surrounding Bigwa village, near Morogoro town, on the lower slopes of the Uluguru Mountains. There, too, villagers eventually won and kept their village. His concerns are different to mine, and he thus pays little attention to the logic behind villagers' protest; when he does, he cites mainly the potential loss of fertile soils as the cause for concern. Such an explanation does not work in the Ihanzu case, since the Kirumi area is commonly acknowledged to be the least fertile in Ihanzu, having been farmed the longest. The locations to which people were supposed to relocate were said to be more fertile, without question.

Chapter 3: Gendered Life-Worlds and Transformative Processes

1 The term *mūlongo* is widely used by Bantu-language speakers across Tanzania and has meanings as varied as its geographical distribution. In all cases the term appears to be associated with patrilineages (Beidelman 1971, 386–7; 1974, 284), with patriclans (Rigby 1969, 81–7), or with the father's matriclan (Lindström 1987, 59–60, 66–8, 191–2). Milongo 'groups' in most societies do not function as collective or corporate entities.

2 A few people I know discussed fertilizing fluids in terms of eggs (*majī*), though this seemed to reflect their training in Western medicine (these

informants were nurses) rather than their fluency in a popular or widely used idiom. Nor would eggs provide a particularly convincing way to imagine procreation: eggs are said to cause infertility (Virginia Adam and Marguerite Jellicoe, n.d. [c. 1961], 'Notes on the Position of Women and Children in Isanzu, Iramba District, Tanganyika.' RH MSS. Afr. s. 2038 [4]). Since Ihanzu male and female seeds are the same, gendered though they may be, there is no notion of seed:male::soil:female as is found among the neighbouring Sukuma (Brandström 1990, 1991) and elsewhere (Ngubane 1976, 275; see also Delaney 1991).

3 There is marked variation among other Tanzanian groups with matrilineal groupings. The Kaguru and Ngulu, for instance, both claim that blood flows in the matriclan (Beidelman 1963a, 328; 1964, 361). Additionally, for the Kaguru, bone, teeth, cartilage, and other solid parts come from a child's father; while soft bits including flesh and blood come from the mother (Beidelman 1973, 136). The Iramba stand this on end, claiming that a child's permanent attributes, such as bones, come from the mother; whereas those less durable body parts, such as flesh and blood, come from the father (Lindström 1987, 57).

4 The Ihanzu do not stand alone in their funerary emphasis on parents. Among the Tanzanian Kaguru, 'both [father's and mother's] sides should contribute the burial cloth (sanda, nursing cloth, womb), thereby not only expressing the past contribution of both the mother and the father in creating the person, but signaling their accord in reaching final disposition of their relations to the dead' (Beidelman 1993, 44).

5 Nor would biological parents (except in the case of infants) ever play the 'parent' roles in funerals. People say they would be too distraught to function properly.

6 Virginia Adam 1962, 'Funerals, Nkangala, Feb. 1962,' in file 1/16, 'Ritual,' BLPES.

7 Gendered rainstones are found widely across Africa (Avua 1968, 29; Cooke and Beaton 1939, 182; Hartnoll 1932, 738; James 1972, 38; Middleton 1971, 196; Packard 1981, 69; Rogers 1927; Williams 1949). The significance of this fact may lie, as in Ihanzu, in the power generated from their combination.

8 Gendered rains and meteorological conditions are common in Africa. See Marshall (1957, 232); Bleek (1933, 308–10).

9 See also Adam, 'Fieldnotes I' (November 1962), p. 21, in file 1/10, BLPES.

10 This gender imagery is strikingly similar to that of a few Southern African groups. Bleek (1933, 308–10) transcribes a /Xam tale: 'You must not arouse a rain-bull, but you must make a she-rain, which is not angry, which rains

gently, because it is a slow shower. It is one that falls gently, softening the ground, so that it may be wet inside the earth. For people are afraid of a he-rain, when they hear it come thundering, as it gets its legs' (see esp. 306–10). Among the !Kung, 'rain itself [like clouds] is male and female ... Male rain breaks the trees and beats down the fruits, the men told us. It is [like] a fight, and may kill a person. Thunder and lightning accompany it, and sometimes hail. Female rain has tiny drops and does not spoil anything; it beautifies the trees and the grass and makes the veldkos grow' (Marshall 1957, 232). Though it is unclear whether the Tswana speak about male and female rains as such, they do associate the sacrifice of female animals with 'soft steady rain (*medupe*) coming from the east without thunder or light-ning' and the sacrifice of a male one with '"strong rain" (*makgomara*) from the north-west' (Schapera 1971, 71). For the Sudanese Uduk, 'the female [rain]stones, in particular, are said to bring steady, gentle rain, and the males to cause dangerous storms' (James 1972, 38).

11 I have not found any Ihanzu stories or myths recounting The Creation. Sev-eral other Bantu-speaking groups in the area – the Luguru (Brain 1983, 18), Rangi (Kesby 1981, 91; 1982, 150–1), Sukuma (Tanner 1956, 46–7), and Gogo (Rigby, personal communication in Kesby 1982, 151) – in a similar vein, have no creation myth. The Iramba, Pender-Cudlip notes, 'regard it as absurd that any man should pretend or expect to know how the human race began' (Pender-Cudlip 1974, 64; also c. 1974, 6–7).

Chapter 4: Annual Rain Rites

1 No rain rites are conducted on Ihanzu's borders, as sometimes happens with similar rites in other parts of Tanzania (see Snyder 1997; Thornton 1982; Fosbrooke 1958; Rigby 1968).

2 See also Wyatt, n.d. (1928?), 'Mkalama: The Back of Beyond,' RH MSS Afr. s. 272.

3 In practice, of course, things are not so simple. For one, the Christian minority frequently refuse to pay grain tribute; also, since some villages are large, and rainmaking assistants are elderly and few, it is impossible to col-lect grain from every homestead.

4 Wyatt, n.d. (1928?), 'Mkalama: The Back of Beyond,' p. 2, RH MSS Afr. s. 272.

Chapter 5: (Wo)men Behaving Badly: Genders within Bodies

1 There are probably two reasons why Swazi *ncwala* rites have been widely

scrutinized while the Zulu women's rites have not (e.g., Apter 1983; Beidelman 1966; Kuper 1972; Lincoln 1987; Makarius 1973). This has to do, first, with the richness of Hilda Kuper's original data on the *ncwala* on which these analyses, Gluckman's included, are based (Kuper 1947, also 1973). Second, Gluckman's own problematic was to explain why such rites did not fundamentally challenge the status quo and thus lead to political revolutions. For this, exploring *ncwala* ceremonies rather than women's rites is perhaps more relevant – or at least this is what the weight of his analysis seems to imply.

2 Harrison (1985) and Hill (1984) provide cases in Melanesia and Venezuela respectively that offer precisely the opposite of this proposition, but that nonetheless maintain the secular–sacred dichotomy. All of these works, but especially Gluckman's, resonate strongly with Victor Turner's work on structure and anti-structure (Turner 1969).

3 Gluckman's argument has been repeatedly challenged and criticized on theoretical, logical, and ethnographic grounds (Norbeck 1963; Krige 1968, 184; Rigby 1968).

4 During menstruation, women may farm, cook, and mind the children and house as usual. They are never confined during menstruation, and menstrual blood itself is, in mundane contexts, unthreatening. It can, however, allegedly be used by witches to make the woman from whom it came infertile.

5 I attended both the 1994 and 1995 dances. The rites and the sequence of events were nearly identical in both years.

6 It is the caves that are of primary importance for these offerings, not the drums.

7 The prominence of obscene songs in various fertility and other rites has been noted across Africa. See, for example Beidelman (1964, 382–4; 1973, 137–9); Krige (1968); and Evans-Pritchard (1929).

8 Virginia Adam, 'Rainmaking 1962 Kirumi,' p. 7, in '1961–1963 Diaries and Other Field Materials,' File 1/29 BLPES.

9 Schoeman was given an identical explanation for Swazi rainmaking rites, though he failed to make any sense of it. In a footnote he writes: 'On asking my informants why females play such an important part in the rain-ceremonies, one of them ... answered: [...] it is done for the sake of the earth, so that the rain clouds will gather, and get soft, i.e., rainy, because it is a female person, and she (a female) is wet (has a uterus). When I asked him to explain what he meant [...] he just shrugged his shoulders and walked off' (Schoeman 1935: 172n). I would have thought his informant's comments were fairly self-explanatory.

10 Menstrual blood is not spoken of as 'wet,' nor is it associated with fertility as is water.

11 None of this is to deny that in many African societies it is men, not women, who control vital economic, political, legal, and symbolic resources. I only wish to imply that the complexities of people's ideas about gender and gender behaviours in ritual and everyday contexts have not always been fully appreciated. In this respect, more subtle explorations of African gender epistemologies are long overdue.

Chapter 6: Ancestral Rain Offerings: Genders without Bodies

1 Diviners commonly visit other diviners to diagnose communal and personal problems. People say this is because, as the saying goes, 'a doctor cannot treat himself' (*ūsūnswī shanga wīnunaa*). Ideally, I was often told, diviners should be unaware of the issues at hand so that they can establish their credibility and mystical merit through divination.

2 For an overview of some of these works and debates, see Morris (1995).

3 For a description of a very similar ancestral offering to heal cattle (*ipolyo la ndwala*), see Sanders (1999).

4 One grandson and the granddaughter were themselves members of the royal clan section, while the other grandson was an Anyansuli clan member. For royal offerings, this is the usual division: at least one grandchild of the royal clan section who is also a member of that section; and one Anyansuli clan member.

5 I have attended a total of nineteen similar offerings at homes and at clan sites around Ihanzu and Iramba, most of them for personal afflictions. I recorded the details of many more offerings and have had many discussions with men and women about the varied rites and their significance. The offering outlined here is typical of Ihanzu ancestral offerings in general. Interestingly, when Erich Obst visited Ihanzu in 1911, he attended an ancestral offering to cure his malaria. His exceedingly detailed observations are by all measures accurate and make clear that, as far as these particular rites go, things have changed little since the turn of the last century (Obst 1912a, 115–17; 1923, 221–2; also Adam 1963b).

6 I attended three other offerings for personal afflictions at this site, and at all of them people sat in these relative positions. Not all clan sites, given their variability, offer the same topological possibilities – some sites, for instance, are flat – but of those that had a decline, for all the offerings I attended, men invariably sat above women. Obst (1912a, 116n) stated clearly that men and women sat separately during ancestral offerings.

7 Before Islam reached Ihanzu, sacrificial animals were suffocated to death (Obst 1912a: 116). Slitting their throats is a relatively recent ritual innovation that probably began either in the late 1930s under Chief Sagilū, the first Muslim Ihanzu chief, or in the 1940s under Chief Gunda, who was also a Muslim. Everyone I spoke with claimed that Islam and their 'traditional' religious practices are perfectly compatible.

8 The events recounted on the final day are not from this offering, but another royal offering, to cure dying cattle, that took place earlier in the year. Of all the offerings I attended, this was the only time the final day was omitted. This was because the male rainmaker, who likes his beer more than most, was keen to attend a beer party in a distant village. This significant ritual omission later returned to haunt him, when people began saying he had ruined the ritual and hence the rain by not completing it properly.

9 As Beidelman notes of another Tanzanian group: 'For Kaguru, kindling a fire clearly alludes to sexual intercourse. In making fire with firesticks, Kaguru use an active stick of hardwood and a passive stick of soft and easily combustible wood. The passive stick, the one drilled, is the female' (Beidelman 1997, 205). In spite of the manifest similarities with the Ihanzu, it appears that the Kaguru construct firemaking as a domain that implies male domination (Beidelman 1997, 205).

References

Abrahams, Ray G. 1981. *The Nyamwezi Today: A Tanzanian People in the 1970s*. Cambridge: Cambridge University Press.

Adam, Virginia. 1961. Preliminary Report on Fieldwork in Isanzu. Conference Proceedings from the East African Institute of Social Research, Makerere College.

– 1962. Social Composition of Isanzu Villages. Conference Proceedings from the East African Institute of Social Research, Makerere College.

– 1963a. Migrant Labour from Ihanzu. Conference Proceedings from the East African Institute of Social Research, Makerere College.

– 1963b. Rain Making Rites in Ihanzu. Conference Proceedings from the East African Institute of Social Research, Makerere College.

Admiralty War Staff (Intelligence Division). 1916. *A Handbook of German East Africa*. London: H.M.S.O.

Africa Development Bank. 2000. *African Development Report 2000*. New York: Oxford University Press (for the African Development Bank).

Agbasiere, Joseph Thérèse. 2000. *Women in Igbo Life and Thought*. London: Routledge.

Alpers, E.A. 1969. The Coast and the Development of the Caravan Trade. In *A History of Tanzania*, ed. I.N. Kimambo and A.J. Temu. Nairobi: East African Publishing House.

Amadiume, Ifi. 1987. *Male Daughters, Female Husbands: Gender and Sex in an African Society*. London: Zed Books.

– 1997. *Reinventing Africa: Matriarchy, Religion and Culture*. London: Zed Books.

Ampofo, Akosua Adomako, Josephine Beoku-Betts, Wairimu Ngaruiya Njambi, and Mary Osirim. 2004. Women's and Gender Studies in English-Speaking Sub-Saharan Africa: A Review of Research in the Social Sciences. *Gender and Society* 18 (6): 685–714.

Apter, Andrew. 1983. In Dispraising of the King: Rituals against Rebellion in South-East Africa. *Man* 18:521–34.

Archetti, Eduardo P. 1996. Playing Styles and Masculine Virtues in Argentine Football. In *Machos, Mistresses, Madonnas: Contesting the Power of Latin American Gender Imagery,* ed. Marit Melhuus and Kristi Anne Stølen, 34–55. London: Verso.

Århem, Kaj. 1985. The Symbolic World of the Maasai Homestead. *Working Papers in African Studies* 10: African Studies Programme, University of Uppsala.

– 1991. The Symbolic World of the Maasai Homestead. In *Body and Space: Symbolic Models of Unity and Division in African Cosmology and Experience,* ed. Anita Jacobson-Widding, 51–80. Uppsala: Almqvist and Wiksell International.

Amfred, Signe. 2002. Simone De Beauvoir in Africa: 'Women = the Second Sex?' Issues of African Feminist thought. *Jenda: A Journal of Culture and African Women Studies* 2 (1). Available online at: http://www.jendajournal.com/vo2.1/arnfred.html (accessed 13 April 2007).

– ed. 2004. *Re-thinking Sexualities in Africa.* Uppsala: Nordiska Afrikainstitutet.

Atkinson, R.R. 1994. *The Roots of Ethnicity: The Origins of the Acholi of Uganda before 1800.* Philadelphia: University of Pennsyslvania Press.

Avua, L. 1968. Droughtmaking among the Lugbara. *Uganda Journal* 32 (1): 29–38.

Bank, L. 1995. The Failure of Ethnic Nationalism: Land, Power and the Politics of Clanship on the South African Highveld, 1860–1990. *Africa* 65:565–91.

Bastian, Misty L. 2000. Young Converts: Gender and Youth in Onitsha, Nigeria 1880–1929. *Anthropological Quarterly* 73 (3): 145–58.

– 2003. 'Diabolic Realities': Narratives of Conspiracy, Transparency and 'Ritual Murder' in the Nigerian Popular Print and Electronic Media. In *Transparency and Conspiracy,* ed. Harry G. West and Todd Sanders. Durham, NC: Duke University Press.

Beidelman, Thomas O. 1963a. The Blood Covenant and the Concept of Blood in Ukaguru. *Africa* 33:321–42.

– 1963b. Witchcraft in Ukaguru. In *Witchcraft and Sorcery in East Africa,* ed. John Middleton and E. Winter, 57–98. London: Routledge and Kegan Paul.

– 1964. Pig (*Guluwe*): An Essay on Ngulu Sexual Symbolism and Ceremony. *Southwestern Journal of Anthropology* 20:359–92.

– 1966. Swazi Royal Ritual. *Africa* 36:373–405.

– 1971. Kaguru Descent Groups (East-Central Tanzania). *Anthropos* 66:373–96.

– 1973. Kaguru Symbolic Classification. In *Right and Left: Essays on Dual Symbolic Classification,* ed. Rodney Needham, 128–66. Chicago: University of Chicago Press.

– 1974. Kaguru Names and Naming. *Journal of Anthropological Research* 30: 281–93.
– 1978. Chiefship in Ukaguru: The Invention of Ethnicity and Tradition in Kaguru Colonial History. *International Journal of African Historical Studies* 11:227–46.
– 1993. *Moral Imagination in Kaguru Modes of Thought.* Washington: Smithsonian Institution Press.
– 1997. *The Cool Knife: Imagery of Gender, Sexuality, and Moral Education in Kaguru Initiation Ritual.* Washington, DC: Smithsonian Institution Press.
Berger, Iris, and E. Frances White. 1999. *Women in Sub-Saharan Africa: Restoring Women to History.* Bloomington: Indiana University Press.
Berglund, Axel-Ivar. 1976. *Zulu Thought-Patterns and Symbolism.* London: Hurst and Company.
Blacking, John. 1977. *The Anthropology of the Body.* New York: Academic Press.
Bleek, D.F. 1933. Beliefs and Customs of the /Xam Bushman, Part 5: The Rain. *Bantu Studies* 7:297–312.
Bloch, Maurice. 1987. Descent and Sources of Contradiction in Representations of Women and Kinship. In *Gender and Kinship: Essays toward a Unified Analysis*, ed. Jane Fishburne Collier and Sylvia Junko Yanagisako, 324–37. Stanford: Stanford University Press.
Blystad, Astrid. 1999. Dealing with Men's Spears: Datooga Pastoralists Combating Male Intrusion on Female Fertility. In *Those Who Play with Fire: Gender, Fertility and Transformation in East and Southern Africa*, ed. Henrietta L. Moore, Todd Sanders, and Bwire Kaare, 187–223. London: Athlone.
Boddy, Janice. 1989. *Wombs and Alien Spirits: Women, Men and the Zar Cult in Northern Sudan.* Madison: University of Wisconsin Press.
Boris, Eileen 2007. Gender After Africa! In *Africa After Gender?* ed. Catherine Cole, Takyiwaa Manuh, and Stephan F. Miescher. Bloomington: Indiana University Press.
Bourdieu, Pierre. 1977. *Outline of a Theory of Practice.* Cambridge: Cambridge University Press.
– 1990. *The Logic of Practice.* Stanford: Stanford University Press.
– 2001. *Masculine Domination.* Cambridge: Polity Press.
Brain, James L. 1983. Basic Concepts of Life According to the Luguru of Eastern Tanzania. *Ultimate Reality and Meaning* 6:4–21.
Brandström, Per. 1990. Seeds and Soil: The Quest for Life and the Domestication of Fertility in Sukuma-Nyamwezi Thought and Reality. In *The Creative Communion: African Folk Models of Fertility and the Regeneration of Life*, ed. Anita Jacobson-Widding and Walter van Beek, 167–86. Uppsala: Acta Universitatis Upsaliensis.

– 1991. Left-Hand Father and Right-Hand Mother: Unity and Diversity in Sukuma-Nyamwezi Thought. In *Body and Space: Symbolic Models of Unity and Division in African Cosmology and Experience*, ed. A. Jacobson-Widding. Uppsala: Acta Universitatis Upsaliensis.

Broch-Due, Vigdis. 1993. Making Meaning out of Matter: Perceptions of Sex, Gender and Bodies among the Turkana. In *Carved Flesh, Cast Selves: Gendered Symbols and Social Practices*, ed. Vigdis Broch-Due, Ingrid Rudie, and Tone Bleie, 53–82. Oxford: Berg.

Brooke, C. 1967. The Heritage of Famine in Central Tanzania. *Tanzania Notes and Records* 67:15–22.

Busby, Cecilia. 2000. *The Performance of Gender: An Anthropology of Everyday Life in a South Indian Fishing Village*. Athlone: London.

Butchart, Alexander. 1998. *The Anatomy of Power: European Constructions of the African Body*. London: Zed.

Butler, Judith. 1990. *Gender Trouble: Feminism and the Subversion of Identity*. London: Routledge.

– 1993. *Bodies That Matter: On the Discursive Limits of 'Sex.'* London: Routledge.

Buxton, Jean. 1963. Mandari Witchcraft. In *Witchcraft and Sorcery in East Africa*, ed. J. Middleton and E.H. Winter. London: Routledge and Kegan Paul.

Campbell, A.C. 1968. Some Notes on Ngwaketse Divination. *Botswana Notes and Records* 1:9–13.

Caplan, Pat. 1989. Perceptions of Gender Stratification. *Africa* 59:196–208.

– ed. 1987. *The Cultural Construction of Sexuality*. London: Tavistock.

Capron, J. 1965. Univers religieux et cohesion interne dans les communautés villageoises Bwa traditionnelles. In *African Systems of Thought*, ed. Meyer Fortes and G. Dieterlen, 291–313. London: Oxford University Press.

Carnell, W.J. 1955. Sympathetic Magic among the Gogo of Mpwapwa District. *Tanganyika Notes and Records* 39:25–38.

Cliggett, Lisa. 2005. *Grains for Grass: Aging, Gender, and Famine in Rural Africa*. Ithaca: Cornell University Press.

Cohen, D.W., and E.S. Atieno Odhiambo. 1989. *Siaya: The Historical Anthropology of an African Landscape*. Nairobi: Heinemann Kenya.

Cole, Catherine M., Takyiwaa Manuh, and Stephen F. Miescher, eds. 2007. *Africa after Gender?* Bloomington: Indiana University Press.

Colson, Elizabeth. 1961. Plateau Tonga. In *Matrilineal Kinship*, ed. David M. Schneider and Kathleen Gough. Berkeley and Los Angeles: University of California Press.

Comaroff, Jean. 1985. *Body of Power, Spirit of Resistance: The Culture and History of a South African People*. Chicago: University of Chicago Press.

Comaroff, Jean, and John L. Comaroff, ed. 1993. *Modernity and Its Malcontents:*

Ritual and Power in Postcolonial Africa. Chicago: University of Chicago Press.

Cooke, R.C., and A.C. Beaton. 1939. Bari Rain Cults: Fur Rain Cults and Ceremonies. *Sudan Notes and Records* 22:181–203.

Cory, Hans. 1944. Sukuma Twin Ceremonies – *Mabasa*. *Tanganyika Notes and Records* 17:34–43.

– 1951. *The Ntemi: The Traditional Rites in Connection with the Burial, Election, Enthronement and Magic Powers of a Sukuma Chief*. London: Macmillan.

Coulson, A. 1982. *Tanzania: A Political Economy*. Oxford: Clarendon.

Crehan, K. 1997. *The Fractured Community: Landscapes of Power and Gender in Rural Zambia*. Berkeley and Los Angeles: University of California Press.

Creider, Jane Tapsubei, and Chet A. Creider. 1997. Gender Inversion in Nandi Ritual. *Anthropos* 92:51–8.

Culwick, A.T. 1931. Some Rock-Paintings in Central Tanganyika. *Journal of the Royal Anthropological Institute* 61:443–53.

Danielson, E.R. 1957. Proverbs of the Waniramba People of East Africa. *Tanganyika Notes and Records* 47–8:187–97.

– 1977. *Forty Years with Christ in Tanzania, 1928–1968*. New York: World Mission Interpretation (Lutheran Church in America).

Declich, Francesca. 2000. Fostering Ethnic Reinvention: Gender Impact of Forced Migration on Bantu Somali Refugees in Kenya. *Cahiers d'études africaines* 157 (40/1): 25–53.

Delaney, C. 1991. *The Seed and the Soil: Gender and Cosmology in Turkish Village Society*. Berkeley and Los Angeles: University of California Press.

Deutches Kolonialblatt. 1901. Vol. 12, no. 24, 15 December.

– 1902. Vol. 13, no. 23, 1 December.

– 1903. Vol. 14, no. 18, 15 September.

Devisch, René. 1991. Symbol and Symptom among the Yaka of Zaire. In *Body and Space: Symbolic Models of Unity and Division in African Cosmology and Experience*, ed. A. Jacobson-Widding. Uppsala: Acta Universitatis Upsaliensis.

– 1993. *Weaving the Threads of Life: The Khita Gyn-Eco-Logical Healing Cult among the Yaka*. Chicago: University of Chicago Press.

Dieterlen, Germaine. 1965. L'initiation chez les pasteurs peul (Afrique occidentale). In *African Systems of Thought*, ed. Meyer Fortes and Germaine Dieterlen, 314–27. London: Oxford University Press.

Douglas, Mary. 1969. Is Matriliny Doomed in Africa? In *Man in Africa*, ed. Mary Douglas and Phyllis M. Kaberry, 121–35. London: Tavistock.

– 1982 [1970]. *Natural Symbols: Explorations in Cosmology*. New York: Pantheon Books.

Eiselen, W.M. 1928. Die eintlike reëndiens van die baPedi. *South African Journal of Science* 25:387–92.

– 1932. The Art of Divination as Practiced by the Bamasemola. *Bantu Studies* 6:1–29.

Emanatian, M. 1996. Everyday Metaphors of Lust and Sex in Chagga. *Ethos* 24:195–236.

Errington, Shelly. 1990. Recasting Sex, Gender, and Power. In *Power and Difference: Gender in Island Southeast Asia*, ed. Jane Monnig Atkinson and Shelly Errington. Stanford: Stanford University Press.

Evans-Pritchard, E.E. 1929. Some Collective Expressions of Obscenity in Africa. *Journal of the Royal Anthropological Institute* 59:311–31.

– 1937. *Witchcraft, Oracles, and Magic among the Azande*. Oxford: Clarendon.

– 1940. *The Nuer: A Description of the Modes of Livelihood and Political Institutions of a Nilotic People*. Oxford: Clarendon.

– 1951. *Kinship and Marriage among the Nuer*. London: Oxford University Press.

– 1970. Sexual Inversion among the Azande. *American Anthropologist* 72: 1428–34.

Feddema, J.P. 1966. Tswana Ritual Concerning Rain. *African Studies* 25:181–95.

Feierman, Steven. 1990. *Peasant Intellectuals: Anthropology and History in Tanzania*. Madison: University of Wisconsin Press.

Feldman-Savelsberg, Pamela. 1994. Plundered Kitchens and Empty Wombs: Fear of Infertility in the Cameroonian Grassfields. *Social Science and Medicine* 39:463–74.

– 1999. *Plundered Kitchens, Empty Wombs: Threatened Reproduction and Identity in the Cameroon Grassfields*. Ann Arbor: University of Michigan Press.

Forde, Daryll, ed. 1991 [1954]. *African Worlds: Studies in the Cosmological Ideas and Social Values of African Peoples*. London: Oxford University Press.

Fosbrooke, H.A. 1958. Blessing the Year: A Wasi/Rangi Ceremony. *Tanganyika Notes and Records* 50:21–29.

Foucault, M., ed. 1972. *Power/Knowledge: Selected Interviews and Other Writings, 1972–1977*. New York: Pantheon.

– 1973. *The Order of Things: An Archaeology of the Human Sciences*. New York: Vintage.

Gausset, Q. 2002. The Cognitive Rationality of Taboos on Production and Reproduction in Sub-Saharan Africa. *Africa* 72 (4): 628–54.

Geiger, Susan. 1997. *Tanu Women: Gender and Culture in the Making of Tanganyikan Nationalism, 1955–1965*. Oxford: James Currey.

Geschiere, Peter. 1997. *The Modernity of Witchcraft: Politics and the Occult in Postcolonial Africa*. Charlottesville: University Press of Virginia.

Geurts, Kathryn Linn. 2002. *Culture and the Senses: Bodily Ways of Knowing in an African Community.* Berkeley and Los Angeles: University of California Press.

Ginindza, T. 1997. Labotsibeni/Gwamile Mduli: The Power behind the Swazi Throne 1875–1925. In *Queens, Queen Mothers, Priestesses, and Power: Case Studies in African Gender,* ed. F.E.S. Kaplan, 135–58. New York: New York Academy of Sciences.

Gluckman, Max. 1956. The Licence of Ritual. In *Custom and Conflict in Africa,* 109–36. Oxford: Basil Blackwell.

– 1963. Rituals of Rebellion in South-East Africa. In *Order and Rebellion in Tribal Africa,* 110–36. London: Cohen and West.

Goheen, Miriam. 1996. *Men Own the Fields, Women Own the Crops: Gender and Power in the Cameroon Grassfields.* Madison: University of Wisconsin Press.

Graham, J.D. 1976. Indirect Rule: The Establishment of 'Chiefs' and 'Tribes' in Cameron's Tanganyika. *Tanzania Notes and Records* 77–78:1–9.

Gray, Robert F. 1955. The Mbugwe Tribe: Origin and Development. *Tanganyika Notes and Records* 38:39–50.

– 1963. Some Structural Aspects of Mbugwe Witchcraft. In *Witchcraft and Sorcery in East Africa,* ed. J. Middleton and E.H. Winter, 143–73. London: Routledge and Kegan Paul.

Green, Maia. 1996. Medicines and the Embodiment of Substances among Pogoro Catholics, Southern Tanzania. *Journal of the Royal Anthropological Institute* 2 (3): 485–98.

– 1999. Women's Work Is Weeping: Constructions of Gender in a Catholic Community. In *Those Who Play with Fire: Gender, Fertility and Transformation in East and Southern Africa,* ed. Henrietta L. Moore, Todd Sanders, and Bwire Kaare. London: Athlone.

– 2003. *Priests, Witches and Power: Popular Christianity after Mission in Southern Tanzania.* Cambridge: Cambridge University Press.

Greene, S.E. 1996. *Gender, Ethnicity, and Social Change on the Upper Slave Coast: A History of the Anlo-Ewe.* London: James Currey.

Grosz-Ngaté, Maria. 1997. Introduction. In *Gendered Encounters: Challenging Cultural Boundaries and Social Hierarchies in Africa,* ed. Maria Grosz-Ngaté and Omari H. Kokole, 1–21. London: Routledge.

Gupta, Akhil, and James Ferguson. 1992. Beyond 'Culture': Space, Identity, and the Politics of Difference. *Cultural Anthropology* 7 (1): 6–23.

Gutmann, M.C. 1997. Trafficking in Men: The Anthropology of Masculinity. *Annual Review of Anthropology* 26:385–409.

Gwassa, G.C.K. 1969. The German Intervention and African Resistance in Tanzania. In *A History of Tanzania,* ed. I.N. Kimambo and A.J. Temu. Nairobi: East African Publishing House.

– 1970. The Outbreak and Development of the Maji Maji War, 1905–1907. PhD thesis, University of Dar es Salaam.

Hacking, Ian. 1982. Language, Truth and Reason. In *Rationality and Relativism*, ed. Martin Hollis and Steven Lukes. Oxford: Blackwell.

Håkansson, N. Thomas. 1998. Rulers and Rainmakers in Precolonial South Pare, Tanzania: Exchange and Ritual Experts in Political Centralization. *Ethnology* 37 (3): 263–83.

Hammond-Tooke, W.D. 1974. World-View. In *The Bantu-Speaking Peoples of Southern Africa*, ed. W.D. Hammond-Tooke. London: Routledge and Kegan Paul.

Handelman, Don, and Galina Lindquist, ed. 2005. *Ritual in Its Own Right: Exploring the Dynamics of Transformation*. New York: Berghahn.

Harrison, Simon. 1985. Ritual Hierarchy and Secular Equality in a Sepik River Village. *American Ethnologist* 12:413–26.

Hartnoll, A.V. 1932. The Gogo Mtemi. *South African Journal of Science* 29:737–41.

– 1942. Praying for Rain in Ugogo. *Tanganyika Notes and Records* 13:59–60.

Hartwig, G.W. 1976. *The Art of Survival in East Africa: The Kerebe and Long-Distance Trade, 1800–1895*. New York: Africana Publishing House.

Hassin, Shireen. 2003. The Gender Pact and Democratic Consolidation: Institutionalizing Gender Equality in the South African State. *Feminist Studies* 29 (3): 505–28.

Hastrup, Kirsten. 1993. The Native Voice – and the Anthropological Vision. *Social Anthropology* 1 (2): 173–86.

– 2004. Getting It Right: Knowledge and Evidence in Anthropology. *Anthropological Theory* 4 (4): 455–72.

Hatley, Barbara. 1990. Theatrical Imagery and Gender Ideology in Java. In *Power and Difference: Gender in Island Southeast Asia*, ed. Jane Monnig Atkinson and Shelly Errington, 177–207. Stanford: Stanford University Press.

Hauenstein, A. 1967a. Rites et coutumes liés au culte de la pluie parmi différentes tribus du sud-ouest de l'Angola. *Boletim do Instituto de Angola* 27:5–23.

– 1967b. Rites et coutumes liés au culte de la pluie parmi différentes tribus du sud-ouest de l'Angola. *Boletim do Instituto de Angola* 29:5–27.

Heald, Suzette. 1999. *Manhood and Morality: Sex and Violence in Gisu Society*. London: Routledge.

Herbert, Eugenia W. 1993. *Iron, Gender, and Power: Rituals of Transformation in African Societies*. Bloomington: Indiana University Press.

Herskovits, M. 1937. A Note on 'Woman Marriage' in Dahomey. *Africa* 10 (3): 335–41.

Hill, Jonathan D. 1984. Social Equality and Ritual Hierarchy: The Arawakan Wakuénai of Venezuela. *American Ethnologist* 11:528–44.

Hodgson, Dorothy L. 1999. Pastoralism, Patriarchy and History: Changing Gender Relations among Maasai in Tanganyika, 1890–1940. *Journal of African History* 40:41–65.

– 2001. *Once Intrepid Warriors: Gender, Ethnicity, and the Cultural Politics of Maasai Development.* Bloomington: Indiana University Press.

– 2005. *The Church of Women: Gendered Encounters between Maasai and Missionaries.* Bloomington: Indiana University Press.

Hodgson, Dorothy L., and Sheryl McCurdy. 1996. Wayward Wives, Misfit Mothers, Disobedient Daughters: 'Wicked' Women and the Reconfiguration of Gender in Africa. *Canadian Journal of African Studies* 30 (1):1–9.

– 2001. *'Wicked' Women and the Reconfiguration of Gender in Africa.* Portsmouth: Heinemann.

Hoehler-Fatton, Cynthia. 1996. *Women of Fire and Spirit: History, Faith, and Gender in Roho Religion in Western Kenya.* New York: Oxford University Press.

Hoernlé, A.W. 1922. A Hottentot Rain Ceremony. *Bantu Studies* 1:20–1.

Holas, B. 1949. Pour faire tomber la pluie (nord du Togo). *Notes Africaines* 41:13–14.

Holmes, C.F., and R.A. Austen. 1972. The Precolonial Sukuma. *Journal of World History* 2:377–405.

Hunter, G. 1953. Hidden Drums in Singida District. *Tanganyika Notes and Records* 34:28–32.

Iliffe, John. 1967. The Organisation of the Maji Maji Rebellion. *Journal of African History* 8:485–512.

– 1969. *Tanganyika under German Rule, 1905–1912.* Cambridge: Cambridge University Press.

– 1979. *A Modern History of Tanganyika.* Cambridge: Cambridge University Press.

Itandala, B. 1980. Nilotic Impact on the Babinza of Usukuma. *Transafrican Journal of History* 9 (1–2): 1–17.

Ittameier, Rev. Everth. 1912. Reise ins neue Missionsgebiet. *Evangelisch-lutherisches Missionsblatt für die evangelish-lutherisches Missions zu Leipzig*: 152–6.

– 1922. Das Christentum als Lebensmacht in unseren heidenchristlichen Gemeinden. *Evangelisch-lutherisches Missionsblatt für die evangelisch-lutherische Mission zu Leipzig*: 92–6.

– 1922–3. Abriss einer Lautlehre und Grammatik des Kinilamba. *Zeitschrift für Kolonialsprachen* 8:1–47.

Jackson, Michael. 1989. *Paths toward a Clearing: Radical Empiricism and Ethnographic Inquiry.* Bloomington: Indiana University Press.

Jackson, R.H., and G. Maddox. 1993. The Creation of Identity: Colonial Society in Bolivia and Tanzania. *Comparative Studies in Society and History* 35:263–84.

Jacobson-Widding, Anita. 1984. African Folk Models and Their Application. Working Papers in African Studies, African Studies Programme, University of Uppsala 1.

– 1985. Private Spirits and the Ego: A Psychological Ethnography of Ancestor Cult and Spirit Possession among the Manyika of Zimbabwe. Working Papers in African Studies, African Studies Programme, University of Uppsala 24.

– 1990. The Fertility of Incest. In *The Creative Communion: African Folk Models of Fertility and the Regeneration of Life*, ed. Anita Jacobson-Widding and Walter van Beek, 47–73. Uppsala: Acta Universitatis Upsaliensis.

– 1991. Subjective Body, Objective Space: An Introduction. In *Body and Space: Symbolic Models of Unity and Division in African Cosmology and Experience*, ed. Anita Jacobson-Widding. Uppsala: Acta Universitatis Upsaliensis.

– 2000. *Chapungu: The Bird That Never Drops a Feather: Male and Female Identities in an African Society.* Uppsala: Acta Universitatis Upsaliensis.

James, Wendy. 1972. The Politics of Rain Control among the Uduk. In *Essays in Sudan Ethnography: Presented to Sir Edward Evans-Pritchard*, ed. Ian Cunnison and Wendy James, 31–57. London: C. Hurst.

Jellicoe, Marguerite. 1969. The Turu Resistance Movement. *Tanganyika Notes and Records* 70:1–12.

– 1978. *The Long Path: Social Change in Tanzania*. Nairobi: East African Publishing House.

Jellicoe, Marguerite, Philip Puja, and Jeremiah Sombi. 1967. Praising the Sun. *Transition* 31 (6):27–31.

Jellicoe, Marguerite, Vincent Sima, and Jeremiah Sombi. 1968. The Shrine in the Desert. *Transition* 34 (7):43–9.

Johnson, Frederick. 1923–6. Notes on Kiniramba. *Bantu Studies* 2:167–92, 233–63.

– 1931. Kiniramba Folk Tales. *Bantu Studies* 5:327–56.

Johnson, V. Eugene. 1934. *The Augustana Lutheran Mission of Tanganyika Territory, East Africa*. Rock Island: Board of Foreign Missions of the Augustana Synod.

– 1948. *Pioneering for Christ in East Africa*. Rock Island: Augustana Book Concern.

– 1951–2. The Rebirth of a People. *East African Annual:* 61–66.

– 1954. African Harvest Dance. *Tanganyika Notes and Records* 37:138–42.

Kachapila, Hendrina. 2006. The Revival of *Nyau* and Changing Gender Relations in Early Colonial Central Malawi. *Journal of Religion in Africa* 36 (3–4): 319–45.

Kaiser, Paul J. 1996. Structural Adjustment and the Fragile Nation: The Demise of Social Unity in Tanzania. *The Journal of Modern African Studies* 34 (2): 227–37.

Kaplan, F.E.S., ed. 1997. *Queens, Queen Mothers, Priestesses, and Power: Case Studies in African Gender*. New York: New York Academy of Sciences.

Kaspin, Deborah. 1996. A Chewa Cosmology of the Body. *American Ethnologist* 23 (3): 561–78.

Keane, Webb. 2005. Signs Are Not the Garb of Meaning: On the Social Analysis of Material Things. In *Materiality*, ed. Daniel Miller, 182–205. Durham, NC: Duke University Press.

Keeler, Ward. 1990. Speaking of Gender in Java. In *Power and Difference: Gender in Island Southeast Asia*, ed. Jane Monnig Atkinson and Shelly Errington, 127–52. Stanford: Stanford University Press.

Kesby, John D. 1981. *The Rangi of Tanzania: An Introduction to Their Culture*. New Haven, CT: HRAF.

– 1982. *Progress and the Past among the Rangi of Tanzania*. New Haven, CT: HRAF.

Kidamala, D., and E.R. Danielson. 1961. A Brief History of the Waniramba People up to the Time of the German Occupation. *Tanganyika Notes and Records* 56:67–78.

Kimambo, I.N. 1991. *Penetration and Protest in Tanzania: The Impact of the World Economy on the Pare, 1860–1960*. London: James Currey.

Kjekshus, H. 1977. *Ecology Control and Economic Development in East African History*. London: Heinemann.

Klima, George J. 1970. *The Barabaig: East African Cattle-Herders*. Prospect Heights, IL: Waveland.

Kohl-Larsen, Ludwig L. 1943. *Auf den Spuren des Vormenschen (Deutsche Afrika-Expedition 1934–1936 und 1937–1939)*. Stuttgart: Strecher und Schröder.

Kohl-Larsen, Ludwig L., and M. Kohl-Larsen. 1938. *Felsmalereien in Innerafrika*. Stuttgart: Strecker und Schröder.

– 1958. *Die Bilderstrasse Ostafrikas*. Eisenach and Kassel.

Kolawole, Mary. 2004. Re-Conceptualizing African Gender Theory: Feminism, Womanism, and the Arere Metaphor. In *Re-Thinking Sexualities in Africa*, ed. Signe Arnfred, 251–66. Uppsala: Nordiska Afrikainstitutet.

Koponen, J. 1988. *People and Production in Late Precolonial Tanzania: History and Structures*. Jyväskylä: Scandinavian Institute of African Studies.

Kratz, Corinne A. 1994. *Affecting Performance: Meaning, Movement, and Experience in Okiek Women's Initiation*. Washington, DC: Smithsonian Institution Press.

Krige, Eileen Jensen. 1968. Girls' Puberty Songs and Their Relation to Fertility, Health, Morality and Religion among the Zulu. *Africa* 38:173–98.

Krige, Eileen Jensen, and Jack D. Krige. 1943. *The Realm of a Rain-Queen: A Study of the Pattern of Lovedu Society.* London: Oxford University Press.

Kulick, Don. 1997. The Gender of Brazilian Transgendered Prostitutes. *American Anthropologist* 99 (3): 574–85.

Kuper, Hilda. 1947. *An African Aristocracy: Rank among the Swazi.* London: Oxford University Press.

– 1972. A Royal Ritual in a Changing Political Context. *Cahiers d'études africaines* 48:593–615.

– 1973. Costume and Cosmology: The Animal Symbolism of the Ncwala. *Man* 8:613–30.

Lakoff, George, and M. Johnson. 1980. *Metaphors We Live By.* Chicago: University of Chicago Press.

Lambek, Michael. 1996. The Past Imperfect: Remembering as Moral Practice. In *Tense Past: Cultural Essays in Trauma and Memory,* ed. Paul Antze and Michael Lambek, 235–54. New York: Routledge.

– 2002. *The Weight of the Past: Living with History in Mahajanga, Madagascar.* New York: Palgrave-Macmillan.

Lan, David. 1985. *Guns and Rain: Guerrillas and Spirit Mediums in Zimbabwe.* Berkeley and Los Angeles: University of California Press.

Langley, Myrtle S. 1979. *The Nandi of Kenya: Life Crisis Rituals in a Period of Change.* London: C. Hurst.

Laqueur, T. 1990. *Making Sex: Body and Gender from the Greeks to Freud.* Cambridge, MA: Harvard University Press.

Laydevant, F. 1933. The Praises of the Divining Bones among the Basotho. *Bantu Studies* 7:341–73.

Leakey, L.S.B. 1977. *The Southern Kikuyu before 1903, Vol. 1.* London: Academic Press.

Lebeuf, Annie. 1965. Le système classificatoire des Fali (nord-Cameroun). In *African Systems of Thought,* ed. Meyer Fortes and Germaine Dieterlen, 328–40. London: Oxford University Press.

Lewis-Williams, J.D. 1977. Led by the Nose: Observations on the Supposed Use of Southern San Rock Art in Rain-Making Rituals. *African Studies* 36 (2): 155–9.

Lienhardt, Godfrey. 1951. Some Notions of Witchcraft among the Dinka. *Africa* 21 (4): 303–18.

Lincoln, Bruce. 1987. Ritual, Rebellion, Resistance: Once More the Swazi Ncwala. *Man* 22:132–56.

Lindsay, Lisa, and Stephan Miescher, eds. 2003. *Men and Masculinities in Modern Africa.* Portsmouth: Heinemann.

Lindström, Jan. 1987. Iramba Pleases Us: Agro-Pastoralism among the Plateau Iramba of Central Tanzania. PhD thesis, University of Göteborg.

– 1988. The Monopolization of a Spirit: Livestock Prestations During an Iramba Funeral. In *On the Meaning of Death: Essays on Mortuary Rituals and Eschatological Beliefs*, ed. S. Cederroth, C. Corlin, and J. Lindström, 169–83. Uppsala: Acta Universitatis Upsaliensis.

Llewelyn-Davies, Melissa. 1981. Women, Warriors, and Patriarchs. In *Sexual Meanings: The Cultural Construction of Gender and Sexuality*, ed. S.B. Ortner and H. Whitehead, 330–58. Cambridge: Cambridge University Press.

Lock, Margaret. 1993. Cultivating the Body: Anthropology and Epistemologies of Bodily Practice and Knowledge. *Annual Review of Anthropology* 22:133–55.

Lonsdale, John. 1977. When Did the Gusii (or Any Other Group) Become a 'Tribe'? *Kenya Historical Review* 5:123–33.

Lorber, Judith. 1994. *Paradoxes of Gender*. New Haven, CT: Yale University Press.

Lugalla, Joe L.P. 1995. The Impact of Structural Adjustment Policies on Women's and Children's Health in Tanzania. *Review of African Political Economy* 63:43–53.

– 1997. Development, Change, and Poverty in the Informal Sector during the Era of Structural Adjustment in Tanzania. *Canadian Journal of African Studies* 31 (3): 424–51.

Lwoga, C. 1985. Bureaucrats, Peasants and Land Rights: A Villagers' Struggle for Self-Determination. In *Villagers, Villages and the State in Modern Tanzania*, ed. Ray Abrahams. Cambridge: African Studies Centre.

MacCormack, Carol P. 1980. Proto-Social to Adult: A Sherbro Transformation. In *Nature, Culture and Gender*, ed. Carol P. MacCormack and Marilyn Stathern, 95–118. Cambridge: Cambridge University Press.

MacCormack, Carol, and Marilyn Strathern, eds. 1980. *Nature, Culture and Gender*. Cambridge: Cambridge University Press.

Maddox, Gregory H. 1986. Njaa: Food Shortages and Famines in Tanzania between the Wars. *International Journal of African Historical Studies* 19:17–34.

– 1988. Leave Wagogo, You Have No Food: Famine and Survival in Ugogo, Tanzania, 1916–1961. PhD dissertation, Northwestern University.

– 1990. Mtunya: Famine in Central Tanzania, 1917–1920. *Journal of African History* 31 (2): 181–98.

Makarius, Laura. 1973. Une interprétation de l'incwala Swazi: Étude du symbolisme dans la pensée et les rites d'un peuple africain. *Annales* 28 (6): 1403–22.

Manicom, Linzi. 1992. Ruling Relations: Rethinking State and Gender in South African History. *Journal of African History* 33:441–65.

Marshall, L. 1957. N!Ow. *Africa* 27:232–40.

Marwick, Max G. 1968. Notes on Some Cewa Rituals. *African Studies* 27 (1): 3–14.

Masao, F.T. 1979. *The Late Stone Age and Rock Paintings of Central Tanzania*. Wiesbaden: Franz Steiner.

Masquelier, Adeline. 2002. Road Mythographies: Space, Mobility, and the Historical Imagination in Postcolonial Niger. *American Ethnologist* 29 (4): 829–56.

Matory, J. Lorand 2003. Gendered Agendas: The Secrets Scholars Keep about Yorùbá – Atlantic Religion. *Gender and History* 15 (3): 409–39.

Mbembe, Achille. 2001. *On the Postcolony*. Berkeley and Los Angeles: University of California Press.

Mbilinyi, Marjorie. 1990. 'Structural Adjustment,' Agribusiness, and Rural Women in Tanzania. In *The Food Question: Profits versus People?* ed. Henry Bernstein et al., 111–24. London: Earthscan.

Meigs, Anna. 1990. Multiple Gender Ideologies and Statuses. In *Beyond the Second Sex: New Directions in the Anthropology of Gender*, ed. P.R. Sanday and R.G. Goodenough, 99–112. Philadelphia: University of Pennsylvania Press.

Melhuus, Marit. 1996. Power, Value and the Ambiguous Meanings of Gender. In *Machos, Mistresses, Madonnas: Contesting the Power of Latin American Gender Imagery*, ed. Marit Melhuus and Kristi Anne Stølen, 230–59. London: Verso.

Middleton, John. 1963. Witchcraft and Sorcery in Lugbara. In *Witchcraft and Sorcery in East Africa*, ed. John Middleton and E.H. Winter, 257–75. London: Routledge and Kegan Paul.

– 1971. Prophets and Rainmakers: The Agents of Social Change among the Lugbara. In *The Translation of Culture: Essays to E.E. Evans-Pritchard*, ed. T.O. Beidelman, 179–201. London: Tavistock.

Mikell, Gwendolyn, ed. 1997. *African Feminism: The Politics of Survival in Sub-Saharan Africa*. Philadelphia: University of Pennsylvania Press.

Millroth, Bertha. 1965. *Lyuba: Traditional Religion of the Sukuma*. Uppsala: Almqvist and Wiksells Boktryckeri AB.

Molet, L. 1965. Kanda et sangere, génies Yakoma. In *African Systems of Thought*, ed. Meyer Fortes and G. Dieterlen, 158–64. London: Oxford University Press.

Moore, Henrietta L. 1986. *Space, Text and Gender: An Anthropological Study of the Marakwet of Kenya*. Cambridge: Cambridge University Press.

– 1988. *Feminism and Anthropology*. Cambridge: Polity.

– 1994. *A Passion for Difference: Essays in Anthropology and Gender*. Cambridge: Polity.

Moore, Henrietta L., and Megan Vaughan. 1994. *Cutting Down Trees: Gender, Nutrition, and Agricultural Change in the Northern Province of Zambia, 1890–1990*. London: James Currey.

Moore, Henrietta L., and Todd Sanders. 2001. Magical Interpretations and Material Realities: An Introduction. In *Magical Interpretations, Material Reali-*

ties: Modernity, Witchcraft and the Occult in Postcolonial Africa, ed. Henrietta L. Moore and Todd Sanders, 1–27. London: Routledge.

– 2006. Anthropology and Epistemology. In *Anthropology in Theory: Issues in Epistemology*, ed. Henrietta L. Moore and Todd Sanders, 1–21. Oxford: Blackwell.

Moore, Henrietta L., Todd Sanders, and Bwire Kaare, eds. 1999. *Those Who Play with Fire: Gender, Fertility and Transformation in East and Southern Africa*. London: Athlone.

Moore, Sally Falk. 1976. The Secret of the Men: A Fiction of Chagga Initiation and Its Relation to the Logic of Chagga Symbolism. *Africa* 46:357–70.

– 1986. *Social Facts and Fabrications: 'Customary' Law on Kilimanjaro, 1880–1980*. Cambridge: Cambridge University Press.

Morris, R.C. 1995. All Made Up: Performance Theory and the New Anthropology of Sex and Gender. *Annual Review of Anthropology* 24:567–92.

Mosko, Mark S. 2005. Introduction: A (Re)Turn to Chaos: Chaos Theory, the Sciences, and Social Anthropological Theory. In *On the Order of Chaos: Social Anthropology and the Science of Chaos*, ed. Mark S. Mosko and Frederick H. Damon. New York: Berhahn.

Mudimbe, V.Y. 1988. *The Invention of Africa: Gnosis, Philosophy, and the Order of Knowledge*. Bloomington: Indiana University Press.

Murray, Colin. 1975. Sex, Smoking and the Shades: A Sotho Symbolic Idiom. In *Religion and Social Change in Southern Africa: Anthropological Essays in Honour of Monica Wilson*, ed. M.G. Whisson and M. West, 58–77. Cape Town: David Philip.

– 1980. Sotho Fertility Symbolism. *African Studies* 39:65–76.

Myhre, Knut Christian. 2006. Family Resemblances, Practical Interrelations, and Material Extensions: Understanding Sexual Prohibitions, Production and Consumption in Kilimanjaro. Paper delivered 24 March, Department of Anthropology, University of Toronto.

Nadel, S.F. 1952. Witchcraft in Four African Societies: An Essay in Comparison. *American Anthropologist* 54 (1): 18–29.

Needham, Rodney. 1972. *Belief, Language, and Experience*. Oxford: Blackwell.

– 1973. *Right and Left*. Chicago: University of Chicago Press.

Newell, Stephanie. 2005. Devotion and Domesticity: The Reconfiguration of Gender in Popular Christian Pamphlets from Ghana. *Journal of Religon in Africa* 35 (3): 296–323.

Ngubane, H. 1976. Some Notions Of 'Purity' And 'Impurity' among the Zulu. *Africa* 46:274–84.

Norbeck, E. 1963. African Rituals of Conflict. *American Anthropologist* 65:1254–79.

Ntarangwi, Mwenda, Mustafa Babiker, and David Mills. 2006. Introduction: Histories of Training, Ethnographies of Practice. In *African Anthropologies: History, Critique and Practice*, ed. Mwenda Ntarangwi, David Mills, and Mustafa Babiker, 1–48. London: Zed.

Ntudu, Yakobo. 1939. The Position of Rainmaker among the Wanyiramba. *Tanganyika Notes and Records* 7:84–7.

Nzegwu, Nkiru 2001. Gender Equity in a Dual-Sex System: The Case of Onitsha. *Jenda: A Journal of Culture and African Women Studies* 1 (1). Available online at http://www.jendajournal.com/vol1.1/nzegwa.html (accessed 13 April 2007).

Obbo, Christine. 2006. But We All Know It! African Perspectives on Anthropological Knowledge. In *African Anthropologies: History, Critique and Practice*, ed. Mwenda Ntarangwi, David Mills, and Mustafa Babiker, 154–69. London: Zed Books.

O'Brien, Dan. 1983. Chiefs of Rain – Chiefs of Ruling: A Reinterpretation of Pre-colonial Tonga (Zambia) Social and Political Structure. *Africa* 53:23–42.

Obst, Erich. 1912a. Die Landschaften Issansu und Iramba (Deutsch-Ostafrika). *Mitteilungen der geographischen Gesellschaft in Hamburg* 26:108–32.

– 1912b. Von Mkalama ins Land der Wakindiga. *Mitteilungen der geographischen Gesellschaft in Hamburg* 26:1–45.

– 1915. Das abflußlose Rumpfschollenland im nordöstlichen Deutsch-Ostafrika (Teil I). *Mitteilungen der geographischen Gesellschaft in Hamburg* 29:7–105.

– 1923. Das abflußlose Rumpfschollenland im nordöstlichen Deutsch-Ostafrika (Teil II). *Mitteilungen der geographischen Gesellschaft in Hamburg* 35:1–330.

Odner, K. 1971. An Archaeological Survey of Iramba, Tanzania. *Azania* 6:151–98.

Ofcansky, T.P. 1981. A History of Game Preservation in British East Africa, 1895–1963. PhD dissertation, West Virginia University.

Ortner, Sherry B. 1996. Gender Hegemonies. In *Making Gender: The Politics and Erotics of Culture*, 35–80. Boston: Beacon.

Ortner, Sherry B., and Harriet Whitehead. 1981a. Introduction: Accounting for Sexual Meanings. In *Sexual Meanings: The Cultural Construction of Gender and Sexuality*, ed. Sherry B. Ortner and Harriet Whitehead, 1–27. Cambridge: Cambridge University Press.

– eds. 1981b. *Sexual Meanings: The Cultural Construction of Gender and Sexuality.* Cambridge: Cambridge University Press.

Ouzgane, Lahoucine, and Robert Morrell, eds. 2005. *African Masculinities: Men in Africa from the Late Nineteenth Century to the Present.* New York: Palgrave Macmillan.

Oyewumi, Oyeronke. 1997. *The Invention of Women: Making an African Sense of Western Gender Discourses.* Minneapolis: University of Minnesota Press.

– 2002. Conceptualizing Gender: The Eurocentric Foundations of Feminist Concepts and the Challenge of African Epistemologies. *Jenda: A Journal of Culture and African Women Studies.*

– 2003. Introduction: Feminism, Sisterhood, and Other Foreign Relations. In *African Women and Feminism: Reflections on the Politics of Sisterhood*, ed. Oyeronke Oyewumi, 1–24. Trenton, NJ: Africa World Press.

Packard, Randall M. 1981. *Chiefship and Cosmology: An Historical Study of Political Competition.* Bloomington: Indiana University Press.

Parkin, D. 1991. *Sacred Void: Spatial Images of Work and Ritual among the Giriama of Kenya.* Cambridge: Cambridge University Press.

Peel, J.D.Y. 2002. Gender in Yoruba Religious Change. *Journal of Religion in Africa* 32 (2): 136–66.

Peletz, Michael G. 1994. Neither Reasonable nor Responsible: Contrasting Representations of Masculinity in a Malay Society. *Cultural Anthropology* 9 (2): 135–78.

Pender-Cudlip, Patrick. 1974. The Iramba and Their Neighbours. In *Foreign Relations of African States*, ed. K. Ingham, 55–66. London: Butterworths.

– c. 1974. God and the Sun: Some Notes on Iramba Religious History. Unpublished manuscript at British Institute in Eastern Africa, Nairobi.

Petermann, W. 1985. *Regenkulte und Regenmacher bei Bantu-sprachigen Ethnien Ost- und Südafrikas.* Berlin: EXpress Edition.

Peters, C. 1891. *New Light on Dark Africa: The German Emin Pasha Expedition.* London: Ward, Lock.

Piot, Charles. 1999. *Remotely Global: Village Modernity in West Africa.* Chicago: University of Chicago Press.

Ponte, Stefano. 1998. Fast Crops, Fast Cash: Market Liberalization and Rural Livelihoods in Songea and Morogoro Districts, Tanzania. *Canadian Journal of African Studies* 32 (2): 316–48.

Potash, Betty. 1989. Gender Relations in Sub-Saharan Africa. In *Gender and Anthropology: Critical Reviews for Research and Teaching*, ed. S. Morgen, 189–227. Washington, DC: American Anthropological Association.

Power, Camilla, and Ian Watts. 1997. The Woman with the Zebra's Penis: Gender, Mutability and Performance. *Journal of the Royal Anthropological Institute* 3:537–60.

– 1999. First Gender, Wrong Sex. In *Those Who Play with Fire: Gender, Fertility and Transformation in East and Southern Africa*, ed. Henrietta L. Moore, Todd Sanders, and Bwire Kaare. London: Athlone.

Prince, von T. 1895. Deutsch-Ostafrika, von der Station Kilimatinde. *Deutsches Kolonialblatt* 6:243–344.

Quinn, Naomi, and Wendy Luttrell. 2004. Psychodynamic Universals, Cultural Particulars in Feminist Anthropology: Rethinking Hua Gender Beliefs. *Ethos* 32 (4): 493–513.

Ranger, Terence. 1968a. Connexions between 'Primary Resistance' Movements and Modern Mass Nationalism in East and Central Africa: Part I. *Journal of African History* 9 (3): 437–53.

– 1968b. Connexions between 'Primary Resistance' Movements and Modern Mass Nationalism in East and Central Africa: Part II. *Journal of African History* 9 (4): 631–41.

– 1983. The Invention of Tradition in Colonial Africa. In *The Invention of Tradition*, ed. E. Hobsbawm and T. Ranger, 211–62. Cambridge: Cambridge University Press.

– 1993. The Invention of Tradition Revisited: The Case of Colonial Africa. In *Legitimacy and the State in Twentieth-Century Africa*, ed. Terence Ranger and Olufemi Vaughan, 62–111. London: Macmillan.

Reche, O. 1914. *Zur Ethnographie des abflußlosen Gebietes Deutsch-Ostafrikas.* Hamburg: L. Friederichsen.

– 1915. Dr Obst's ethnographische Sammlung aus dem abflußlosen Rumpfschollenland des nordöstlichen Deutsch-Ostafrika. *Mitteilungen der geographischen Gesellschaft in Hamburg* 29:251–65.

Reiter, R.R. 1975. *Toward an Anthropology of Women.* New York: Monthly Review.

Richards, Audrey. 1956. *Chisungu: A Girl's Initiation Ceremony among the Bemba of Zambia.* London: Routledge.

Rigby, Peter. 1966. Dual Symbolic Classification among the Gogo of Central Tanzania. *Africa* 36 (1): 1–17.

– 1968. Some Gogo Rituals of 'Purification': An Essay on Social and Moral Categories. In *Dialectic in Practical Religion*, ed. Edmund R. Leach, 153–78. Cambridge: Cambridge University Press.

– 1969. *Cattle and Kinship among the Gogo: A Semi-Pastoral Society of Central Tanzania.* Ithaca: Cornell University Press.

– 1971. Politics and Modern Leadership Roles in Ugogo. In *Colonialism in Africa, 1870–1960: Vol. 3, Profiles of Change: African Society and Colonial Rule,* ed. V. Turner. Cambridge: Cambridge University Press.

Roberts, A. 1970. Nyamwezi Trade. In *Pre-Colonial African Trade: Essays on Trade in Central and Eastern Africa before 1900,* ed. Robert Gray and D. Birmingham. London: Oxford University Press.

Rodemann, H.W. 1961. Tanganyika, 1890–1914: Selected Aspects of German Administration. PhD dissertation, University of Chicago.

Rogers, F.H. 1927. Notes on Some Madi Rain-Stones. *Man* 27:81–7.

Rogers, Susan. 1990. The Symbolic Representation of Women in a Changing Batak Culture. In *Power and Difference: Gender in Island Southeast Asia*, ed. Jane Monnig Atkinson and Shelly Errington, 307–44. Stanford: Stanford University Press.

Roosens, E. 1994. The Primordial Nature of Origins in Migrant Ethnicity. In *The Anthropology of Ethnicity*, ed. H. Vermeulen and C. Govers. Amsterdam: Het Spinhuis.

Sanders, Todd. 1997. Rainmaking, Gender and Power in Ihanzu, Tanzania, 1885–1995. PhD thesis, London School of Economics and Political Science, London.

– 1998. Making Children, Making Chiefs: Gender, Power and Ritual Legitimacy. *Africa* 68 (2): 238–62.

– 1999. 'Doing Gender' in Africa: Embodying Categories and the Categorically Disembodied. In *Those Who Play with Fire: Gender, Fertility and Transformation in East and Southern Africa*, ed. Henrietta L. Moore, Todd Sanders, and Bwire Kaare, 41–82. London: Athlone Press.

– 2000. Rains Gone Bad, Women Gone Mad: Rethinking Gender Rituals of Rebellion and Patriarchy. *Journal of the Royal Anthropological Institute* 6 (3): 469–86.

– 2001a. Save Our Skins: Structural Adjustment, Morality and the Occult in Tanzania. In *Magical Interpretations, Material Realities: Modernity, Witchcraft and the Occult in Postcolonial Africa*, ed. Henrietta L. Moore and Todd Sanders, 160–83. London: Routledge.

– 2001b. Territorial and Magical Migrations in Tanzania. In *Mobile Africa: Changing Patterns of Movement in Africa and Beyond*, ed. M. de Bruin, Rijk van Dijk, and D. Foeken. Leiden: Brill.

– 2002. Reflections on Two Sticks: Gender, Sexuality and Rainmaking. *Cahiers d'études africaines* 166 (42/2): 283–315.

– 2003a. Invisible Hands and Visible Goods: Revealed and Concealed Economies in Contemporary Tanzania. In *Transparency and Conspiracy: Ethnographies of Suspicion in the New World Order*, ed. Harry G. West and Todd Sanders. Durham, NC: Duke University Press.

– 2003b. Reconsidering Witchcraft: Postcolonial Africa and Analytic (Un)Certainties. *American Anthropologist* 105 (2):338–52.

Sanderson, G.M. 1955. The Use of Tail-Switches in Magic. *Nyasaland Journal* 8 (1): 39–56.

Schapera, Isaac. 1971. *Rainmaking Rites of Tswana Tribes*. Cambridge: African Studies Centre.

Schoeman, P.J. 1935. The Swazi Rain Ceremony. *Bantu Studies* 9:169–75.

Scott, James C. 1985. *Weapons of the Weak: Everyday Forms of Peasant Resistance.* New Haven, CT: Yale University Press.

Senior, H.S. 1938. Sukuma Salt Caravans to Lake Eyasi. *Tanganyika Notes and Records* 6: 87–90.

Sharp, Lesley A. 2000. The Commodification of the Body and Its Parts. *Annual Review of Anthropology* 29:287–328.

Sheridan, Michael J. 2002. An Irrigation Intake Is Like a Uterus: Culture and Agriculture in Precolonial North Pare, Tanzania. *American Anthropologist* 104 (1): 79–92.

Sick, E. von. 1915. Die Waniaturu (Walimi): Ethnographische Skizze eines Bantu-Stammes. *Baessler-Archiv* 5:1–62.

Simonsen, Jan Ketil. 2000. Webs of Life. PhD Dissertation, University of Oslo.

Snyder, Katherine. 1997. Elders' Authority and Women's Protest: The *Masay* Ritual and Social Change among the Iraqw of Tanzania. *Journal of the Royal Anthropological Institute* 3:561–76.

– 2005. *The Iraqw of Tanzania: Negotiating Rural Development.* Cambridge, MA: Westview.

Spencer, Paul. 1988. *The Maasai of Matapato: A Study of Rituals of Rebellion.* Bloomington: Indiana University Press.

Spire, F. 1905. Rain-Making in Equatorial Africa. *Journal of The African Society* 5:15–21.

Stambach, Amy. 2000. *Lessons from Mount Kilimanjaro: Schooling, Community, and Gender in East Africa.* New York: Routledge.

Steinmetz, George. 2005. Positivism and Its Others in the Social Sciences. In *The Politics of Method in the Human Sciences: Positivism and Its Epistemological Others,* ed. George Steinmetz. Durham: Duke University Press.

Stoller, Paul. 1995. *Embodying Colonial Memories: Spirit Possession, Power, and the Hauka in West Africa.* New York: Routledge.

Stølen, Kristi Anne. 1996. The Power of Gender Discourses in a Multi-Ethnic Community in Rural Argentina. In *Machos, Mistresses, Madonnas: Contesting the Power of Latin American Gender Imagery,* ed. Marit Melhuus and Kristi Anne Stølen, 159–83. London: Verso.

Strathern, Marilyn. 1980. No Nature, No Culture: The Hagen Case. In *Nature, Culture and Gender,* ed. Carol P. MacCormack and Marilyn Strathern, 174–222. Cambridge: Cambridge University Press.

– 1988. *The Gender of the Gift: Problems with Women and Problems with Society in Melanesia.* Berkeley and Los Angeles: University of California Press.

– 1990. Negative Strategies. In *Localizing Strategies: Regional Traditions of Ethnographic Writing,* ed. Richard Fardon, 204–16. Washington: Smithsonian Institution Press.

Strobel, Margaret. 1982. African Women: A Review Essay. *Signs* 8 (1): 109–31.

Stuhlmann, F. 1894. *Mit Emin Pascha ins Herz von Afrika*. Berlin: Dietrich Reimer.

Sunseri, T. 1997. Famine and Wild Pigs: Gender Struggles and the Outbreak of the Majimaji War in Uzaramo (Tanzania). *Journal of African History* 38: 235–59.

Swantz, L.W. 1974. The Role of the Medicine Man among the Zaramo of Dar es Salaam. PhD thesis, University of Dar es Salaam.

Swantz, Marja-Liisa, with Salome Mjema and Zenya Wild. 1995. *Blood, Milk and Death: Body Symbols and the Power of Regeneration among the Zaramo of Tanzania*. Westport, CT: Bergin and Garvey.

Tamale, Sylvia. 2004. Gender and Trauma in Africa: Enhancing Women's Links to Resources. *Journal of African Law* 48 (1): 50–61.

Tanner, R.E.S. 1956. An Introduction to the Northern Basukuma's Idea of the Supreme Being. *Anthropological Quarterly* 29 (4): 45–56.

– 1957. The Installation of Sukuma Chiefs in Mwanza District, Tanganyika. *African Studies* 16 (4): 197–209.

Taylor, Christopher. 1992. *Milk, Honey and Money: Changing Concepts in Rwandan Healing*. Washington: Smithsonian Institution Press.

Temu, Andrew E., and Jean M. Due. 2000. The Business Environment in Tanzania after Socialism: Challenges of Reforming Banks, Parastatals, Taxation and the Civil Service. *Journal of Modern African Studies* 38 (4): 683–712.

Ten Raa, Eric. 1968. Bush Foraging and Agricultural Development: A History of Sandawe Famines. *Tanzania Notes and Records* 69:33–40.

– 1969. The Moon as a Symbol of Life and Fertility in Sandawe Thought. *Africa* 39 (1): 24–53.

Thornton, Robert J. 1980. *Space, Time, and Culture among the Iraqw of Tanzania*. New York: Academic.

– 1982. Modelling Spatial Relations in a Boundary-Marking Ritual of the Iraqw of Tanzania. *Man* 17:528–45.

Thurnwald, R.C. 1935. *Black and White in East Africa: The Fabric of a New Civilization*. London: George Routledge and Sons.

Tomikawa, M. 1970. The Distribution and Migration of the Datoga Tribe. *Kyoto University African Studies* 5:1–46.

Tripp, Aili Mari. 1997. *Changing the Rules: The Politics of Liberalization and the Urban Informal Economy in Tanzania*. Berkeley and Los Angeles: University of California Press.

Tsing, Anna Lowenhaupt. 1990. Gender and Performance in Meratus Dispute Settlement. In *Power and Difference: Gender in Island Southeast Asia*, ed. Jane Monnig Atkinson and Shelly Errington, 95–125. Stanford: Stanford University Press.

– 1993. *In the Realm of the Diamond Queen: Marginality in an Out-of-the-Way Place*. Princeton, NJ: Princeton University Press.

Turner, Victor. 1955. The Spatial Separation of Adjacent Genealogical Generations in Ndembu Village Structure. *Africa* 25:121–37.

– 1967. *The Forest of Symbols: Aspects of Ndembu Ritual*. Ithaca: Cornell University Press.

– 1969. *The Ritual Process: Structure and Anti-Structure*. Chicago: Aldine.

– 1974. *Dramas, Fields, and Metaphors: Symbolic Action in Human Agency*. Ithaca: Cornell University Press.

Turshen, Meredeth, and Clotilde Twagiramariya, ed. 1998. *What Women Do in Wartime: Gender and Conflict in Africa*. New York: Palgrave.

Udvardy, Monica. 1989. Gender Metaphors in Maladies and Medicines: The Symbolism of Protective Charms among the Giriama of Kenya. In *Culture, Experience and Pluralism: Essays on African Ideas of Illness and Healing*, ed. Anita Jacobson-Widding and David Westerlund, 45–57. Uppsala: Acta Universitatis Upsaliensis.

Vail, Leroy, ed. 1989. *The Creation of Tribalism in Southern Africa*. London: James Currey.

Vijfhuizen, C. 1997. Rain-Making, Political Conflicts, and Gender Images: A Case from Mutema Chieftaincy in Zimbabwe. *Zambezia* 24 (1): 31–49.

Visweswaran, K. 1997. Histories of Feminist Ethnography. *Annual Review of Anthropology* 26:591–621.

Waller, Richard. 1978. The Lords of East Africa: The Maasai in the Mid-Nineteenth Century (c. 1840–1885). PhD thesis, University of Cambridge.

Ward, Robert E. 1999. *Messengers of Love*. Kearney, NE: Morris.

Watt, J.M., and N.J. Warmelo. 1930. The Medicines and Practices of a Sotho Doctor. *Bantu Studies* 4:47–63.

Weatherby, J. 1979. Raindrums of the Sor. In *Chronology, Migration, and Drought in Interlacustrine Africa*, ed. J.B. Webster, 317–31. London: Longman and Dalhousie University Press.

Weil, Peter M. 1976. The Staff of Life: Female Fertility in a West African Society. *Africa* 46: 182–95.

Weiss, Brad. 1996. *The Making and Unmaking of the Haya Lived World*. Durham: Duke University Press.

Werbner, Richard. 1990. Bwiti in Reflection: On the Fugue of Gender. *Journal of Religion in Africa* 20 (1): 63–91.

Werther, C.W. 1894. *Zum Victoria Nyanza: eine Antisklaverei-Expedition und Forschungsreise*. Berlin: Gergonne.

– 1898. *Die mittleren Hochländer des nördlichen Deutsch-Ost-Afrika*. Berlin: Hermann Paetel.

West, C., and D.H. Zimmerman. 1987. Doing Gender. *Gender and Society* 1 (2): 125–51.

Williams, F.R.J. 1949. The Pagan Religion of the Madi. *Uganda Journal* 13: 202–10.

Willis, Justin. 1992. The Making of a Tribe: Bondei Identities and Histories. *Journal of African History* 33:192–208.

Willis, Roy. 1991. The Body as Metaphor: Synthetic Observations on an African Artwork. In *Body and Space*, ed. Anita Jacobson-Widding. Uppsala: Acta Universitatis Upsaliensis.

Wilson, Monica. 1957. *Rituals of Kinship among the Nyakyusa*. London: Oxford University Press.

– 1970 [1951]. Witch-Beliefs and Social Structure. In *Witchcraft and Sorcery*, ed. Max G. Marwick, 276–85. London: Penguin.

Winter, Edward H. 1955. Some Aspects of Political Organization and Land Tenure among the Iraqw. Conference Proceedings from the East African Institute of Social Research, Makerere College.

Wolputte, Steven Van. 2004. Hang on to Your Self: Of Bodies, Embodiment, and Selves. *Annual Review of Anthropology* 33:251–69.

Woodburn, James. 1979. Minimal Politics: The Political Organisation of the Hadza of North Tanzania. In *Politics in Leadership: A Comparative Perspective*, ed. W.A. Shack and P.S. Cohen. Oxford: Clarendon Press.

– 1988a. African Hunter-Gatherer Social Organisation: Is It Best Understood as a Product of Encapsulation? In *Hunter and Gatherers: History, Evolution and Social Change*, ed. Tim Ingold, David Riches, and James Woodburn, 31–64. Oxford: Berg.

– 1988b. Hunter-Gatherer 'Silent Trade' with Outsiders and the History of Anthropology. Fifth International Conference on Hunting and Gathering Societies, Darwin, Austalia.

Yanagisako, Sylvia Junko, and Jane Fishburne Collier. 1987. Toward a Unified Analysis of Gender and Kinship. In *Gender and Kinship: Towards a Unified Analysis*, ed. Jane Fishburne Collier and Sylvia Junko Yanagisako, 14–50. Stanford: Stanford University Press.

Young, R., and H.A. Fosbrooke. 1960. *Land and Politics among the Luguru of Tanganyika*. London: Routledge and Kegan Paul.

Zimon, H. 1974. *Regenriten auf der Insel Bukerewe (Tanzania)*. Freiburg: Universitätsverlag Freiburg.

Index

ANTHROPOLOGICAL HORIZONS

Editor: Michael Lambek, University of Toronto

Published to date: